TAKING UP SPACE

TAKING UP SPACE
Exploring the Design Process

Tiiu Poldma

Université de Montréal / University of Montreal

Fairchild Books

New York

EXECUTIVE EDITOR Olga T. Kontzias

EDITORIAL DEVELOPMENT DIRECTOR Jennifer Crane

SENIOR DEVELOPMENT EDITOR Joseph Miranda

PRODUCTION DIRECTOR Ginger Hillman

ASSOCIATE PRODUCTION EDITOR Andrew Fargnoli

ASSOCIATE ART DIRECTOR Erin Fitzsimmons

COPY EDITOR Susan Hobbs

TEXT DESIGN Dutton & Sherman Design

COVER DESIGN Erin Fitzsimmons

Library of Congress Catalog Card Number: 2008931783

ISBN: 978-1-56367-628-4

GST R 133004424

Printed in the United States of America

TP09

To my husband, Alar, and my son, Julius

Contents

Extended Contents

Chapter 4

Scenarios, Design Briefs, and Users 99

Chapter 5

Contextualizing Interior Design Problems 139

Preface

Throughout this book there are sources of inspiration, images, ideas, and concepts about the design process. These are inspired by conversations about design and exploring the process with the intention of designing interior space. This book is about *taking up space*, about using design thinking to create interior spaces for people in dynamic situations, as they live, work, and play in interior environments.

We work with people when we design, whether it is designing products or environments, buildings, or systems. For interior designers, we design interior environments that thrive with human activity and exist within a broader framework of building, urban environment, and society. We respond to clients' needs, study user requirements, and creatively explore possibilities. We research functional requirements and conceptualize space, source-appropriate products and materials, and consider light, form, and color. We orchestrate multiple players and contexts, negotiate contracts, and solve problems of human interactions with objects and space, whether creative or aesthetic, functional, or situational. We respond to needs and requirements, often within the constraints of buildings, existing codes, or legislative rules, whether local, national, or international. And we are in the business of creating designed environments for particular purposes that are economical in nature.

We do all of these things *exploring the design process*. This book is about how the design process is explored from an interior design perspective. What is the design process to an interior designer? How do we design interior space? Why write a book about it? The "design process" has been explored by many people in fields from architecture to engineering to art, and we use these perspectives already. However, for each discipline (and the many others in between) the meaning of what constitutes the design process changes and molds to the particular contexts, circumstances and needs of the profession that is represented. The design process is appropriated, used, and understood to be many things by many different disciplines, and each one appropriates process in its own way.

Multiple contexts integrate two somewhat distinct elements: dynamic human activities and static and physical spaces within which these activities occur. The nature of designing interior space is somewhat contemporary and evolving with the advent of information and communication technologies. Interior space that once might have been designed for one purpose and for a long time period is now often designed for multiple and changing uses that can alter in a few minutes over the course of a day. These spaces are housed within physical structures that both confine and create the spaces. As you will see, even this is somewhat treacherous terrain, as "space" can be physical or virtual, real or imagined.

This design process is difficult to explore within the confines of the written word or visual images alone. Much of what we do as interior designers is to dialogue with people—clients, suppliers, consultants, and colleagues—to end up with the best design for a given situation and space. Therefore, it is important to understand what makes the design process come alive, whether as a design student or young professional, and that designing goes well beyond creating sketches or models. While these form the backbone of the communication in designing, they are supported by multiple dimensions we explore herein.

The book is organized to present and explore the design process both in its circular form and also as a systematic process. We begin, in Chapters 1 and 2, by examining the generic concept of design process and how this is informed by design methods, processes, and views from both within and outside of the field of interior design. Different aspects of the design process are explored as these weave around the primary concept of the process itself and how this is transformed within the realm of the execution of the design of the space.

Chapters 3, 4, and 5 break down the design process, introducing the building blocks of designing. It shows how design is circular, interactive, and constantly changing. The building blocks are steps you can use to explore the process, and hopefully appropriate it in your own way. There is no right or wrong, no prescribed way, and this, although difficult to understand at times, is actually the most liberating aspect of the process. When you use the building blocks, and when you explore designing in multiple ways, you "see" the world a little differently.

A parallel component of the design process is the development of the design program/brief for the client and the design requirements relative to the project and the user. The dynamic interrelationship among the client, the interior designer, and the design environment cannot be underestimated. Chapters 2 through 7 explore this interrelationship through the use of case studies, visual examples, and theoretical references that support the idea being explored.

Creating design programs and briefs, researching and documenting the design requirements, developing the design concept, and then transforming the concept into the built reality are all elements of this evolution.

Chapter 6 looks at the design process from the creative perspective, and suggests that creativity manifests itself in many forms. Chapters 4, 5, and 7 show how thinking and doing design are mutual concepts, as concepts and theoretical ideas in the book are always explored with concrete examples to show you what the ideas mean.

A fundamental component of this book is the inclusion of extensive case studies of projects done by both students and designers. Whereas the design projects by professionals are included to instruct and suggest ways to see the design process in action, the student projects are presented with two ideas in mind: to show you how the process evolves from very rough ideas, and to inspire you with the final results that are often done from very rough beginnings. The case studies are referenced often more than once so that you can see how the design evolves through different stages, from different perspectives, and with different end goals.

Finally, Chapters 8 through 10 introduce the broader and more complex issues that guide design thinking in a global world, because these have an impact on decisions made during the design process. Ethics, sustainability, and social, global issues all have an impact on both the design process itself and on how the various aspects are played out in the decision making that is needed to design appropriately. Questions of service and care are juxtaposed with responsibility and introduce concepts about the evolution of knowledge through design research. Design research and how it differs from the actual process is explored toward the end of the book, in the broader, more academic sense.

Design and the design process never change. How we do design and how we design for clients is changing constantly. Although in Chapters 1 and 2 we try to look at the phasing of design work and understand the design process in a series of concepts, maybe even steps, in the real world of interior design, things change rapidly and the complexity of each problem dictates the steps. Budget, time, and situational constraints drive the design problem and the design situation at all times. There will never be a "step-by step" method that will suit every situation and every design problem. Just recently I have had the opportunity to consult with clients for projects and we have changed the design quickly and deliberately, and the design process has almost happened in reverse of the steps described in this book. This is the simultaneous beauty and frustration of designing, and subsequently trying to pin it down into a series of steps.

More and more clients need the vision first, and then want to develop the practical details later. This is becoming an acceptable reality in the design world. Therefore, this is a book about puzzle pieces and building blocks, and you can use these in order, out of sync, and in any way that you like, to achieve your goals. The main thing to glean out of reading and using this book is that you, and only you, can be the interior designer, and you are one who can appropriate and use the design process in your own way.

Do not lose sight of what it is to be an interior designer, and that we are asked to perform a service for a client and to design interiors to service people and their myriad of activities in the dynamic sense. Objects and time are virtual and tangible concepts that aid us in this plan making.

In the end, we create spaces for people, and in the process, we design, we "make a plan," and deliberately go about using what we learn and come to know, to better the human condition. This book takes you on this journey of discovery.

Acknowledgments

The primary source of inspiration for this book comes from having conversations with many people who are passionate about design. These conversations have pushed my own thinking about the design process and creating dynamic interior spaces.

Words will never adequately express the gratitude I have for the support and inspiration I have gained from friends and colleagues worldwide. Over the past 25 years I have had the privilege to work with many students and colleagues developing and discussing interior design, art, architecture, and education, and it is from these perspectives that many of the ideas within this book flow.

I owe a great debt to all of the students, teachers, and colleagues that I have worked with, whether in theory classes, in design studios, in cafés, or in cyberspace chat rooms, locally and around the world. Students inspire me by what they accomplish every year in the courses that I teach, while the act of designing itself brings sheer joy, especially when projects are actualized and the client-designer relationship has been productive and positive. There have been hundreds of friends and colleagues over the years, from the worlds of industrial and interior design, the visual arts, architecture, education, and philosophy who have been sources of inspiration, conversation, and consultation and in these few pages, I can only name a few.

I wish to thank those whose voices have helped the emergence of this book. Among the students, colleagues, fellow researchers, designers, relatives, and friends with whom I have had the privilege of having conversations, there are those who have helped me to shape the ideas that emerge within this book. Many years ago I had several conversations with then student (and now friend) Hélène Caouette on how students see and use the design process. Since then I often chat with students after they have left school, to see how they feel about design, their profession, or the larger world of design and architecture. Our conversations fed my desire to express the ideas within this book.

I am grateful to all of the students that I have taught in the past 20-some-odd years who have contributed in some way to the evolution of this book. They so generously allowed me to access their ideas, explore their concepts of interior design, and so willingly assisted me in compiling many of the visual examples in this book.

I acknowledge the generosity of friend and colleague Michael Joannidis, with whom conversations about pushing the design process to its fullest are a constant source of inspiration. I thank him for his input, dialogue, and discussion throughout the development of the book. His professional insights in the world of design practice and design education were vital to the ideas that I wanted to develop in this book.

Namely, that the process of thinking as a designer is about theory and process as much as about the implementation of the design into the actual world we live in. His highest standards of how we design permeate his words and actions, and are a daily source of inspiration for students and teachers alike. Many of the contexts within this book are thanks to our ongoing exploration of the design process with students through the design studios we teach together.

I thank my colleagues in the Interior Design Program at the University of Montreal. I wish to thank Dr. Jacqueline Vischer, Richard Martel, Jean Therrien, and Dr. Rabah Bousbaci, as we have all together over these past eight years worked to develop the unique program we teach that pushes the limits of the design process and creates dynamic interior designers every year.

I gratefully acknowledge Kersti Leetmaa's work in reading and editing the manuscript in its earliest stages and offering constructive criticism. My heartfelt thanks to Sylvie Belanger, whose research work was thorough and whose enthusiasm is neverending.

The resources of the University of Montreal, Faculty of Environmental Design Library, and McGill University's library system have been particularly important in the compilation of material for this book, and I thank the staff for their support.

I am grateful to several friends and research colleagues with whom I could talk about the design process from other disciplines, notably AARRC, and to Susann, Lynn, Neomi, Pam, and Mary. They constantly challenged me to think and explore my ideas from their perspective.

I am also thankful to the clients who so graciously allowed their stories to be told, for future students and designers to learn about the complex contexts of designing interior space.

Sources of inspiration have been many and almost too numerous to mention. Although this book is not about design research, the writings of Ken Friedman, Klaus Krippendorff, Erik Stolterman, and Harold Nelson have been particularly useful and meaningful in helping the ideas explored become a little more inquiry based.

Some time ago I was a student at Ryerson University, where I met Drew Vasilevich. I am grateful to Drew, who many years later allowed me to pick his brain and become a source of inspiration for me. When I first began to teach, I used his words (embedded in my brain) to push my own students to be the best that they could be—to explore designing to its fullest, and to become, as he says, "great thinkers."

I am grateful to friend and colleague Giovanni De Paoli, Dean of the Faculty of Environmental Design (Aménagement), who encouraged me to pursue this book alongside my academic responsibilities. Also to my University of Montreal fellow colleagues, who, in one form or another, have pushed my intellectual thinking in the past eight years. In particular, I am grateful to Michel Gariepy and Irene Cinq-Mars, with whose encouragement I completed the Doctor of Philosophy at McGill University.

I am grateful to Joe Miranda, my development editor, with whom this work has evolved in a collaborative sense, and whose editing has only improved the quality of the writing. His input and encouragement have made the process of writing this book a pleasure.

Grateful acknowledgement to Olga Kontzias, executive editor; Jennifer Crane, senior development editor; and Andrew Fargnoli, Erin Fitzsimmons, and Noah Schwartzberg and the staff at Fairchild Books, whose unwavering support has been valuable and encouraging . . . and to Melanie Sankel, account manager, who gave me the courage to pursue this in the first place!

Taking Up Space

Chapter One

INTRODUCTION TO DESIGN PROCESSES

Objective

This first chapter introduces the fundamental concepts of design as understood by various designers from different disciplines. Why might this be interesting? Because designing interior space involves a multitude of approaches. We think about the design, put ideas down on paper, and create something that becomes "real." And yet each designer does this very differently.

In our world, we look around us and see many things that people have created. We see physical objects, such as buildings and their interiors, artwork, cars, and video games. We get up in the morning and brush our teeth, drink from a cup, and sit in a chair. We listen to songs, talk to our friends on the Internet or on the phone, and we move around the world in a heartbeat, both physically and virtually. We accomplish all of this using designed objects within a designed interior environment or outside in a designed world.

Design is a very broad activity that encompasses everything from designing objects like a fork or a sneaker to designing a computer system or a game, the interior of a building, or a search engine. Designers of all types from different backgrounds make objects, create programs, and design environments where human beings interact, take shelter, and live their daily lives. And yet, we experience and enjoy interior spaces every day and we respond to them emotionally.

WHAT IS DESIGN?

Design is all around us and, whether we realize it or not, it affects our life experiences on a daily basis. Designing interior space is part of the larger world of design. The space may be as small as a playroom for a child or as large as the corporate offices of an investment banker. It may be a shelter for a homeless person, or a home for a family, a restaurant, a mall, a hospital, a hotel, or any one of a myriad of inhabited spaces. Spaces come in different sizes, in different places, and in different contexts. What they all have in common is that they are occupied by a variety of people. It is the people—you and I—each with personal and social activities that make these spaces come alive. Without the different people we call users, interior space would not be very interesting, nor would it be of much use. (See Figure 1.1.)

These spaces also have in common the act of someone thinking about them and designing them using design processes. It is the interior designer or the architect who uses design processes to transfer ideas and concepts from a virtual and conceptual

I am sitting at a table in a marina. It is a beautiful place, on the shores of the Atlantic Ocean. The ocean is a deep blue, set against a bright and clear sky and the intense green of fir trees. The marina is built out of pine and beech timber, and the winds swirl around this sturdy building that sits by the edge of the sea. From the full-height glass doors and windows you can see the bay, the old brick cathedral, and the local town amid the boats and docks and walkways of the marina.

It is a beautiful and bright sunny day in July, and the building is empty and quiet except for my typing on the keyboard. Some passersby climb up to this post-and-beam open mezzanine to look around, interrupting my solitude. They begin an animated conversation with the manager who has accompanied them, and exclaim how beautiful it is. The manager says that one little girl he showed this place to called it her "house of dreams!" We acknowledge each other with a smile as they continue their chat with the manager about the interior space. Their conversation disappears as they leave. As I sit here, I realize how the space becomes still and quiet, and although the beauty still exists, it really rests in the interactions and comments that I have heard and the perceptions and experiences of

Sketch of the marina

the little girl and the others who have come into this space. It is the presence of the people, their conversations, their awe, and their reactions that create the beauty of their personal experiences. The interior comes alive in that moment. I think to myself, "that's what I want my students to understand as I help them experience the design process . . . that's what I want my clients to feel about spaces that I create for them?"

(July 25, 2002, at a marina on the East Coast of Canada)

entity into something tangible, built and experienced by people.

DEFINING DESIGN

We are interior designers, and we operate in the much larger framework called society and the world. The idea of *design* is understood by many different people to mean many different things. Many years ago, Kurt Hanks, Larry Belliston, and Dave Edwards (1977) wrote in their book *Design Yourself!*:

> Design is an elusive concept. Depending on who is defining it and the context in which it is used, design can mean many things.

> . . . Design is one of the most important factors in our lives, but often one of the most neglected. If a person does not design he is at least ruled by the designs of others. . . . Design is finding the optimum in a particular set of circumstances. (pp. 3–4)

As the authors point out, there are as many definitions and ideas about design as there are ways to be in the world. When we make a decision to do something, we might very well be designing.

The dictionary definition of design is multifaceted. The best place to begin with any definition is the dictionary. The *Oxford Dictionary Thesaurus* (2001) defines design thus:

design noun 1. plan or drawing produced to show the look and function or workings of something before it is built or made. 2. the art or action of producing such a plan or drawing. 3. underlying purpose or planning . . . 4. a decorative pattern. verb 1. conceive and produce a design for. 2. plan or intend for a purpose. (p. 329)

This same dictionary also provides synonyms for design as follows:

design noun 1. a design for the office plan, blueprint, drawing, sketch, outline, map, plot, diagram, draft, representation, scheme, model . . . intention, aim, purpose, plan, intent, objective, object, goal, end, target, hope, desire, wish, dream, aspiration, ambition. (p. 329)

As we can see from these definitions, design is the act of making a drawing to express or represent an idea, but it is also an intentional act done by someone to produce something. The word *design* also implies desire, creation, purpose, dreams, ambition, objectives, and many other goals we aspire to in our society and in our lives.

Design is a general term that describes what we do specifically as interior designers. We practice interior design, and this means that we intentionally design interior environments. Design also implies the notion of "fit." We design things to fit a purpose, to respond to a situation, to solve a problem. Designing is a fundamental aspect of human nature. Everything we create or make is designed to some extent or another.

Figure 1.1 • Student interior concept for a retail space

Talk of the Town Food Court, Charlottetown, PEI, Canada

This first case study is one we will see at different points in the book. This is a food court design, found within a larger interior commercial shopping center complex that is housed in a downtown business in an historic city. Here we see an example of how a design concept is first generated through conversation with a client and sketches of an idea in its earliest conceptual stages in Figure A. Then we see how the final concept appears in built form in Figure B.

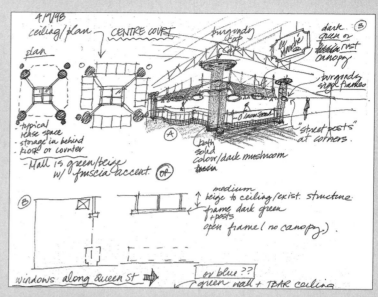

Figure A • Food court concept, Charlottetown, PEI

Figure B • Final design concept for food court, 2006

THE ACT OF DESIGNING

Even though some things that we see in our world might not be formally designed, design is all around us, whether in other cultures, in nature, or in our experiences of daily life. We capitalize on our own sense of design when we are inspired by the world around us.

Any time we create an object, design an interior, or raise a building, we are designing. Harold Nelson and Eric Stolterman (2003) examine this in their seminal book, *The Design Way*:

Design is . . . the ability to imagine that-which-does-not-yet-exist, to make it appear in concrete form as a new, purposeful addition to the real world . . . things that really count, and are highly valued, come from design, when not directly from nature. (p. 10)

When we speak of design, we consider it here as both an art and a science.

Design can be many things:

- Design is artistic: We use hand-drawn and computer-aided means to artistically show our ideas.
- Design is creative: We create a design that shows someone how an interior space might be used.
- Design is functional: We lay out spaces and put things into three dimensions to see what is possible, and to help people live and work better.
- Design is practical: We create designs to satisfy specific needs.
- Design is thinking about new possibilities: We create new ways to help people experience interior space.

However, we often mistake design for art or for creative innovation. Although we hope to innovate and create something new, there are often parameters that must be respected. David Pye (1978) suggests that the distinction between art and design is one of the limits imposed:

The thing which sharply distinguishes useful design from such arts as painting and sculpture is that the practitioner of design has limits set

upon his freedom of choice. A painter can choose any imaginable shape. A designer cannot. If the designer is designing a bread knife it must have a cutting edge and a handle. . . . These are the limitations that arise, as anyone can tell, from the "function" of the thing being designed. (p. 11)

We are paid, as interior designers, to perform a service: to design an interior space, to respond to certain needs, functional requirements, and desired ambiances, as well as to conform to certain budgets.

Design Issues and Problems

When we create designs for interior spaces, we are hired to improve an interior environment, look at a design issue, or solve an interior design problem. In the world of architecture and design, interior designers become part of a team to build an interior, whether it is to furnish a home, renovate a hotel lobby, or build new, innovative environments for recreation, work, or play.

Design is misunderstood in popular culture. People think that design happens quickly and that if anything is designed, it must be done perfectly, without error or consequence. However, design takes time and requires understanding of the different aspects of the processes that are used to complete it thoroughly and well. You evaluate the situation, understand the context, and respond using your design skills.

Designing interior space means understanding people and how they live. It is a complex process, and designers need to understand human nature and the different things that affect people in their living and working environments. Design issues arise when we are given a problem or confronted with something that doesn't work, could be made better, or needs a design-thinking process.

For example, I might be an 85-year-old woman with arthritis, still living in my home where I have lived for the past 45 years. When I was younger, the house suited me, but as I age, my arthritic hands may not be able to turn the round knob on my bathroom door.

An interior designer might think about:

- how I move my hands and what ergonomic issues are present
- what support I need to be able to lean on the door to open it.
- the direction of the swing of the door
- what I need to see well (lighting), how to avoid falling (contrast in materials and large surface finishes), and how to get safely from the hall to the bathroom (movement and circulation)
- the form and material of the handle

An industrial designer might think about:

- the grip of the handle and the issues related to the ergonomic function of the hand at 85 years of age
- the form of the handle as responding to hand function
- the movement of the handle
- the material

The architect might consider:

- the form and direction of the handle
- the material of the handle
- the direction of the swing of the door
- the ability to safely exit from the home if there is a fire

Each one considers the issues surrounding the 85-year-old woman and the door handle, but from their specific perspective, or stance.

Simple and Complex Design Issues

This is a relatively simple example. We design a lever door handle to solve this particular problem. The scale is small and intimate, and the result not only gives the woman the functional ability to enter a space but the ability to move around independently. Whereas the industrial designer might design the handle, the interior designer thinks about the best handle for the user, and the architect considers these issues and the user's ability to exit from the building.

A more complicated design issue might indirectly involve global warming. At the outset of a project we can examine what is already in the space and through our choices, we can make a difference. Even if our client wants everything to be new, we can recycle

aspects of the existing interior space to recoup materials and avoid waste.

Design Problems

When we design interior spaces, we do so essentially to solve problems; however, this is not always evident. We may be asked to design a space for a client to make more money, to help workers be more productive, or to help people organize their living space for a particular purpose. Sometimes these problems might seem insurmountable, and sometimes they are simply situations requiring our assistance. Therefore, although we often refer to designing as problem solving, it is also many other things. When we are asked to design interior spaces, we might be asked to:

- create an interior space for a particular purpose
- work on a new way to accommodate activities in a space
- create something new (which has never existed before), or something innovative
- help solve a problem a new way (perhaps a space was poorly designed and we are asked to use our skills to fix the problem)
- develop a different way to put spaces together or look at how people should use a space differently
- understand and see the designed space in a new, innovative, or different way

There are many design problems, design situations, and design solutions. In this book we cannot study them all. But we can identify what they are, learn to design for a better interior environment, and develop the thinking and doing skills to make this happen.

Design Situations

A design situation might be a problem to be solved, a condition that needs a new eye, a creative issue that needs new insights, or something that needs a fresh application of design thinking. In his seminal book, *By Design*, Ralph Caplan wrote in 1982:

> Design at its best is a process of making things right. That is, the designer, at his best, or hers, makes things that work. But often things do not work. And making things right is not just a gene-

rative but a corrective process—a way of righting things, of straightening them out. (p. 11)

As Caplan suggests, we design to improve objects, situations, and, in the case of interior design, the quality and comfort of human-occupied interior space. But quite often, whereas we may have the best intentions, our designs do not work. Why?

Generally it is because design methods alone will not help you to solve a problem. Rather, it is knowing what questions to ask, what to search for, and what to think about that will help you understand how to solve the problem at hand. This means that you must understand:

- the constraints or issues
- the problem and its parameters
- the client and the activities of the space
- the goals of the user/client/stakeholder
- the desires and needs of the occupants
- the nature of the space
- the intention for the space and its users

This requires thinking about the design using the design process.

DESIGN PROCESSES

Designing interior space means understanding and using different design processes. Different contexts should be considered when designing an interior space. Interior designers might do the following:

- We may speak to the people who live in the space; we may talk to the clients who pay for the space to be built.
- We look at the space itself: What are the characteristics, what are the window or door openings, which way does the interior face relative to the sun?
- We look at the characteristics of the space: What are the existing elements and parts that we need to keep, discard, or consider?
- We look at the contexts of the project: What is the budget, and what are the needs of the people who will use the space?

> **BUILDING BLOCK** • *As you begin to try the design process, think about what you are doing and why. Why do we need the design process, one that is used by many different designers in many different areas, as compared to an architect, for instance? All designers, be they architects, planners, or interior designers, use logic, intuition, problem-solving skills, and creative skills to solve design problems and create spaces that suit various human situations in the built environment.*

- We look at the wants and desires of the people who will occupy the space: How will they work or live? What do they need to do? Who will they interact with? What do they like and dislike? What do they want and need to be comfortable, happy, and productive in this space?
- What religious or cultural issues might be salient in the project?
- What sensitivities do people have to color, light, or other aspects of the project?
- How much time will they spend in the space?
- What are the security and safety issues?
- What are the specific storage or equipment needs?
- What image do they want to project to the outside world? Do they interact with others in society? If so, how?

Although simple, these questions are very broad based. But they must be addressed, and you will see as we move along in the book that the questions change and become more complicated, depending on the design project.

What We Do and How We Do It

What we do is implement the design process steps through research and analysis, the design program we create, and the built project we complete. The different design activities are situated within the larger framework of both the built environment and society. Our role as interior designers is to create a functional and aesthetically pleasing space that is stimulating, inviting, and pushes ideas about how our built environment might be conceived in a sustainable world. The emphasis is on who we are and what we do in the larger society, not from a professional practice perspective but as an engaged citizen of the world. We not only design for the little girl and her house of dreams at the marina, we also design for corporate executives, Alzheimer's patients, you, and me.

Design Thinking

To be able to visualize, design, and create interior spaces, you must understand what you are doing and for what purpose. You need to ask questions, in both your professional and personal lives. You need to examine the world through open eyes and see things as they are. Design thinking encompasses ways of doing and seeing as well as ways of understanding the world around us, both as sources of inspiration and critically understanding what works and what does not.

There are as many ways to understand designing as there are ways to design. The key is to develop the thinking tools that will enable you to sift through all the choices and make the right decisions. This book will not give you a list of how-to's; rather, it will show you diverse ways of tackling issues in interior design, and how to best choose the method, process, or concept for the project at hand.

You will also read about the world of design in a larger sense. Design thinking requires understanding the complexity inherent in interior design problems, both in the nature of the designed interior space and how the human aspect affects it.

About Thinking in General

Before we can design an interior, we need to think about the processes involved and the ways we might go about designing the project. Learning to think may require different perspectives, depending on what you want to accomplish. You may need to design a small space for a client, but cannot see how you can fit in everything that they want. Or you may have an open-ended client list of activities and requirements, and no understanding of how these can all be accommodated. Each problem or issue requires you to think.

There are productive ways to think depending on the problem at hand, and we apply different thinking skills to each issue or problem. In the book *Teach Yourself to Think*, Edward De Bono (1996) suggests that there are five basic thinking processes. He lists them as follows:

1. Broad/Specific
2. Projection
3. Attention/directing
4. Recognition
5. Movement

Each way of thinking will take you in a different direction, depending upon your goal. For example, we can consider the client who comes to us and asks us to design a store for selling widgets. We ask the following questions, and each one leads us deliberately to think in a different way.

1. Broad: What type of store do you want, and how do you want to sell the widgets? What type of feeling do you want to project to prospective widget buyers?
   Specific: I will design the store to fit ten widgets so I can sell at least five at a time. (See Figure 1.2.)
2. Projection: What would happen if we filled the space with widgets from wall to ceiling, or projected them from an LED screen onto the floors and walls? (See Figure 1.3.)
3. Attention/directing: What is a widget? How is it used? How much will it sell for? (See Figure 1.4.)
4. Recognition and fit: Would this widget be best sold if it is displayed on the wall using a projected light? Can we fit ten widgets on the wall in a row,

Figure 1.2 • Sketch elevation of a storefront design

Figure 1.3 • Photoshop sketch of a widget store concept

and would that assist the salesperson? (See Figure 1.4.)

5. Movement and alternatives: Can we have some widgets on the wall and some on the counter, to encourage impulse buying? Or alternatively, can we drop some widgets from the ceiling and have them above the sales counter so people can see how they work?

And this final sketch is actually the one that began the concept in the first place. We have an idea, a possibility, and this comes directly from two designers speaking to each other, exploring the possibilities of a widget/gadget store design. (See Figure 1.6.)

We began by talking about widgets, and then we evolved to gadgets. The concept evolves from one idea to the next, each time changing both our conception of it and how we see it in our minds, and in the actual space where it occurs. Note that each way of thinking brings a different way to see the problem. De Bono suggests that these ways can overlap. Indeed, when we design, we might use some or all of these different ways of thinking, one at a time, some of the time, or all at once. Each thinking process translates

Figure 1.4 • Detail view of display areas for a widget

into a sketch on paper or in your computer. When we think as designers, we put down our thoughts in sketch form. We need sketching as part of our thinking process because we need a way to express the thoughts that we have in our head.

Rudolf Arnheim talks about the function and nature of sketching as a means to visualize concepts in the design process (in Margolin & Buchanan, 2000):

> The function and nature of sketches is inseparable from that of the design it serves. The creative

process of designing, being an activity of the mind, cannot be directly observed. The sketches, done for the eyes and directed by them, make some of the design plans visible. They not only supply the designer with tangible images of what his or her mind is trying out in the dimness of its own freedom, but they also permit the observer or theorist to catch a few stop-motion glimpses of the flow of creation. (p. 74)

As you can see from the widget/gadget example, we can come up with different ways to see an issue,

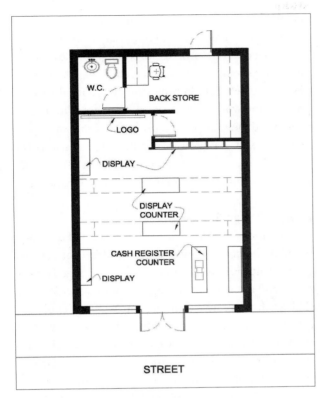

Figure 1.5 • Plan sketch of the widget store design.

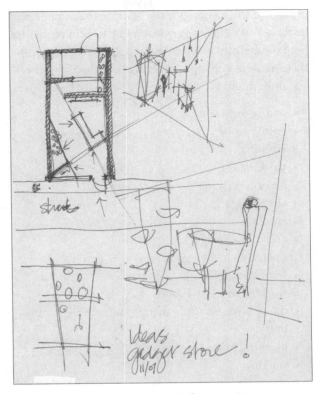

Figure 1.6 • Series of small sketches of movement

understand a problem, or apply design thinking. We do so with our mind thinking about it and our hand or computer sketching it out. We see the possibilities and express them through line, sketch, and form.

Why is this type of thinking important? Early on in your design thinking, you want to open your mind to different possibilities. We have a "flow of creation," as Arnheim suggests, and we also need to try out our ideas. As De Bono (1996) states, "The value of seeking further alternatives is obvious. The first way is not necessarily the best way. A range of alternatives allows us to compare and assess them and choose the best" (p. 41).

The increased complexity of today's world requires us to apply different methods of thinking in different situations. We live in a post-industrial society, meaning that we no longer go to school solely to learn a skill. Rather, we learn to think, with the aim of using this thinking to design appropriately and creatively in various life situations.

In his book *Think!,* Michael LeGault (2006) talks about the importance of this shift in learning: "The spoils of this post-industrial world will not go to the people, companies, and nations winging it and relying on snap judgments and gut feelings, but the ones sweating the details and doing the best critical and creative thinking" (p. 73).

Design processes are exactly this: ways of critical and creative thinking that can change the situations we find ourselves in. It means developing the knowledge and thinking skills necessary to adapt interior spaces to specific and changing situations.

INTERIOR DESIGN IN TODAY'S COMPLEX SOCIETY

Interior design happens when designers create interior space for constantly changing needs and purposes. The interior environment can be compared to a theatre stage that becomes the backdrop for a certain set of activities. A stage is constantly changing to suit the scene; so is the interior space, in most instances. We "fit" the environment around particular human activities in a particular point in time, and these activities change and evolve constantly. These activities might include:

- eating together
- eating alone
- sleeping
- working
- entertaining
- shopping
- relaxing
- creating a design
- operating in a surgical unit
- watching a play
- working in a hotel room
- doing business while flying from one city to another
- listening to music
- walking

These activities might be done:

- alone
- in a group
- in real time in a physical space
- in virtual space
- in movement

Case Study 1.2 helps us understand these ideas.

Phases of Design Work

As we see from the children's toy store case study, the design process evolves from the concept to the built environment. Generally, an interior designer proceeds by setting up specific phases of the work to give a system or logic to the design process. Designers usually begin by interviewing the client to determine their project ideas and get a sense of what the client wants to do. They investigate all the parameters of the problem, including interviewing users, studying the existing space and building constraints, and investigating particular aspects of the problem at hand.

After the research is done, the designer establishes needs and develops design criteria to use as

guidelines for the design. The project is designed, priced for construction, and built to become reality. The project (design process "product") is followed diligently through these stages and then evaluated post-construction to improve the design for the next project. The work is always done in phases, but these may vary depending on the project and the way a particular interior designer works. But all professionally designed projects are planned in stages or phases. We will look at this concept in more detail in Chapter 2.

Interior Design Stance

If we consider interior design and the role of design in today's society, we must also consider what constitutes an interior design stance. Interior design is both an art and a science, meaning we combine artistic skills such as creative thinking and aesthetic choices, with scientific components such as research and analysis of the problem. Two concepts are specific to an interior design stance: the way we see the interior space and project, and the notion of design as a service aimed at human needs and desires.

Design, as we have seen, has existed for thousands of years, whereas interior design, as it is practiced in today's society, has evolved from a modern amalgamation of the influences of art, architecture, and many different sciences. Mary Knackstadt (1995) suggests that:

> Interior design may have started as a child of the decorative arts and architecture, but that was over a hundred years ago, and many sciences have contributed to the body of knowledge. . . . Interior design is a service industry, and practicing interior designers are trained observers, just like doctors, sociologists, and other scientists. Behavioral psychologists make recommendations based on their observations; so do interior designers. Art creates a mood; so do theatrical set design and interior design. (p. 73)

When we design interiors, we are asked to do so by an individual, a business, an institution, or a family. We are given a set of needs and wants, constraints or contexts. These different contexts set the limits on

Figure A • Store interior concept

A Children's Toy Store Concept

In this concept we explore the ways that we might experience the future space for a retail store. The concept is for a children's toy store, organized in a meandering layout that captures the attention of children and parents alike. (See Figures A and B.)

Figure B • Store interior concept

what we can (or cannot) do as interior designers. We have a specific stance that is guided by this idea of service, and we provide services related to our particular stance.

THE ROLE OF THE DESIGNER

Design is done by people for people. As we have seen in the previous discussions, we design as a service for people in a dynamic relationship. The space we design is the envelope within which people live, work, or play; we influence that space through our design thinking. We will look at this concept in terms of who we are, what we do as interior designers, and what our role is in both the built environment and within society.

Design is a concept that has existed since the dawn of mankind. The role of the designer throughout history has been to effect change using skills and know-how coupled with a bit of creative thinking. This creative thinking centers on a special combination of imagining and changing something virtual (an idea in one's head) into a real, tangible product. In *The Design Way*, Nelson and Stolterman (2003) unfold a philosophy centered on this concept of design existing all around us. They state:

> Humans did not discover fire—they designed it. The wheel was not something our ancestors merely stumbled over in a stroke of good luck; it, too, was designed. . . . Design is the ability to imagine *that-which-does-not-yet-exist*, to make it appear in concrete form as a new, purposeful addition to the real world. (p. 9)

Design is all around us, both in nature and in the things we have and use every day. Our homes, our possessions, and the way we get around every day, whether in shoes or with bicycles or cars—all of these things were designed.

To use an example of how a professional sees design, I will tell you about Michael Joannidis, who looks at interior design as something that exists all around us and yet that we create. He sees design as a universal concept and that people are designing all the time. An international interior designer who has

traveled the world, Michael considers this important aspect of design as a universal phenomenon. He suggests that design comes from ideas, and that these are neither necessarily unique nor original. He suggests that design is all around us, and that design ideas are often inspired by the everyday things that we see. Figure 1.7 shows an example of the inspiration he uses from his trips abroad.

The merchant setting up his wares in the marketplace is as much a designer in that he deliberately plans how he will present his goods for sale. Through the creative means available to him, the merchant designs a pleasing concept that he feels will generate business.

As we saw earlier in this chapter, to design is to make a deliberate plan to create. This deliberate plan comes with ideas, processes, needs, concepts, and design programs, all created by the designer. There are many ways to design something, and many choices to be made. The designer must make these choices systematically and deliberately, and hone his creative skills to integrate the various contexts of a given project.

The *Oxford Thesaurus Dictionary* also defines designer as follows: *designer* noun 1. a person who design things. The thesaurus suggests several synonyms: *designer* noun 1. *a designer of farmhouses* creator, planner, deviser, inventor, originator, maker, architect, builder. So by definition, the interior designer creates, plans, and devises alternative or new ways of living, working, or playing within interior spaces.

Interior designers create interior spaces to house the social and personal activities of people from different walks of life, from different backgrounds and cultures, and with different and specific needs. We design for all stages of life, from birth to death, each demanding a unique way of seeing and negotiating interior spaces. We help people to realize their needs using design processes.

The Nature of the Design Process as Two Experiences

The interior design experience occurs when the designer uses design processes to create spatial

Figure 1.7 • Design inspiration

experiences. There are two types of experiences going on when we design. The first is the personal and creative act of design. The second experience is the social aspect of design existence, when the design is put out into the real world where people will use and live with it, judge it, and respond to it.

We create a design in our heads, conceptualizing something from nothing in the most personal sense, but using technical and artistic know-how. We design from inside ourselves. When conceived, our designs are built and become applied into society. They become real places where real people live and work. The designs are made to suit what people need. In this way, interior design is a service we provide to create interior environments for people for their personal or social use.

The Interior Designer as Artist and Problem Solver

Designers use artistic skills to create interior spaces for a particular use or function. Interior designers also design as a service to a client. We can design interior spaces for altruistic purposes or for ourselves, but more often we design for a client who has hired us. A certain responsibility comes with this role. In the seminal book *The Nature and Aesthetics of Design*, David Pye (1978) discusses the responsibility of the designer, and challenges the commonly held belief that the designer creates designs either for beauty or to solve a problem, but not both. Many people believe that designers are artists, and therefore can do what they want. Others believe that the designer must always solve a problem, precluding the creative process. Pye challenges these ideas when he writes about the role of the designer:

> The modern designer is seldom paid to be an artist. He is paid to solve a problem to help make somebody a profit. . . .
>
> Design is neither a problem-solving activity nor an art. It is both. . . . Every good designer is made up of both . . . nor does he think of art as God and problem-solving as Mammon, but thinks of the two as inseparable parts of one whole, like the mind and body of man, each dependent upon the other and each affecting the other. (pp. 93–95)

The Interior Designer's Role within the Built Environment Disciplines

Being an interior designer is not the same as being an architect, an electrical engineer, or an artist. Although interior designers do design within buildings as architects do, the scale and level of human interest is different. Architects are concerned with the building and how it fits into a larger urban context. They are also concerned with the ways that people move toward the interior space and are engaged by it. Industrial designers are concerned with the object and its relationship to the human user within this built environment. They are concerned with the systems and components that constitute the object and its life from process to production.

Interior designers are concerned with the human/object/space relationship as this relates to interiors, and whether within buildings, within larger spaces in buildings, or outside. Interior designers worry about the details of the space, the fit of the space, and its contexts with people and how to integrate the space and the objects in it with their more "intimate" needs. Interior designers have a more specific concern for the more small-scale, intimate needs, and how the design proposed suits these needs.

The Relationship with Architecture, Art, and the Social Sciences

The interior designer is a player within the built environment. Our role is often misunderstood, and yet when it comes to designing spaces, it is a vital one. We understand what people need, and consider the human, intimate aspects of spaces, whether interior or exterior. These understandings are based on interior-design-specific knowledge that we acquire, and knowledge found in other disciplines such as architecture, industrial design, psychology, sociology, and various other disciplines. In Figure 1.8, we see the role of the architect and the interior designer, and how these might unfold with regards to the building.

While we do not always deal with architects, we do always deal with those people who control the use of the building. For example, in the home it would be the client or architect; in an exhibition design it would be the conference center owner. In other buildings it is a series of stakeholders, including architects, building administrators or landlords, and tenants. We will explore these different stakeholders in more detail in subsequent chapters.

The Interior Designer as Team Player

Because we do not design alone and are always working with clients and various stakeholders in a project, we are by necessity team players. We design for a client, and work with architects and engineers to determine the structural, mechanical, or building aspects of the space. We deal with contractors or project managers to build the interior, and we work with cabinetmakers and suppliers to develop the

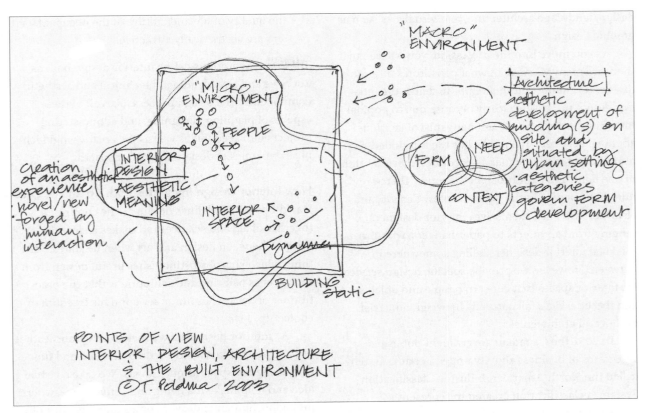

Figure 1.8 • Sketch of relationship of interior design to the built environment

details, and select and install finishes and fitments. We design, supervise, create, build, and coordinate. Designing means learning how to juggle many concepts at once. As a novice designer you need to learn critical thinking skills for problem solving as well as artistic creativity and know-how. These skills are contradictory yet complementary in nature. Roberto Rengel (2003) notes differences between interior design and other allied professions, positioning interior design in this context:

> Engineers use their knowledge to provide practical and efficient solutions based on the physical laws of nature. Builders use their knowledge to construct projects that are structurally sound and well crafted. The dominant trait of designers is their knowledge and ability to create designs that touch the human heart in ways that neither the engineer's design nor the builder's construction can. (p. 4)

Interior designers work with many different stakeholders, both designers and clients alike. As team players, each time we embark on a design project, we work together to help develop the project from concept to reality. We will examine the different types of roles and stakeholder responsibilities later on. Let's examine the role of the interior designer in a little more detail first.

Defining What Interior Designers Do Today

Over the past 45 years, interior design has evolved into a profession in its own right, and this evolution has also forged an education and research knowledge base in the United States and overseas. But interior design remains a relatively young profession, when compared with law or architecture. Interior design is a profession that forms part of the built environment, and as such, is part of a larger group of disciplines, including architecture, industrial design, urban design, landscape architecture, and visual arts such as graphic design.

As you move into the profession, you will see that there are many versions of what constitutes interior design. It is important to attempt to define the interior design profession clearly because due to popular media and culture, there are many misconceptions about what we do. The public has the misguided notion of interior designer as decorator, fabric swatch in one hand and paintbrush in the other. There are numerous people in the United States, Canada, and elsewhere who call themselves interior designers, ranging from architects to paper hangers, with professional interior designers falling somewhere in between. However, we provide specific design services for interior spaces that concern people and objects, and these services fall naturally between industrial design and architecture.

In 2001 the Canadian government published categories of business activity under a coding system called the North American Industry Classification System, a classification created to represent professions in the United States and Canada under the North American Free Trade Agreement. The definition of interior design services within this document reads as follows:

> Interior design services . . . establishments primarily engaged in planning, designing and administering projects in interior spaces to meet the physical and aesthetic needs of people, taking into consideration building codes, health and safety regulations, traffic patterns and floor planning, mechanical and electrical needs, and interior fittings and furniture. (p. 7)

This is a clear if somewhat pragmatic definition. The current North American National Council for Interior Design Qualification (NCIDQ) definition (2007) is a formal description of the interior design profession. It reads as follows:

> Interior design is a multifaceted profession in which creative and technical solutions are applied within a structure to achieve a built interior environment. These solutions are functional, enhance

the quality of life and culture of the occupants, and are aesthetically attractive.

These two definitions define interior design both as a service and as a blending of technical and aesthetic components. The design process takes all of these aspects of planning, designing, and administering projects into account, as well as the creative and technical dynamics of designing interior spaces.

How Interior Design Integrates Both Art and Science

David Pye (1978) defines design as the coming together of art and science, and makes a clear distinction between design and art when he states, "The thing which sharply distinguishes useful design from such arts as painting and sculpture is that the practitioner of design has limits set upon his freedom of choice" (p. 11).

As interior designers, we seek to integrate aesthetics and artistic know-how with both need and function, using the space as our canvas. We take a virtual idea and help make it a living and active space, where intangible human endeavor comes together with physical lived experience. We use what we learn, what we know, and what we have been exposed to as the basis from which to solve complex interior problems (Pye, 1978; Rengel, 2003). Interior design is a complex, multidimensional discipline situated in a context of time, space, and dimension. It is driven by contemporary ways of living and constant change, where function and beauty intersect with broad and complex issues transcending aesthetics or function alone.

Student Understanding of the Role of the Interior Designer

Recently I explored this idea of interior design and intention with students by asking them to examine what it means to be an interior designer in today's society. The students were aware of the complexities inherent in being an interior designer, as they understood the different aspects of the interior design profession. I share their views with you to help you to understand how you can also think about the profession and the role of the interior designer in terms of the design process.

The schematics shown in Figure 1.9 represent their views of interior design, based on articles and readings they were asked to do and discussions that were conducted in class.

As you can see, the responses were varied, but all point to the multifaceted aspects of how the interior designer combines many different components, and at the heart of this is the design process.

Interior Design as Problem Solving

Interior design is about solving problems. There are many parameters to a particular design problem, and they are constantly changing. In my own professional practice I design spaces that vary in size, use, and scope. Each design problem is unique, and the decisions that I make with a client always require the establishment of a new relationship. For example, in Case Study 1.3 we look at designing a trade show booth.

The trade show booth is another example of a design problem. As design professionals, we encounter many different types of problems, each with a different set of parameters and issues. This client has one view; a residential or commercial client would have quite another. We all have personal interpretations of what interior space is and what constitutes a complete interior. It is up to the interior designer to engage the various stakeholders in a common dialogue to achieve the desired goals.

I suggest that interior designers are artists and sculptors of space for the use and enjoyment of everyday life and its myriad functions. Interior design and its processes are an interactive and engaged journey between the designer and the user. These interactions occur on an intimate and very personal level, and gain access to both the public and private lives of people when we design the spaces where they live, work, and play. This relationship is built on the understanding of a complex range of factors that influence—and are influenced by—culture, need, function, use, activity, race, history, relationship, aesthetic, form, psychology, philosophy, and the interrelationships between all of these as processes. Thus space may be seen as personal, psychological, social, or contextual. It is usually understood in this context as either inside, interior space, or intangi-

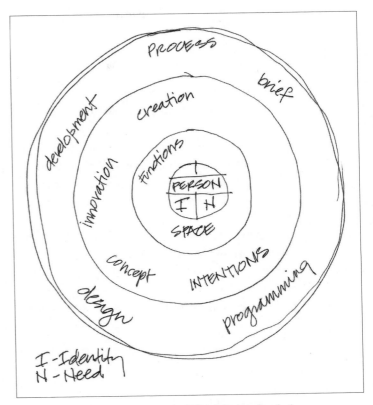

Figure 1.9 • Student ideas about the role of the interior designer

ble space (Tomas, 1964; Grosz, 1993; Ainley, 1998; Bilda & Dimirkan, 2002). Critical interior designers design space with a regard for, and awareness of, many underlying factors and values that shape human endeavour. Finally, we weave all of these factors around the safety and security of the designed and built environment, meeting practical requirements such as building safety codes and regulations.

DESIGN THINKING AS INQUIRY

As you progress in this book, you will at first study design problems and issues on a smaller scale or with a simpler approach. Why inquiry? Because:

- we ask questions to solve problems.
- we identify issues surrounding the particular problem at hand.
- we research questions and issues to understand the reasons and contexts of the design issue at hand.

Designing Trade Shows

The interior designer tells the story:

Creating an exhibition booth design is like organizing and putting a lot of puzzle pieces together. . . . I visualize what the different components will be, who is going to be on the site, and try to put them together like puzzle pieces. I have to be able to visualize both the design and the detail as I create the concept.

I get an idea from my client of what feeling he wants to express, and then I generate sketches and concepts through visualization of the words, phrases, and images he has given me. Inspirations include the company image and logo, the desired corporate theme, and the client's own personal idea for the booth. I also work closely with the trade show publicist to create a cohesive design that integrates the design with the promotional campaign for the show.

I then sit down with all of these cues and explore the design concept possibilities in detail, creating plan views, three-dimensional visualization sketches, and color and material choices that reflect the concept I am trying to express. My ideas are expressed in sketches that show how the booth will look in three dimensions, and the plans and elevations for the space that the booth will occupy. All must remain within the strict rules of the particular conference center. Strategies are proposed to the client in terms of furniture acquisition, construction logistics of the

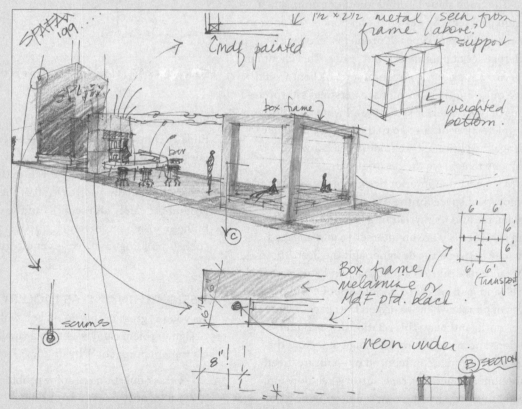

Figure A • Sketch of exhibition space, 1999

Figure B • Built exhibition space, Salt Lake City, USA, 1999

various booth components, and the proposed budget. The exterior and immediate surroundings of the booth are also considered, as well as the ceiling of the conference center, the surrounding exhibits, and the effects of the booth as a mode of attracting the public from a distance. The design concept is then transformed into final design plans and drawings, which explain the different components in detail. I include a three-dimensional walk-through and show the client all of the furnishing components, color, and material suggestions as well as a rendered view. The client approves the design, at which point working drawings are produced, including details of the components, specifications, and sources. Consultants and/or tradespeople get involved, including engineers and architects, and in this case conference trades and organizers as well as the signage and graphics companies. I work on detailed budget or costing with potential contractors. This includes getting competitive bids from the contractors, organizing the booth installation on site, and generating AutoCAD drawings of the booth construction details. I ran this memo by my client and this was how he responded:

. . . To me, the booth is all about environmental branding. You're taking the brand attributes of our firm—and you express them in built form. You could say that that is the reason we've hired a professional interior designer (versus an expo designer or a contractor, or doing it ourselves)—a professional designer works on so many levels and across all disciplines (incorporating architecture, graphics, interiors, decorating, etc.) . . . you get to know what the client is trying to achieve (or what message they're trying to convey) and you express it with materials, textures, colors, and form. (E-mail conversation August 14, 2002, courtesy R. Girard)

• we ask questions to understand the impact of choices we make and the impact of our designs on people.

As you progress chapter by chapter, the issues become a little more challenging and the techniques become more complex. Design is a form of inquiry because we ask questions in order to provide solutions to various problems. We do this for several reasons. Harold Nelson and Eric Stolterman (2003) provide us with some thoughts about this concept as it relates to the effect of design on society. Not only do we want to solve problems, design activities aim to serve humanity. However, as they state:

> Design activities can do and have done great service to humanity. But design has done great harm as well. . . . We cannot know what the unintended consequences of a design will be, and we cannot know, ahead of time, the full . . . effects of a design implementation. (p. 10)

Nelson and Stolterman suggest various motives for designing. Designs can be created to:

survive

improve

develop

thrive

evolve

serve others

make something of lasting quality

create something of real consequence

participate in the never-ending genesis

(Nelson & Stolterman, p. 12)

To achieve some or all of these goals, interior designers must be able to think functionally and creatively, practically and aesthetically. Interior designers must also learn how to ask the right kinds of questions. This is fundamentally inquiry, as we question what we see and seek to design better solutions.

On another level, John Zeisel (2006) considers how design as inquiry is complex due to the very nature of design itself. In his seminal book, *Inquiry By Design*, he suggests that:

> Design is difficult to describe because it includes so many intangible elements such as intuition, imagination and creativity—which are also essential to research. . . .
>
> Physical design inventively mixes together ideas, drawings, information, and many other ingredients to create something where nothing was before. Design can also be seen as an ordered process in which specific activities are loosely organized to make decisions about changing the physical world to achieve identifiable goals. (pp. 19–21)

There are numerous aspects to design thinking as inquiry, much too broad for the scope of this book. Zeisel (2006), Nelson and Stolterman (2003), Caplan (1982), and many others explore the mystery that is designing. In this book we will refer to inquiry as a design process now and then, and we consider inquiry as "investigating" the issues, contexts, and problems that compel or inspire us to design interiors in the first place. As we move through the various components of the design process, you will see how inquiry becomes a fundamental component of designing a space appropriately. We will return to this concept of inquiry in Chapter 10.

Think about design as a means of discovering answers to questions such as:

• What is the best way to think about this problem?
• How can I create something interesting and useful for my client?
• How can I design an interior environment that suits my client and gives the user something new, different, and useful in ways that they could not imagine?
• How can I create that special environment where people can flourish and be at their best?

ABOUT CONVERSATION, DIALOGUE, AND THE DESIGN PROCESS

As a design student, you have probably noticed that we are always talking about design, interior design, and the design process to fellow students, to teachers, and with people. Conversation, dialogue, and the verbal "working through" of ideas about designing are also fundamental to any design process. Throughout this book, we will consider many visual tools as a primary means to communicate our ideas. However, another important component of the design process is the verbal communication and dialogue that we have with the various people involved in the design project. The conversations that we have with potential users of the space, the dialogue we engage in with clients, teachers, or fellow students, all impact on how we understand the design issues and problems we are faced with.

The importance of these conversations and dialogues are not always obvious during the design process. When we design, we do not do it alone. We are always involved at some point with other people. As we suggested earlier on, interior design is a service-oriented profession. We meet with clients, talk to users of the spaces, and discuss our design ideas with our teachers. We are often part of a larger team of designers, architects, specialists, and consultants who are all stakeholders in the project. When we interact with people, we communicate our ideas. We have several ways of doing this, such as:

- conversations/dialogue
- design sketches (virtual or real)
- design drawings (plans, three-dimensional representations of the space)
- artful and visual tools (concept boards, material boards, concept sketches)
- models and actual representations

This is the initial step of the design process, and occurs before any other aspects are considered. The interior designer cannot even begin to conceive of a design without talking to the stakeholders and asking questions. These questions may include the following:

- What is the purpose of the design?
- What is the budget?
- What is the intended reason (goals, use) of the design?
- What feeling do you want to create?
- What image are you intending to convey?
- Who is your clientele?

Each question generates reflections on the part of the designer. And these are not exhaustive by any means. Each project demands a new series of questions.

Let's consider some more case studies here, using student projects. Each example is followed by a sketch of how a student might have considered these questions.

In the next case, we ask questions about designing for the homeless.

We are always designing for someone and have to understand their various needs and activities as well as how they perceive what they need. We need to dialogue with the people for whom we will design. We must also understand the design problems related to a project and become aware of our own prejudices in the process, and be responsive through our creative ideas.

Case studies 1.4 and 1.5 are two very different types of examples of needs for specific users. Let's now look at the design process in more detail in Chapter 2, and explore further how we might go about answering these needs.

A Room for a Child

Questions that we might ask:

- Who is the child? What are his interests? What does he like? Not like?
- How old is the child?
- What equipment needs are there?
- What is the size and shape of the room? The orientation? Views outside?
- Where are the various features of the space—for example, windows, lighting fixed in ceilings or walls, light switches, frames and doors?
- What are the materials in the space—for example, existing flooring, wall type, ceiling type? Are these going to be reused?
- How will the child feel in the space?
- How can we re-create a sense of wonder for the child?
- Do we ask the children what they need? How do we go about researching and designing for this particular need?

Figure A • Sketch of concept for therapeutic children's playroom

A Homeless Shelter

Things we need to consider and reflect upon include:

- What is it like to be homeless?
- Why would we even consider building a homeless shelter?
- What are government agencies doing to solve the problem?
- Where are the homeless in my town? How do they live? What do they think about a shelter?

Put yourself into their situation, and ask yourself these questions:

- What does it mean to be homeless?
- What is it to survive?
- What is meaningful in the state of homelessness?
- What is important?
- What is "dwelling" and "space" in this context? How is this socially motivated?

How do we understand what it might be like to be homeless? What do we need to know to be able to use our design skills to design an appropriate place?

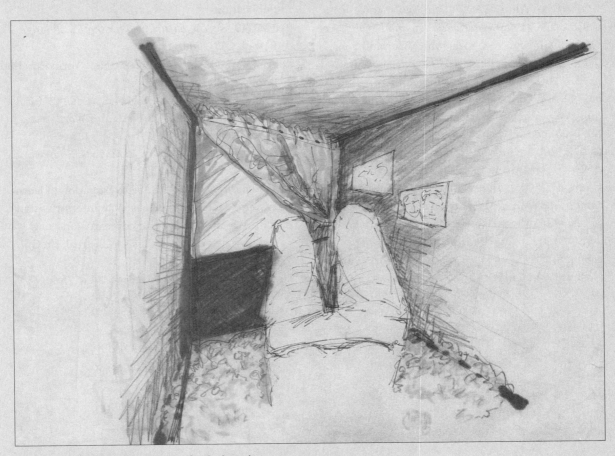

Figure A • Student sketch of concept for the homeless

BIBLIOGRAPHY

Ainley, R. (Ed.). (1998). *New frontiers of space, bodies and gender.* London: Routledge.

Berkerts, G. (1994). *Process and expression in architectural Form.* OK: University of Oklahoma Press.

Bilda, Z., & Demirkan, H. (2003). An insight to designers' sketching activities in traditional versus digital media. *Design Studies, 24*(1) UK: Elsevier Science, Ltd.

Buchanan, R., & Margolin V. (eds.) (1995). *Discovering Design: Explorations in Design Studies.* Chicago: University of Chicago Press.

Caplan, R. (1982). *By design.* New York: McGraw-Hill.

De Bono, E. (1996). *Teach yourself to think.* London: Penguin Books.

Hanks, K., Belliston, L., & Edwards, D. (1978). *Design yourself!* Los Altos, CA: William Kaufmann.

Knackstadt, M. (1995). *Interior design and beyond: Art, science, industry.* New York: John Wiley and Sons.

Koberg, D, & Bagnall. J. (1981). *The universal traveller.* Los Altos, CA: William Kaufmann.

Koenig, P. A. (2000). *Design graphics: Drawing techniques for design professionals.* Upper Saddle River, NJ: Prentice Hall.

Laseau, P. (2001). *Graphic thinking for architects and designers.* New York: John Wiley & Sons.

Le Gault, M. (2006). *Think! Why crucial decisions can't be made in the blink of an eye.* New York: Threshold Editions.

Lin, M. W. (2003). *Drawing and designing with confidence: A step-by-step guide.* New York: Van Nostrand Reinhold.

Margolin, R., Buchanan, (Eds.) (2000). *The idea of design: A design issues reader.* Cambridge, MA: MIT Press.

McDonough, W., & Braungart. M. (2002). *Cradle to cradle: Remaking the way we make things.* New York: North Point Press.

Miller, S. F. (1995). *Design process: A primer for architectural and interior designers.* New York: Van Nostrand Reinhold.

National Council for Interior Design Qualification (2007). Interior design definition. Retrieved from http://www.ncidq.org_07-2004.pdf

Nelson, H., & Stolterman, E. (2003). *The design way: Intentional change in an unpredictable world. Foundations and fundamentals of design competence.* Englewood Cliffs, NJ: Technology Publications.

Pye, D. (1978). *The nature and aesthetics of design.* Bethel, CT: Cambium Press.

Rengel, R. (2003). *Shaping space.* New York: Fairchild Books.

Soanes, C., Waite, M., & Hawker, S. (Eds.) (2001). *Oxford Dictionary, Thesaurus and Wordpower Guide.* Oxford: Oxford University Press.

Tomas, V. (1964). *Creativity in the arts.* Englewood Cliffs, NJ: Prentice Hall.

Vaikla-Poldma, T. (2003). An investigation of learning and teaching processes in an interior design class: An interpretive and contextual inquiry. Unpublished doctoral thesis. Montreal: McGill University, Author.

Zeisel, J. (2006). *Inquiry by design.* New York: W. W. Norton & Company.

Chapter Two

DESIGN PROCESSES FOR INTERIOR DESIGNERS

Objective

The *design process* is a series of ideas, concepts, and methods used to design interior space. You may learn some or all of these methods and processes at school. You may also learn some of them when you enter the profession of interior design or its many related fields in environmental design. When reading the ideas and concepts in this chapter, you will need to temporarily suspend your preconceived thoughts about designing. Why?

- Because you may think that design is a step-by-step process.
- Because you are not sure what the design process is.
- Because you may get different ideas about the design process from different people, sources, and places.
- Because as you learn about the design process, the designing part of the process will become evident (part of what you will do and who you are).

The design process is used and experienced differently depending on the context or circumstances. When we do real-world design projects, we usually break them down into chunks, or phases, to show a client the progress or to keep the project under control. When you work on a design problem in the design studio, you must produce phases of the work. Alternatively, at school you may have a project handout or a design problem statement with a series of deadlines. We will explore these different phases from both a student and a professional perspective, and break them down to explain each part of the process.

We will conclude this chapter with the first steps in generating preliminary ideas for a project. How do we get inspiration for a particular design problem? How can we get going on a project and generate first ideas? We will look at ways to initiate *design thinking*.

METHODS AND APPROACHES IN DESIGN

Designers use many different design methods and processes to create interior spaces. The design process encompasses all of the different activities undertaken by an interior designer, from an initial meeting with a client to the research of a particular problem, to the completion of the project.

The design process can be used to solve only one aspect of a problem, perhaps the renovation of an existing space or a move from one location to another.

Or it may involve all the steps of a design project from the earliest inception before the building is built to halfway through the construction.

The design process might also be used to create a new idea, a different type of environment. Perhaps we want to explore a new way of working, living, or playing. Perhaps we are concerned about how an environment may not be suitable for a particular use. Each time we embark on asking questions, looking around us, seeing the designed environment, and wanting to change what we see, we are engaging in the design process.

When we first begin a design problem, we assume that we are dealing with a space occupied by people. We also tend to immediately think that this is a design problem that must be solved. However, there is no one way to design, nor is there a simple way to solve a design problem. In fact, not all design situations are design problems.

To better understand these ideas, we will explore the following:

- What is a design activity in general?
- What is an interior design activity?
- What is a design method (in general, across many disciplines)?
- What is a design method in interior design? What is the difference between design methods in general and design processes and methods in interior design?
- What is the design process? What are its main components?
- What is the iterative process of design thinking and acting?
- What is an interior design stance, and why is this important to understand?

Another important aspect of this process is the holistic nature of the design process: a holistic way of designing that considers all components of the problem; in the case of interior space, it is a dynamic place with numerous activities. It is a place of movement and change, of temporal experiences and permanent meanings.

SPECIFIC CONCEPTS

Generally speaking, the design process is a way of drawing and expressing ideas that allows a designer to turn ideas into the tangible reality of a space. When designing interior spaces, the design process consists of several concepts, ideas, and steps, some of which are in order and some of which are not. The process involves several potential tools that you will use to solve interior design problems. Some projects require all of the tools available to you, while others need very specific ones. (See Figure 2.1.)

In the seminal book *The Universal Traveller*, Koberg and Bagnall (1981) unfold the design process as a process of analysis and synthesis of a series of steps that take you on a journey for any type of design problem.

accept situation ➔ analyse ➔ define ➔ ideate ➔ select ➔ implement ➔ evaluate

They explore each of these steps and suggest that:

Design can be defined as a process of creative problem solving; a process of creative, constructive behavior. Designers are people who behave creatively relative to problem situations; people who generate uniquely satisfying solutions to such situations . . . the process of design or creative problem solving describes a series or sequence of events, stages, phases, or design stages, as we will call them. (p. 16)

In this book we explore these stages, drawing from many authors, designers, and people from different walks of life, all with ideas about the design process as a general concept. In simple traditional terms, the designer analyzes the problem by collecting data. The designer consults with the people who will use the space, and decides what data is relevant and what needs to be considered when trying new ideas within the space. The designer then interprets the data and synthesizes this in drawing, which, in the case of an interior designer, includes plans and volumetric views of the spaces.

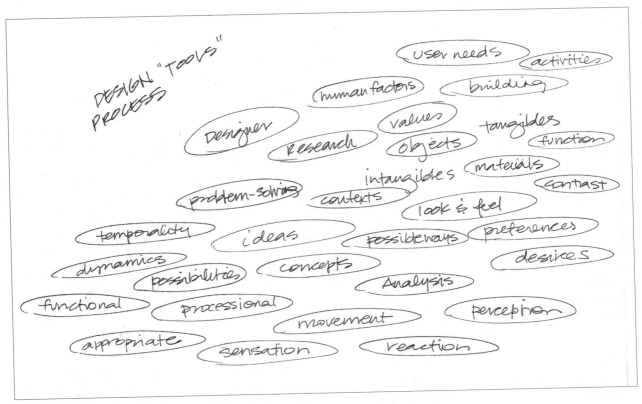

Figure 2.1 • Sketch of design process/thinking tools

The Analysis-Synthesis Approach to Design

Figure 2.2 shows an example of a traditional way that we might think about how we create designs.

The idea that the design evolves from a synthesis of research and analysis done is not new, and has been explored widely in design, architecture, and many other disciplines. This approach suggests that design problems consist mainly of two simple aspects known as *analysis* and *synthesis*. This means that if we research a problem and analyze it long enough, we can create a design that synthesizes the issues and, therefore, solves the problem. However, when we design interior spaces, the design process is not linear or step oriented exclusively. When we use design processes to design interior space, we do a number of different tasks, some in sequence, and some simultaneously, as we evolve a design from an idea toward a reality. We will now take a more in-depth look at the way we do this in interior design.

Different Aspects of the Design Process for an Interior Designer

The design process is about visioning a built reality from something unreal, uncreated, or not yet realized. To get to the built reality for an interior designer means beginning with an in-depth understanding of what is required. The design process is about understanding the parameters of a particular problem or situation by asking questions at each step along the way.

Let's begin with some of the basic steps and see what questions we might ask:

- Research the different aspects of the problem: What is the project about?
- Ask questions about what we see and observe: What do people need in order to accomplish their activities?
- Decide and implement different activities within a space: What is needed to facilitate the move-

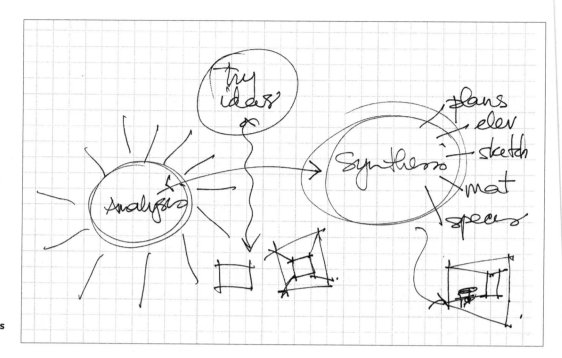

**Figure 2.2 •
Sketch of the
analysis-synthesis
schema**

ment of people, help them to accomplish activities, or improve their sense of well-being?

- Use different types of methods to solve the problem: What tools are needed?
- Define design criteria appropriate for the contexts of the problem: What are the essential elements of the problem or project?
- Develop concepts appropriate for the problem, the human use, and space: What can we envision for this person in his space?
- Evaluate different ideas: What works and what does not in this space?
- Try different things in the space itself: What might this space look like?
- Develop final concepts: What do we need to do to conceptualize the project?
- Communicate our ideas to people who do not understand the design process the way that we do: How do we talk to people to make this happen?
- Transform the project into a built reality: What do we need to make this project happen, on time, on budget, and with the aesthetic intentions we have?

Notice that each question brings with it a different series of issues that we need to tackle. Not only do we ask many questions, we also think about design differently each time we are given a project. Designing a home or kitchen for a household is not the same as designing a restaurant or an office. Each design project brings with it a different approach: There are as many different design methods as there are problems. Each time you meet a new teacher, client, or designer, they will use a different way to understand and solve a certain problem. Depending on the project at hand, we can use a variety of tools, including:

- conversations/interviews/discussions
- lists/programs/diagrams
- concepts/plans/three-dimensional sketches
- presentations/models/computer simulations
- materials/drawings/details
- samples/mock-ups

For an interior designer, the design process is an all-encompassing process that moves from preliminary research and analysis toward the finished product—the interior space. The design process is holistic, dynamic, and constantly in movement.

Figure 2.3 shows all of the different tasks we may (or may not) do during the design project.

If we regroup the tools we listed earlier in this chapter, we can say that this process consists of three primary elements:

1. Understanding the parameters and questions of the design problem (research, information gathering, contexts, issues, parameters, limits, possibilities)
2. Developing design concepts by examining all the contexts, using creative problem solving, and trying out different ways of seeing the potential design. Thorough research and information gathering leads to creative problem solving, allowing you to create interior designs through an *analysis/synthesis* approach that is broad and all-encompassing. You analyze all parts of the problem, search for solutions and concepts, and come back to the analysis to see if what you are considering fits. You weed out the possibilities through reflective thinking and judgment, and finally develop a design solution that fulfills the particular project parameters and/or requirements.
3. Developing a design solution that encompasses both an analysis/synthesis and the tangible/intangible aspects of the problem in the form of a designed interior space.

Three Concepts (Parts) of the Design Process

As we study the design process concept sketch in Figure 2.3, we can dissect the three primary elements even further into three basic parts. We will define

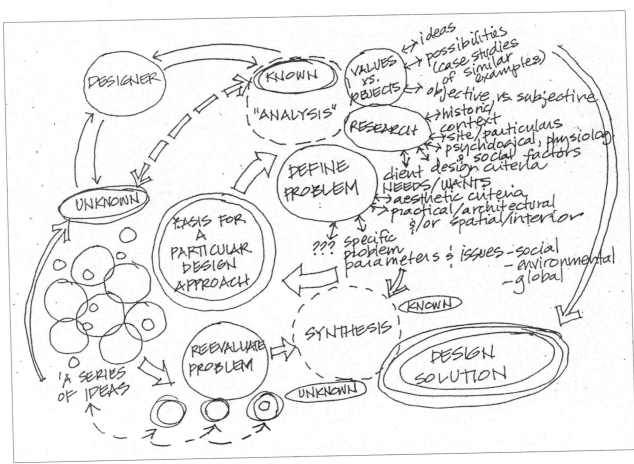

Figure 2.3 • The design process in interior design

each part first and then look at how these concepts are understood in the context of how we actually design a space.

Concept One

We begin the process by trying to understand the parameters and questions of the design problem (the tangible elements). Therefore, we begin by immersing ourselves in the design project. We ask questions, get to know the project, and develop the information gathering we need, as shown in Figure 2.4. In general, researching the different aspects of the problem includes:

- collecting and analysing information (data, pictures, stories, interviews, researched material from books, the Internet)
- asking questions about what we see and observe
- interviewing the people involved, whether the user of the space or the client who has mandated you to do the project

- asking questions about the particulars of the project
- understanding the problem, project, or situation inside and out
- developing design programs and understanding the various requirements of the project

Concept Two

The second concept of the design process is the designing itself, where you can move from the more tangible aspects of a project into the more intangible aspects of the design questions/issues. This includes beginning to conceptualize an interior space using creative and technical techniques, using design elements and principles, and creating design ideas. We move into unknown territory as we try different ideas within the space through planning, sketching, and modeling (see Figure 2.5). This includes:

**Figure 2.4 •
Client meeting
notes: determi-
ning needs for a
café renovation**

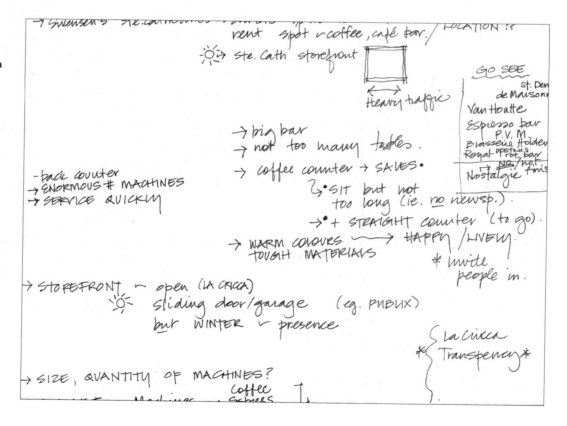

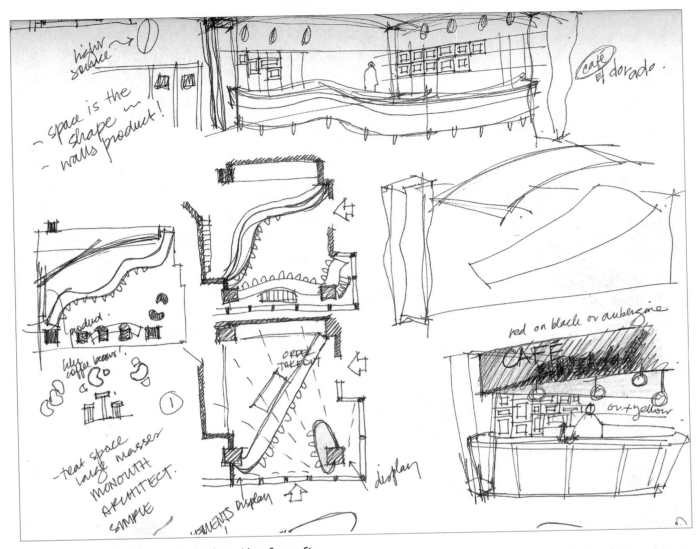

Figure 2.5 • Initial planning and 3-D sketches—ideas for a café

- defining what is appropriate to the context of the problem
- beginning to plan in two dimensions to see what will work and what will not
- trying the 2-D immediately in 3-D to see what effects the two-dimensional planning might have on the space
- developing design concepts and evaluating their appropriateness relative to the research gathered and analyzed
- returning to the analysis to compare the designs with the requirements

Part of this aspect of the design process means selecting appropriate color, lighting, environmental systems, and furnishings, while the space is developed and details begin to take shape. (See Figure 2.6.)

Concept Three

This part of the design process is where decisions are made based on critical judgments. This involves developing a design solution that encompasses the analysis/synthesis and the tangible/intangible aspects of the problem. This is decision time: Some ideas are good, and some are not. Some ideas must be

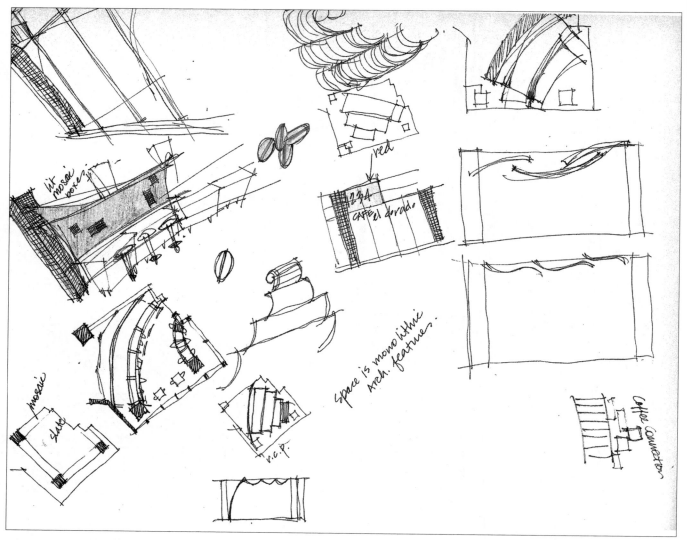

Figure 2.6 • Developing ideas with visual brainstorming

developed, others must be discarded. This is when the final concept is formalized and in-depth aspects are refined. Developing a final concept means:

- deciding on the best course of action based on all the work to date
- proposing a design that you show in two-, three-, or multidimensional form
- preparing detailed development of concepts that might be built

- finalizing plans, elevations, furniture, and fitment concepts, with all materials, lighting, and context-situated project aspects defined
- communicating your ideas to people who do not understand the design process the way that we do (usually in plans and perspective, often with a budget attached)
- creating the drawings and documents necessary to transform the concepts into a built reality (contract documents, drawings, sketches, virtual and real products)

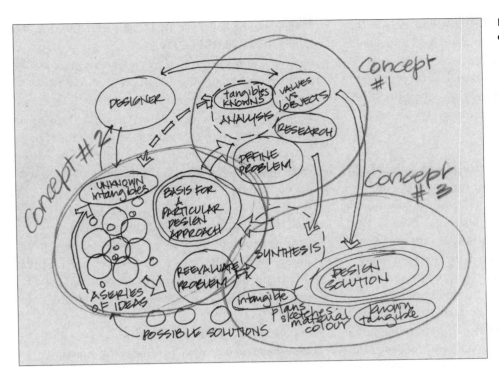

Figure 2.7 • The three basic design process concepts

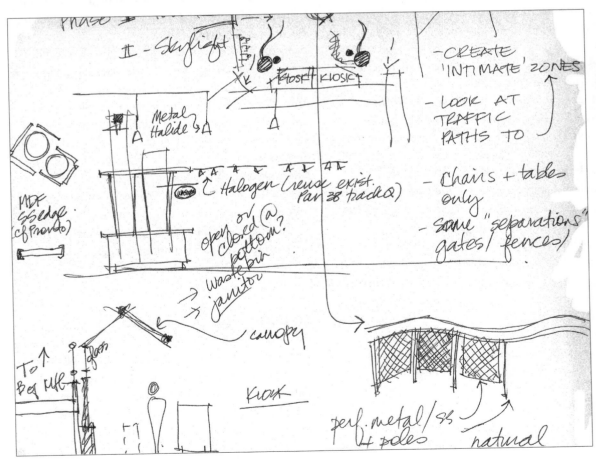

Figure 2.8 • Design process—how concept 1 and concept 2 are situated in the design process through a sketch

DESIGN ACTIVITIES AND PROCESS PHASES

Think of the design process as a series of guidelines, methods, and creative tools that you can use to transform ideas in your head into drawings on paper and then into built interior spaces. These concepts all are part of what designers describe as *design activity.*

What Is a Design Activity?

Quite often in design theory, the idea of a design activity is used to describe any process that a designer engages in that attempts to improve the human condition through the act of designing. This is a very loaded concept, as you will see in the next few pages. Design activities mean many things to many different people. An architect may understand the design activity as it concerns the building and its urban context, whereas an industrial designer may consider the purpose of an object. Interior designers consider the design activity to be the act of designing an interior space to suit the functional and aesthetic needs, wants, and desires of the user/client. This is a very basic understanding, and there are many ways to do this.

Design activities are done using varying methods, and there are as many design methods as there are design types. Each design discipline has its own methods and processes to design for their specific needs. A graphic designer will not have the same toolbox as the interaction designer or the interior designer.

It is difficult to put into words the nature of design activity, partly because of the variety of design tasks, but also because of the very nature of designing itself. As you might have guessed from reading thus far, design moves with the flow of what the project, client, and situation require. This makes interior design a dynamic and changing activity. Each time we design for a new client or user, we are faced with new situations, new problems, or new functions. Each time, we have a new space, new contexts, different people, and different conditions within which we design. Ultimately we try to use our designerly ways to better the conditions of living and working in our daily lives, whether at home, in the work environment, or when we play.

THE PHASES OF THE DESIGN PROCESS FROM DIFFERENT PERSPECTIVES

Because the design process has many variables, it is useful to understand the design process from two perspectives: that of the student and that of the design professional. Let's take a look at the three basic design process steps that we have explored thus far, and develop them in further detail and from two different perspectives—that of the design student, and that of the design professional.

The Design Student and the Studio Class

In the design studio, the design process fundamentally consists of three layers: the research and creative process, the design development process, and the design production process as seen in Figure 2.8.

The Research and Creative Process

The research and creative process is the one most emphasized in design schools. You begin examining the parameters of the design problem by conducting various forms of research; then you explore aesthetic concepts of interior space and develop creative ideas for the design of the space. Sometimes the design is based on research, analysis, and the development of a set of design criteria. Human elements play an important, if not primary, role in meshing creative ideas to social activities. This is where a playful, artistic sense of space is mixed with the student's intentions, and where several initial ideas are explored and alternative possibilities are developed. From this initial creative process, there evolves a design concept. The figures in Case Study 2.1 show three different versions of the same project and three different ways to sketch out the preliminary design ideas after the research has been completed.

The Design Development Process

The design development phase is the transformation of the previous two processes, a first conceptual idea and then trying the idea out in a two-dimensional plan, toward the final design solution. In design schools, this phase means working the design concept in more detail—developing the various views of the space, selecting appropriate materials and furnishings, and developing views of the space that communicate the design intent and scope to the viewer. This design development is manifested in many ways, from real or virtual computer-simulated models to drawings to three-dimensional representations. The production of the final design is then presented in a critique where it is judged by teachers and peers.

The Design Production Process

This final phase varies from project to project. Sometimes the same design concept is developed in the form of contract documents; sometimes this is done outside of the design studio. In either case, the idea of the design production is to transform the design concept into details and drawings that communicate to a builder or contractor the design intent in the form of material and furnishing specifications, developed details of millwork and architectural elements, or systems to be treated within the space. In school this is not possible, so contract documents are learned to simulate this process.

In these three major processes, the emphasis is on creative production and the end result: the design concept.

THE PHASES OF THE DESIGN PROCESS FROM THE PERSPECTIVE OF THE PROFESSIONAL INTERIOR DESIGNER'S STUDIO

In the professional world, the interior designer is faced with the same three processes as the student, but the design process becomes somewhat more complex with the added contexts of real-world issues.

In practice, interior space is developed from a design concept that must exist in the real world. To realize this, the concept must be designed to fit within certain parameters that are concrete and real. For professional designers, the design process is usually broken down into a series of work phases. These include (and are not necessarily limited to):

- the research and programming phase
- the preliminary design phase
- the design development phase
- the contracts documents and production phase
- the project execution phase
- the post-project phase (also known as post-occupancy evaluation phase)

The following example shows one way we can put the design process to work. It lists the range of services that an interior designer can provide a client for a project that varies in scope and intent. This is just one version of the various stages in the design process. This is not a prescriptive or complete list by any means. You will want to explore different ways that designers work and what different terms they may use to describe their services.

Research and Programming Phase

- Prepare a letter of agreement outlining the scope of services to be provided and the fee schedule; signature of contract.
- Explore site requirements, context, and building parameters (physical dimensions of space).
- Establish client needs and requirements for specific project type; develop design program (as required).
- Investigate local, national, and specific zoning/code requirements for specific project type and scope.
- Establish client design criteria and involvement of other consultants such as architects and/or engineers.

Preliminary Design Phase

- Examine existing client plans and requirements for space.
- Identify client needs and requirements based on above research.
- Determine extent of existing or new requirements within space.
- Conduct inventory of existing furnishings and fitments to be reused, if required.
- Conduct product research on new materials and ideas that are to be generated.
- Meet periodically with other professionals throughout all stages to coordinate work as it materializes.

AN ART EXHIBITION SPACE

This is a project with a design concept development for an art-exhibition space in a real building. In this example, three student designers each try different concepts from first research and analysis.

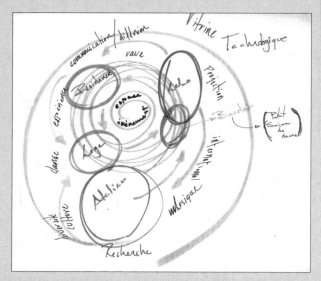

Figure A • Nathalie's first conceptual idea for a project

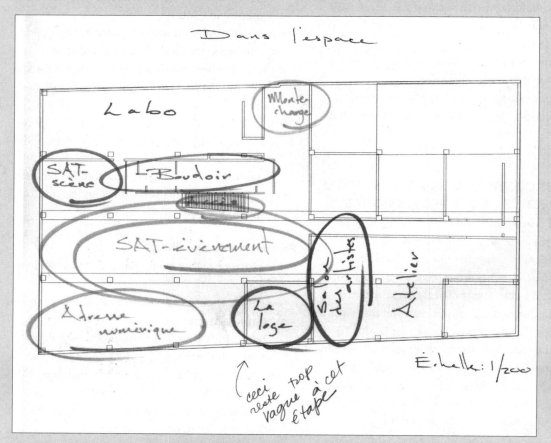

Figure B • Nathalie's first planning with bubbles in sketch

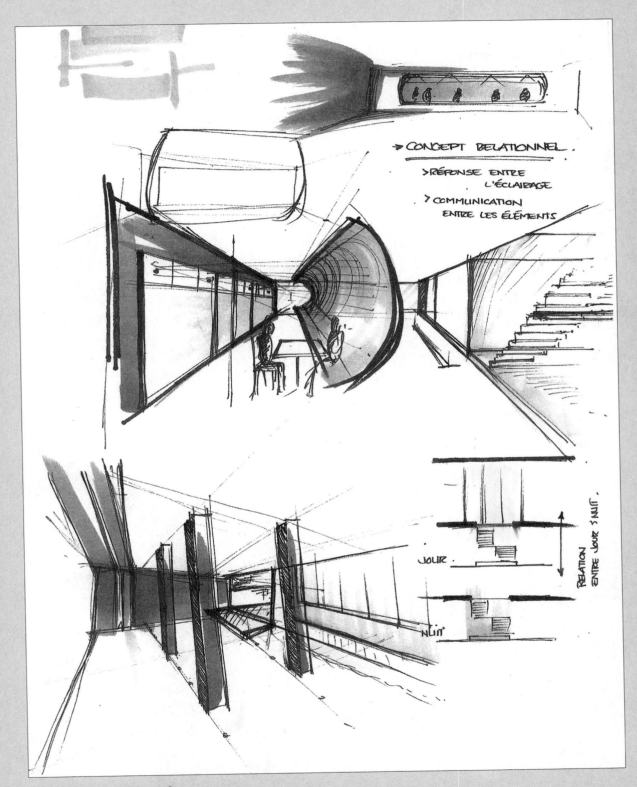

Figure C • Julie's ideas in 3-D form

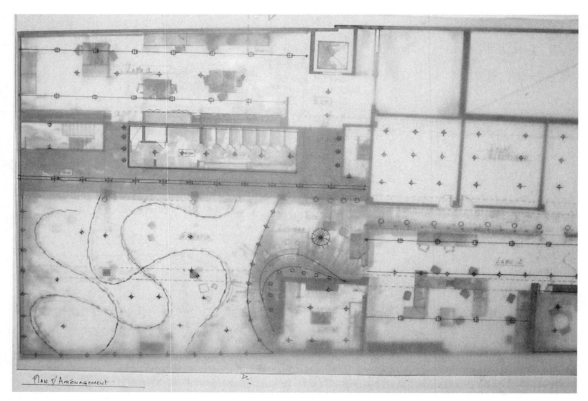

Figure 2.9 • Manon's plan and ceiling plan together

Figure 2.10 • Manon's sketches for concept as derived from model

MULTIPURPOSE ARTISTS' SPACE

This project is unique in that the three-dimensional space can change with user needs within a few hours.

The three perspectives that you see in Figure A are all of the same space that can be changed due to the flexible movement of the design.

Figure A • Julie's ideas in 3-D

- Provide preliminary layouts and space planning.
- Create preliminary conceptual development of two- and three-dimensional ideas for discussion with the client (include sketches, perspectives, elevations, and/or sections).
- Provide preliminary budget figures, if required, for anticipated work and conceptual ideas; may require a developed design program protocol.

Design Development Phase
- Design proposal(s) and final concept including plans, elevations, three-dimensional views, color, material, and lighting development.
- Present design concept to client.
- Submit budget proposal, and get client approval.

Contract Documents and Execution Phase
- Create detailed drawings and specifications, including plans, sections, elevations, and details.
- Coordinate consultants' work as required.
- Coordinate and contract documents for pricing purposes, including coordination of permit requirements.
- Coordinate tender process and pricing of project.
- Prepare necessary documents upon client approval of contractor, and if changes or modifications are required, determine coordination and scheduling of the work to be executed.

Project Administration Phase
- Monitor progress of project and advise client of progress of the work.
- Supervise site and coordinate meetings.
- Advise client of changes on site and coordinate changes with contractor and/or consultants, upon client approval.
- Inspect materials and furnishings as installed according to specifications.

Post-Project Phase (Post-Occupancy Evaluation Phase)
- Review post-occupancy deficiency list with contractor and client.

- Conduct post-occupancy evaluation of the design and the workmanship; reassess design criteria for future projects or work.
- Consider adequacy of design parameters as satisfying the functional and aesthetic needs set out at the outset of the project.
  (Retrieved from 1999 conversations with designers, classwork, and teaching notes)

These are the standard components of an interior designer's scope of services. The actual scope and order of phasing of a project will vary from designer to designer and from one firm to another. Other services may be provided, such as pre-lease layouts for potential tenants in an office building. You will notice that in each example, the actual act of designing is but one aspect of the whole, and that there are many contexts that help formulate the designing part of the work. We will now turn toward a more detailed discussion of the design process as this relates to basic design requirements.

THE TEN BASIC INTERIOR DESIGN PROJECT REQUIREMENTS
As you have seen thus far, the design process includes multiple contexts that must be considered simultaneously. Within the interior design problem, not only are there phases and steps in the design process itself, there are also design requirements. To be able to decide on a particular approach, you need to consider both the different ways that the design process works, as well as the basic requirements that must be fulfilled.

Let us take another look at the design process sketch presented earlier in this chapter, this time with more detail filled in. The sketch, shown in Figure 2.11, develops the design process to include questions to be asked and a more detailed description of various parameters that could be considered.

In the previous section we mapped out the design process and how this is conceptualized in broad concepts, looking at the basic design process steps and phases in different ways. We will now break these down into specific requirements. As we

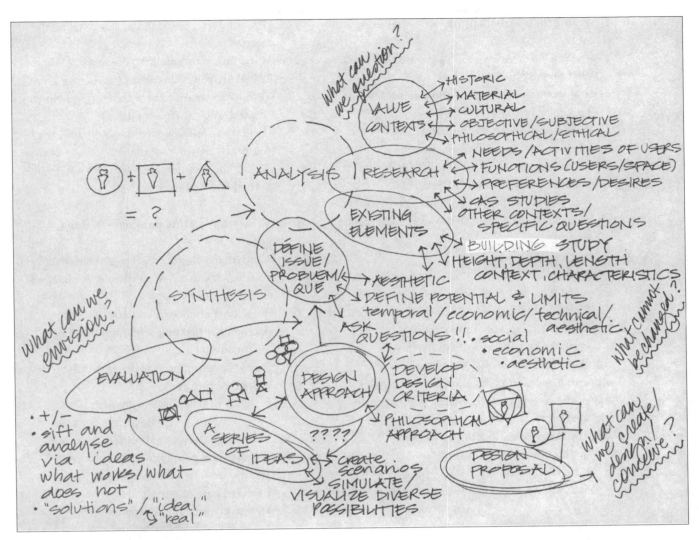

Figure 2.11 • The design process (developed sketch)

develop a design, we must draw from the ten basic interior design requirements. The following outline is a guide that can be used to map out questions you might want to ask on a particular project. You can use these questions as a guideline to develop a design program, a design brief, or just to help situate yourself when beginning your design project. (We will explore design programs and briefs further in Chapters 3 and 4.)

1. **Research/analysis**
   - Establish the parameters of the problem
     - Establish the research contexts; how to find the problem
   - Establish client types: users, owners, administrators
   - Establish client needs and preferences
- Determine what we can question. What can we change? What cannot be changed?

Consider the first questions you ask in terms of design inquiry and design action:
- What is the actual? (What exists in the particular problem at hand?)
- What is the ideal? (What is the ideal way to achieve the solution to the problem?)
- What is the real? (How will I go about finding the problem and the solution?)
(Nelson & Stolterman, 2003, p. 40)

Designing for a particular user and what we need to know:

- Who are we designing for? What do they want? What do they need?
- How do we understand the human user within a space?
- How do we understand human scale?

2. **Information gathering—what are the design approaches particular to this project?**
   - What would we like to do? What can we do?
   - How is what we do tied to the context of the problem?
   - What might be possible?
   - What has been done in this same type of design?

3. **Establish the contexts of the problem**
   What are the specific aspects of the design problem that must be defined to realize an appropriate solution? For each problem, you may draw from any or all of these contexts; you may also create new or unknown contexts along the way.
   - What are the general contexts?
     - Site and building
     - Material (e.g., sustainable design incorporated into design thinking means what?)
   - What are the human contexts?
     - Physical/anthropological, ergonomic
     - Psychological, social
     - Aesthetic
     - Desires and needs
   - What are the specific social and cultural issues surrounding the needs of the user?
     - Intentions and ethics
     - Cultural
     - Economic
     - Social (e.g., user as a part of a particular cultural, economic, or social context)
   - What are the objective and subjective contexts?
     - Philosophical values as applied to the problem (e.g., health and the concept of healing; ideas about "improving the quality of life")

- Point of view of the person to be using the space
- What future or unknown contexts are there?
  - What are the issues arising in the research?
  - What did you not know that might help you understand the issue at hand?
  - What possibilities exist that perhaps are not currently there?
  - What ideas, issues, and elements add to the actual and real contexts?

4. **Establish the existing parameters of the project**
   - What are the characteristics of the site and project as it exists? What cannot be changed?
     - Site characteristics
     - Interior spatial characteristics
     - Elements impacting on design thinking
       ◦ Transitions
       ◦ Fenestrations, architectural features
       ◦ Encumbrances
     - Heights, limits, possible changes

5. **What are appropriate and possible design approaches and problem-solving issues?**
   - Asking questions—learning how?
     - Examine case studies
     - Design criteria development
     - Develop the design program
     - Examine philosophical approach
     - Examine aesthetic approach
     - Examine design intent?
     - Examine other?

6. **Defining the design approach**
   - Tangible elements (known elements; codified knowledge)
     - Economic, technical
     - Human factors
     - Design program, design criteria
     - Possible aesthetic ideas/approaches
   - Intangible elements (unknown elements; tacit knowledge)
     - Potential experiences of the space

- How people feel about what they need; what is important to them
- Possible ways to design the space
- Temporal relationships of activities with spatial forms, installations, and objects (how things move and change with time)
- Human psychological responses (how do they react in terms of their physical responses)
- Human psychological and social relations (how do they react in terms of their psychological responses, territorial needs, and social needs)
- Aesthetic and creative potential of project
- Aesthetic form relationships with human user and activities

7. **Evolving the design concepts**
   - Preliminary designs
   - Overall approaches/exploring possibilities
   - Design intentions and specific directions
   - Refined and clarified design and user activity program
   - Preliminary concept development and evaluation; early design judgments
   - Design direction determined

8. **Design development—developing in-depth aspects of the project**
   - Design production of the design.
   - In-depth development; 2-D and 3-D development.
   - Development of material, color, lighting, and environmental factors.
   - Sculpt the space using spatial organization.
   - Evaluate design development, including critiques and judgments.

9. **Design implementation**
   - Understand when to "stop designing."
   - Design presentation of final concept (schools).
   - Design project production and implementation (practice).
   - Determine project supervision and implementation (scenarios in school and realities of practice).

10. **Post-design responses and thinking**
    - Evaluate the design solution.
    - Project ideas into the future.
    - Learn from past mistakes; learn from design decisions.
    - Understand the iterative nature of design; the design solution is not finite.

THE DESIGN PROCESS AS A DYNAMIC PROCESS

Let us now take a closer look at the complex nature of the design process. While researching the different aspects of a problem, we try to imagine what might be and what is possible, given the real and tangible constraints of a particular building or space, client or user needs, and other known factors. The very fact that we design for human use makes interior design, in the sense we talk about here, a dynamic activity.

This idea of dynamic movement between the tangible and intangible aspects of a design problem is perhaps one of the more difficult aspects of the design process to understand. Whereas different designers, architects, and writers have tried to define it, you must learn on your own how to move from one aspect of the design problem to another and back again.

The very nature of the design process is the movement from one aspect to another. This back-and-forth quality is what eventually moves the design forward. Some call this process iterative (Zeisel, 2006). We can look at the design process as iterative, as well as immersive, dynamic, or temporal. When we sketch out possibilities, we think about the actual project constraints and realities. We immerse ourselves in the project, moving from one aspect of a design to another and back again, each time refining our ideas a little farther. We constantly move between what we see, what we know, and what we do not know. By moving back from the ideas into the more tangible aspects of the design, we test our ideas against what we have researched and what is real. Thus, the design process is a moving process. You move from the creative trying out of ideas toward something more real and physical in terms of actual forms and materials.

Tangible and Intangible Aspects of a Design

We first research and learn about the tangible (known) aspects of the design program. We document everything we can and analyze the best ways that we can use the information we have gathered. We then move into more intangible (unknown) aspects of the design, such as exploring possibilities, creating design ideas or plans, and envisioning concepts. We continue on with ideas and try out different approaches, in the form of sketches or models, both in sketch and virtual forms.

Considering the Real, the Possible, and the Ideal

Each time we undertake a new design problem, we need to try and see it in three ways. We try to explore what is real, what is possible, and what is ideal. These are concepts I always try to explore early in the design process with students. We ask ourselves these questions:

- The real: What exists now in the space? What is the existing condition under which we will design?
- The possible: What are the potential ways that this same design already exists? What is possible in the realm of the design project?
- The ideal: What has never been tried? What would be the best idea if there were no constraints at all? What might be a new or different way to see this design?

Looking at the project or problem in these different ways at the outset helps us to understand what is possible, what ideas have potential, and what ideally could be done. This does not mean that the design will necessarily develop along any of these lines; however, it does mean that we must try to explore the potential of the design in the most contexts possible before we even begin to design within the space itself. As we move along in the design process, we can check back to our initial questions and ideas and see how our first thoughts about the real, the possible, and the ideal are satisfied.

Let's explore each idea in more depth next.

> **BUILDING BLOCK** • *The idea of movement from one stage to another has been explored by many architects and designers in different ways. We move from one type of thinking into another, depending on the aspect of the design we want to explore. When we plan out the space, we are using the "known" aspects of the problem. We know that the user needs x space to perform y task. We know that they must have z amount of space for their employees, for example. We then conceptualize how this space might look. We move toward the "unknown," the murky territory of creating something from nothing.*

The Real

It is here that you first question the tangible aspects of the design. What are the actual existing parameters and contexts of the design problem at hand? What exists out in your community, the urban or rural environment you are a part of, the world around you? How are things done now and what does this consist of?

You can research different aspects of the tangible in the design problem to establish the "real" aspects. What are the things that you know? For example, in a home renovation for a single working mother in an older district of town, you might consider such things as:

- similar projects (case studies)
- historical perspectives (precedents, best practices)
- social issues (how people live or work together; what is it like to be a single mother in the city; what are her daily activities, the work pressures, the home routine)
- physical issues of the house itself (location of the site, building parameters, height, width, depth, openings, window views, orientation of the building and exposure to sunlight during various times and seasons, city location relative to the equator)

The Possible

The possible grows out of the real. As you research the real aspects of the design problem, you will find things that are possible that you may not have thought of at first. These are still the tangible elements, some of which are common knowledge and some of which are known only to you, the designer. For example, perhaps a New Jersey senior's residence is actually similar to a hotel located on the West Coast. What are the possibilities for the design in the context of the problem that you are studying? What is the potential, and what have other designers done in other parts of the country or the world?

In Case Study 2.3, we look at a student project for an interactive science center for teenagers. While the student researches the project parameters and collects information, she also considers what is possible for her project.

The Ideal

Here you enter into the less tangible aspects of the research by asking what might be possible. You consider the ideal situation if the client or user had no budget constraints, no building issues, or no preconceived ideas. The goal here is not to impose the ideal, but rather to think of possibilities and then go back and adapt them to the user and his needs later on. Perhaps you have seen beautiful use of a certain material in a restaurant that would be ideal in the home design you are considering. Or perhaps you envision a spa-like atmosphere for a seniors' community center.

In Case Study 2.4, we examine what students think about as they try to envision an ideal hospital playroom for young cancer patients undergoing chemotherapy. What would the children ideally like to see if they could have a playroom within the hospital?

THE MOVEMENT OF THE DESIGN PROCESS

As you can see from the sketches and case study examples, we move from one activity to another when we design, but we also return to activities we have already done. Why? Because we find out information as we go along that changes our previous ideas. We move from what we know toward what we do not know, and when we do so, we try out different ideas on paper.

The designing happens again and again whenever we evaluate our ideas. We return to the first stages once more and refine the ideas. Figure 2.12 shows an example of how we can summarize this movement of the design process.

Figure 2.3 at the beginning of the chapter has a circular feel because we go from one thing to another, but we may return again to the first aspect in order to move back into the next one. This is how the process becomes iterative, meaning we go back through the stages to refine our ideas. This idea might be expressed as in Figure 2.13.

Information gathering planning designing creating evaluating testing ideas
planning designing creating evaluating designing deciding
implementing evaluating

Figure 2.12 • The movement of the design process

research think create design evaluate research test design evaluate create
evaluate test design refine detail refine design implement test
detail transform design refine implement
return to research

Figure 2.13 • Multiple movements of the design process

An Interactive Science Center

The student is starting her final project. She wants to develop a new concept for an interactive science center for teenagers. She has researched the subject and begun a design program. She has not yet finished her programming, but already has several ideas.

In class, the teachers ask the students to step away temporarily from their research and explore three questions by producing visual representations of the research that they are doing. This exercise will serve as a means to understand what is real, what is possible, and what is ideal within their particular project. They are asked to produce a collage of the three questions answered in whichever way they would like.

The student has completed here preliminary research and has a complete program developed. She is designing an interactive science center for both

Figure A • Design program example and final concept board

Figure B • Collage of ideas (exploring the real, the possible, and the ideal)

teenagers and adults where people can interact with knowledge of science, math, and technologies. She does an extensive design program and brief, where she evaluates the needs and generates ideas in sketch form (see Figure A).

In this short brainstorming collage, she explores the three questions: What is real? What is possible? What is ideal?

She creates the concept map seen in Figure B to answer the questions, and transfers into the visual

her answer, using the collage to identify the overall key issues of the project:

- The constraints of her building, an existing planetarium in need of an upgrade
- The design possibilities from around the world for this type of interactive center
- The ideal: What is being interactive? What is science and interaction for students and adults?

Children in a Therapeutic Playroom

In this case study, groups of two students were asked to design a playroom for children undergoing chemotherapy. The children were confined to their hospital beds around the clock. The students were given the physical parameters of the space: a two-story area accessible from the floor of the cancer ward. The mandate was to provide a playroom, up to two stories in height, within easy access of the patients' rooms. Here parents could leave their children, giving both parent and child a much-needed respite.

In the first part of the project, students were asked to do research on children suffering from illness. They also set out to understand what it is like to be a child between the ages of 6 and 12, whether ill or not. The students needed to get a feel for the children's fantasies and desires to envision an ideal environment for them to play in.

The concept is based on inspiration of what it might be like to be in this situation, and a further exploration of what might be ideally possible as a means to represent the children's desires. The following three figures show how students conceive of a therapeutic playroom, as seen from the vantage point of the child within the space.

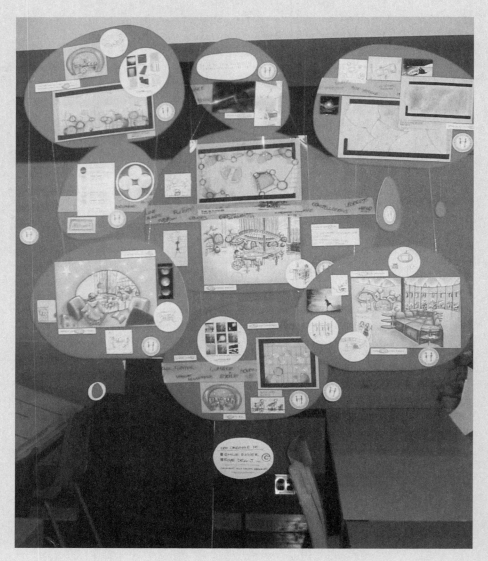

Figure A • Concept presentation

Figure B • Concept sketches from the vantage point of the child

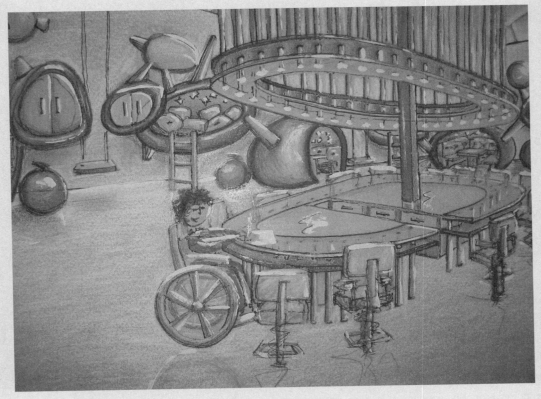

Figure C • Sketches from the vantage point of the child

The process goes through multiple changes, and each time we generate sketches or drawings to explore the specific stage of the design process. Each time we return to the "designing" part of the process, we go through an iteration, and our design (hopefully) becomes a little more refined, a little more complete.

Practicing the Process of Movement in Interior Design

Let's look at Case Study 2.3 again. We saw the collage as a visual representation of possible ways to understand the problem as real, possible, and ideal. In this type of iterative process, the designer started with information gathering and then moved into thinking about the design even before her design program was complete. In this process, certain aspects might overlap. For example, you may be gathering information for a design project, and you come up with some ideas in a concept map format. You then try your idea in plan and perhaps sketch it out in three dimensions. Chances are you may not get it the first time.

This is what the student did in Case Study 2.4. She tried out her ideas in her concept map, then worked on plans but they did not work. So she tried things in a three-dimensional scale model of the space. She then returned to the original concept map and looked at it again, to inspire her while working on her model. From this, she generated three-dimensional sketches of what she saw in the model (Figure 2.14).

Figure 2.14 • Student design concept development in model and sketches

EARLY RESEARCH, ANALYSIS, AND BRAINSTORMING TECHNIQUES

We will conclude this chapter with a few tools and techniques to foster initial thinking about a design project. There are many different methods for developing first ideas, and the goal here is to show you how to generate some first-level thinking before you have even finished the research and analysis phase of the project.

Ideally, while you are doing the research, you can already try, in a parallel way, to foster early creative thinking. In design offices this might be encouraged as a brainstorming session, whereas in a research group this is often done using word and group verbal associations. The idea here is to do the following:

- While doing research, get down ideas on paper as they come into your head . . . design!
- Do not design! At this point you are trying to understand the question, issue, problem, or idea you are working with.
- Use your friends and colleagues as a way to team up and brainstorm using word associations (Figure 2.15).
- Explore the Internet and read books to find sources of inspiration other than the information you are required to research.

You need to get the ideas on paper, but keep an open mind so that you are able to explore all possibilities.

Brainstorming Techniques

Here are some different examples of visual and verbal individual and group brainstorming techniques. These come from many different sources, and they are not exclusive or exhaustive by any means. They are introductory to more ideas we will explore later on in subsequent chapters. Due to the limitations of print, we examine visual media here. However, you can easily build a video or make a moving example using some of these techniques.

Verbal Brainstorming

Alone or in a group, throw out words that relate to the subject at hand. What inspires you or your friends? Put them down in a list.

> **BUILDING BLOCK •** *Designing is a "process" that moves through multiple changes. You start by trying an idea, then perhaps modeling it in the space. The idea, however, is not clear; it is vague, perhaps a little muddled. You return to the plan and try it another way. You adjust and try your new idea again in the space. Again you "see" something from your mind's eye or on paper, and return again to try another idea. Each time you explore an idea from one aspect to another and back again, you "return" to the design process in the interior space.*

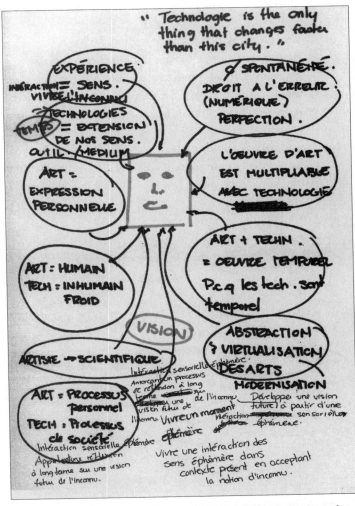

Figure 2.15 • Example of student brainstorming and the sketch created

Word association—Generate words that inspire thinking about the project. Figure 2.16 shows an art exhibition space where word association was used. Before the design began, the student designer got together with fellow students and they developed a series of brainstorming exercises, including a word association collage.

Participatory concept (building ideas)—In this example, the student was asked to make a collage. Rather than create a solo project, this student decided to engage all of her fellow classmates in a concept map building exercise, to stimulate thinking about the idea of art/technology (Figure 2.17). The result is a movement in word association—building ideas.

Visual Brainstorming

Develop collages of images cut out from everyday magazines. Images reflect visual ideas about the themes or subject being explored, and help inspire the representation of meanings and thoughts as they are generated. Figure 2.19 is an example of a constructed wall collage exploring the theme of arts technology for the design proposal of an artist's collective/exhibition and dance space, in a hostile unlit environment.

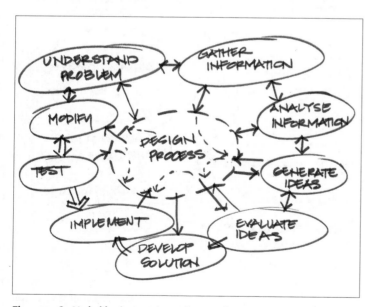

Figure 2.16 • Verbal brainstorming using word association

BUILDING BLOCK • *Always save your sketches, or save your plans in some format, either as JPGs or as PDFs. You need to keep a record of what you design because then the ideas will always be there. You may want to return to the original ideas and see what you were thinking, especially if you get stuck. Whether on paper or disc, keep records of your ideas, however sketchy and loose, good or bad.*

Visual inspiration from nature and the five senses—Designers often use images to represent the five senses and how they evoke meanings about the themes worked on for a particular project. This helps to give sharp visual meanings to the ideas brewing about in your head. For example, a found object can inspire the design of a luminaire in a quick second year light and color project, as we see in Figure 2.20.

Collage as a multidimensional concept—In this version of a collage students use it as a means to develop multiple dimensions to sense the concept that they are exploring.

STUDYING THE DESIGN METHODOLOGIES OF GREAT THINKERS

In interior design, we use and borrow many methods and approaches from other fields. Although we use methods from disciplines such as architecture and industrial design, we must also understand the design process from the perspectives of art, science, and crafts, and from other fields and disciplines such as environmental behavior, sociology, anthropology, and psychology.

Over the years much has been written about design processes and methodologies in many fields/domains. The following excerpts present different views and ideas from a wide range of design disciplines. This sampling is by no means exhaustive. It proves that there is no one method or process in design, no one good or bad way. Hopefully you will be inspired to find out more and read up on many other valuable perspectives.

Figure 2.17 • Student group concept map

Christopher Alexander

In his seminal book, *Notes on the Synthesis of Form* (1971), Christopher Alexander proposes that design comes from the design program and this is grounded in the two fundamental concepts of form and context:

> Physical clarity cannot be achieved in a form until there is some programmatic clarity in the designer's mind and actions; and for this to be possible, in turn, the designer must first trace his design problem to its earliest functional origins and be able to find some sort of pattern in them. . . .
>
> It is based on the idea that every design problem begins with an effort to achieve fitness between two entities: the form in question and its

Figure 2.18 • Student directing the building of the collage (2006)

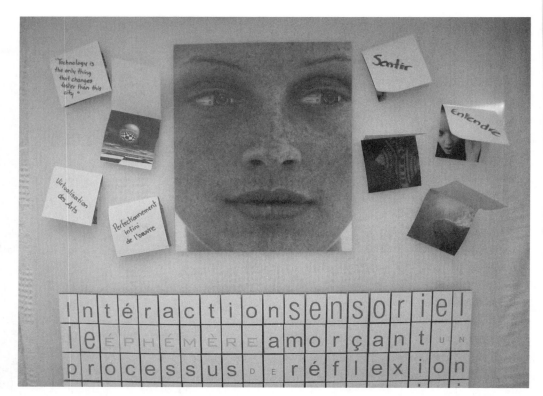

**Figure 2.19 •
Student project for
the design studio
(third-year fall 2003)**

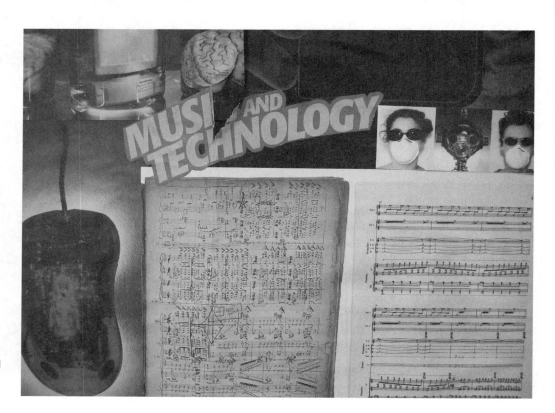

**Figure 2.20 • Visual
inspiration from a
found object**

context. The form is the solution to the problem; the context defines the problem. (pp. 15–16)

Alexander is considered the intellectual father of design thinking, and his ideas are widely examined and studied in a variety of design-related disciplines.

Hanks, Belliston, and Edwards

Hanks, Belliston, and Edwards offer this idea of the design process and its methods:

The design process can take a few minutes to several years. It can be simple or complex. It can involve one person or tens of thousands (or even whole nations or worlds indirectly). Whether simple or complex, the design process can be stated in six easy steps: Problem identification, preliminary ideas, design refinement, analysis, decision, implementation. . . . The design changes with each design problem. You will find that, even though you utilize the six steps of the design process, your process solution will require continual changes. Look for changes and develop your own modified process for each design. (pp. 60–61)

Don Koberg and Jim Bagnall

Koberg and Bagnall provide what they call a "soft-systems" approach to understanding the design process. They cite numerous authors, including John Dewey, when they offer this simple chart for defining the design process and design methods:

A Design Process is
. . . A PROCESS OF maximizing goals
. . . A PROCESS OF optimizing objectives
. . . A PROCESS OF realizing intentions
. . . A PROCESS OF giving form to intentions
. . . A PROCESS OF making dreams come true
. . . A PROCESS OF anticipatory improvement
. . . A PROCESS OF bridging analysis to synthesis via concept
. . . A PROCESS OF taking apart, comprehending and putting together

Figure 2.21 • Collage in 360-degree round—sensing the 3-D

. . . A PROCESS OF organizing data into improved reality
. . . A PROCESS OF fulfilling a prophesy

Design methods are
. . . TECHNIQUES FOR SUCCESS
. . . TOOLS FOR PROBLEM-SOLVING
. . . STRATEGIES FOR TRICKS
. . . SUB-PROCEDURES

A SUCCESSFUL SOLUTION IS ONE THAT
. . . enhances a defined purpose
. . . achieves the pre-stated end(s)
. . . satisfies a conscious intent
. . . frees the problem-solver for other activities
. . . helps to further clarify value and purpose
(p. 29)

Ralph Caplan

Caplan suggests that design can "make things right" when used appropriately. He speaks about industrial design and its processes as he suggests that design can be useful and positive when used appropriately and with depth:

There is a disease called dermatomiocitis, a collagen deficiency that causes the body's cells to become unstuck. A comparable affliction—the ungluing of the social system—affects the body politic.

Design could help, for design at its best is a process of making things right. That is, the designer, at his best, or hers, makes things work. (p.11)

Styling is superficial design, but since the design process operates below the surface, superficial design is a contradiction in terms. It is a contradiction we live with, for design (most of it superficial) is pervasive. . . . [O]ur problems are situational. They always have been. (pp. 13–15)

Ellen Shoskes

Ellen Shoskes (1989) describes the design process as a series of project phases. In *The Design Process*, she takes an architectural approach to the building process, developing it as a series of steps situated in planning, urban site analysis, building program development and design. She presents the design process as follows:

The design process has a certain mystique. It is hard to describe moments of inspiration. But architecture is both an art and a science. The architectural design process . . . integrates analysis with intuition. Architect Robert Geddes has described the architect as composer: Indeed, getting almost any project done today requires a collaborative effort orchestrated with as much innovation and imagination as the creative act of design itself. Design is decision making, and the key to successful projects lies not only in the final form but in the process leading up to it. Poor design decisions can be costly to correct or have lasting social implications. The design of the process must be as carefully considered as the design of the form. (p. 8)

The standard project phases typically consist of planning, programming, schematic design, design development, contract documentation, and contract administration. . . .

During the planning stage goals are defined, nondesign issues are raised, part lessons are evaluated, and the location of the project is determined. Programming defines the specific objectives of the project and describes the functional, physical, social and budget requirements to be met. (p. 12)

Stanley Abercrombie

In his seminal book, *A Philosophy of Interior Design*, Abercrombie suggests how we can achieve the design process:

The concept that guides our pencil and that later will guide our eye in equipment furniture and fabric selection is itself guided by such practical considerations as functions to be served, the space to be used and the budget to be met. It is also guided by a less tangible consideration, the determination and appropriate personality for each job. . . . The designer can easily offer particularity (indeed, can hardly avoid it) when working for a known client with known needs and tastes. . . .

Just as the success of any design will be limited by the wisdom of the concept it follows, the wisdom of any concept is limited by the vision and knowledge of the designer who conceives it. . . . [T]he amount of technical knowledge needed by the designer continues to proliferate. More is needed as well: the fluency in what is, after all, a visual language, the designer will need a superior degree of visual literacy, reading easily the subtleties with which plans, rooms, furniture and ornament all speak to us. And still more is needed: the designer needs to care deeply for the design's users, even when those users are anonymous, and for a design's effects. (pp. 63–65)

John Chris Jones

Seminal in the world of industrial design, John Chris Jones has been at the forefront of exploring the design process and design methods. Here in the book *Designing Designing* he explores the design process as a dynamic ongoing experience:

Building is a form of living and living is a form of building. That's one way of realizing that there are no products, no fixtures, only continuous flux. And that designing, making, and using are all process that are added to, and interact with, the natural processes of where those activities occur. (p. 162)

Aims, purposes, requirements, functions: these are words for how we see what's needed. But when we name we tend to exclude the main part, the least predictable ourselves, our minds, and how they change, once we experience something. It's ourselves, not our words, that are the real purpose of designing. The biggest mistake is to take the product alone as the aim. It's always secondary, always a means, to process, to what we're doing now or what we're doing later. (p. 212)

Harold Nelson

As an architect and designer, Harold Nelson has developed some clear ideas about the design process. With Eric Stolterman, he has coauthored an authoritative book on the foundations of design entitled *The Design Way* (2003). In the following interview, Nelson (2004) is asked about his idea of the design process as bound in the idea of intention:

I differentiate between design capacity and design competence. I include both capacity and ability as essential elements of design competence. (p. 170)

I think design competence enables humans to be purposeful, teleological beings in an unpredictable environment . . . as design competent human beings we create the world rather than merely noticing, reflecting and reacting to the world. Design competence allows humans to act with intention, to create intentional change. This is in clear distinction to the types of change science struggles with which are chance and necessity. (pp. 170–171)

Ranulph Granville

Ranulph Granville, in the book *Mind the Gap!*, considers the design process as a process of circular thinking:

I am interested in design as a way of thinking rather than a mechanism that creates output. . . .

For me, design involves circular thinking (circular causality) and science tries to get rid of these circles (hence, linear causality). In any interactive world, then, design is central. I consider design—as I understand it—as a good model for this sort of thinking. Or rather for understanding and characterizing this sort of thinking. (p. 126)

John Zeisel

In his seminal book, *Inquiry by Design* (2006), John Zeisel explores in-depth the diverse aspects of design, inquiry, and the design process from an environment/behavior perspective:

Design begins when an individual or team first thinks about the project—for example, a building, an open-space plan, or an object. It includes a stage when detailed working drawings of a project are given to contractors instructing them how the designers expect the project to be built. It includes a stage when contractor and designer negotiate changes in the design to respond to problems that arise during construction. The process formally ends when construction is completed. Designers conventionally break down this process into contractually binding stages: programming, preliminary design, final design, working drawings, and construction supervision.

Design is difficult to describe because it includes so many intangible elements such as intuition, imagination and creativity—which are also essential to research. (p. 19)

. . . [D]escribing the design process may help designers and teachers of design understand their own behavior and thereby improve their design ability. Analysis is also useful for researchers and designers who want to work together. (p. 21)

This has been an introductory sampling only. There are many other perspectives that you can explore by investigating designers and thinkers. As we move along in the book, we will also explore some current and future ideas about the design process and methods.

BIBLIOGRAPHY

Abercrombie, S. (1990). *A philosophy of interior design.* New York: Harper & Row.

Alexander, C. (1971). *Notes on the synthesis of form.* Cambridge, MA: Harvard University Press.

Caplan, Ralph. (1982). *By design.* New York: McGraw-Hill.

Ching, F. (2004). *Interior design illustrated* (2nd ed.). New York: Van Nostrand Reinhold.

Glanville, R. (2004). Interview with Ranulph Glanville—The other way around: Science as design. In W. Jonas & J. Meyer-Veyden (Eds.), *Mind the gap! On knowing and not-knowing in design.* Bremen, Germany: Hauschild Verlag.

Hanks, K., Belliston, L., & Edwards, D. (1978). *Design yourself!* Los Altos, CA: William Kaufmann.

Jones, C. J. (1991). *Designing designing.* London: Architecture, Design & Technology Press.

Karlen, M. (1993). *Space planning basics.* New York: Van Nostrand Reinhold.

Knackstadt, M. (1995). *Interior design and beyond: Art, science, industry.* New York: John Wiley & Sons.

Koberg, D., & Bagnall, J. (1981). *The all new universal traveller: A soft-systems guide to creativity, problem-solving and the process of reaching goals* (rev. ed.). Los Altos, CA: William Kaufmann.

Laseau, P. (2001). *Graphic thinking for architects and designers.* New York: John Wiley & Sons.

Malnar, J. M., & Vodvarka, F. (1992). *The interior dimension: A theoretical approach to enclosed space.* New York: Van Nostrand Reinhold.

Margolin, V., & Buchanan, R. (2000). *The idea of design: A design issues reader.* Cambridge, MA: MIT Press.

Miller, S. F. (1995). *Design process: A primer for architectural and interior designers.* New York: Van Nostrand Reinhold.

Mitchell, C. T. (1993). *Refining designing: From form to Experience.* New York: Van Nostrand Reinhold.

Nelson, H. (2004) Holism: Design as the basis of human civilization; interview with Harold Nelson. In W. Jonas & J. Meyer-Veyden (Eds.), *Mind the gap! On knowing and not-knowing in design.* Bremen, Germany: Hauschild Verlag.

Poldma, T. (1999). *Gender, Design and Education: The Politics of Voice.* Unpublished Master's thesis. Montreal: McGill University, Author.

Pye, D. (1978). *The Nature and Aesthetics of Design.* London: Cambium Press.

Shoskes, Ellen (1989). *The design process.* New York: Whitney Library of Design.

Zeisel, J. (2006). *Inquiring by design* (Rev. ed.). New York: W. W. Norton & Company.

Chapter Three

THE INTERIOR DESIGN PROJECT

Objective

In the following chapters, we will begin to explore the design process by studying its different components. We will look at the initial questions that need to be asked when getting to know the client and the parameters of the project. We will also examine the relationship between the client and the designer. What are the intentions of the interior designer at the outset of a design project? How do we understand the client and user in the context of a design problem? We will also introduce typically used research and analysis tools.

Concepts such as defining the design problem, understanding our role as a designer with design intentions, and understanding the nature of the user in an intimate context are initial things we need to grasp. We will look at the earliest stages of the design task and understanding the parameters of the problem. When these are understood, we meet with the client and then move on to developing the design program and brief, within which the design criteria are developed. Fostering initial design ideas will also be explored, as this initiates design thinking.

We will concentrate on smaller-scale projects and the person as an intimate user of the interior space. We will use case studies situated in residential and institutional design from designers and students alike. We will look at small design program development and simple analysis tools. The concept of constraint as a positive trigger for design thinking is explored, using the building and its physical contexts as the point of departure. Team and individual brainstorming methods are introduced as part of the early research and analysis stage of the project, as well as ways to understand the user as a person with very intimate needs.

As we saw in Chapter 2, the design process for interior designers includes many different contexts and factors that must be considered. Not only are we concerned with the project and its parameters, we do research and collect information, sifting through it to see what is important. Like driving a car, we first start up the engine and then shift into gear. When we have completed gathering our information, we shift into another gear, start to design the space, and plan it out.

GETTING INTO THE DESIGN PROJECT

Our first contact with the design project is through the potential client. This client may also be the user, or merely the one who is paying for the design. At an initial meeting we must be prepared to ask numerous questions to determine if the project is the right one for us. It is at this time that we begin to acquaint ourselves with the parameters of the project and the client's needs and desires. We are on a quest to understand the scope of the project, the issue at hand, or the situation that requires our services as an interior designer.

Questions that can be asked immediately include (and are not limited to):

- Who is the client? Who is the user?
- What is the space? Will the design be in the existing space or a new space?
- What activities are going on in the space? What is happening around the space or in the nearby community that affects the space?
- What is the size of the space?
- What do the people want for the space? Are they working in it or living in it?
- What type of space is it?
- Who are the people? What are their needs?
- What do they want or desire for their space?

THE STAGES OF THE DESIGN PROCESS

To understand the complexities of the design process, it is best to break it into stages. From what we learned in Chapter 2, we can now suggest organizing the design process into three primary parts. These are (in simple terms):

- pre-process
- design process
- post-design process

As you move from one stage to another, you do different tasks and try different things along the way. At each stage of the process, you employ specific elements or notions, or use the same element during several stages. But each time you move from one stage

to another, you are in the process of doing an activity specific to that step in the overall design process.

When things go well, documentation may seem unnecessary; however, if ideas do not work out, this becomes an essential paper trail. On a more positive note, documentation of each aspect of the design process allows us to remember the things we think about. Sometimes a design idea that may not work in a particular project can be useful at another time or in another design.

Pre-Process

This stage covers understanding the client needs and project parameters prior to the research phase. The components of this stage include:

- learning about the project and the client
- testing the ground, before taking on the project
- understanding the different contexts and parameters of the design problem/issue at hand

Design Process

This is the information gathering stage, where a lot of the research analysis takes place. The components of this stage include:

- understanding the client needs and project parameters
- researching all aspects of the project and contexts specific to the problem
- breaking down the problem into parts
- studying precedents or case studies within and beyond the project themes

Developing a Design Brief and Program Components

- Activities, needs, preliminary space types and sizes
- Evolution of the required components of the project (lists, research)

Establishing Design Criteria Components

- Fine-tuning the required components (psychological, social, spatial needs related to activities; fixed and temporal components; lighting, color, and material choices as these relate to budget,

technical requirements, ambiance, environmental comfort issues, ergonomic or anthropometric needs)
• Developing initial design ideas

Planning Process Components

• Reconfiguring the parts of the research
• Analyzing and grouping together the research into client and project-related elements (charts, matrix analysis, spatial allocations)
• Developing initial plans and preliminary sketch ideas

Designing Process Components (developing ideas, testing and evaluating ideas, finding the final solution, developing the design concept)

• Designing the interior space itself by developing design ideas and concepts
• Testing and evaluating ideas
• Deciding on a particular design approach
• Developing the design concept
• Evaluating the concept in depth toward a final solution

Creative Process Components (developing ideas, testing and evaluating ideas, including intuitive and creative thinking)

• Developing the design ideas aesthetically
• Designing in different dimensions
• Visioning the space: modeling and creating three-dimensional views, detail thinking from the outset, visualizing the space in movement
• Developing the concepts for the project

Evaluation Process/Thinking Process Components

• Working through the design concept
• Testing ideas by walking through the space visually
• Developing design elements and details that consider all the senses
• Working the developed detailed ideas and concepts (millwork, lighting, ambiance) through the choices and integration of innovative uses of materials, colors, forms

The Implementation Process Components

• Implementing the final design into technical or construction plans and executing it through pricing and construction
• Implementing the final design concept
• Creating the means by which contractors can build on the site (plans, details, modeling)
• Understanding changes as part of the implementation process

Post-Design Process

The components of this include:

• Evaluating the design once it is finished/built
• Evaluating post-occupancy (after people have moved in, looking at and assessing the viability of the design)
• Planning for the next project; integrating feedback on the actualized design

UNDERSTANDING THE DESIGN PROCESS IN ACTION

Designing is a process in action, and we have just listed the process as a series of steps. You may find that this process is not always done in a step-by-step fashion. Figure 3.1 shows you how an interior designer moves from one stage to the next.

Depending on the project context and the complexity of the problem, you may work on each stage systematically only once, or you may move through each stage two or three times. Problems vary from the simple and straightforward to the more complete, with different issues and contexts. Let's look at these differences in terms of first- and second-level design problems next.

First-Level Design Problems: Developing Simple Design Projects

In simple terms, a first-level approach to a design problem might be examined as a series of steps in the overall design process. Here is one approach that you might take:

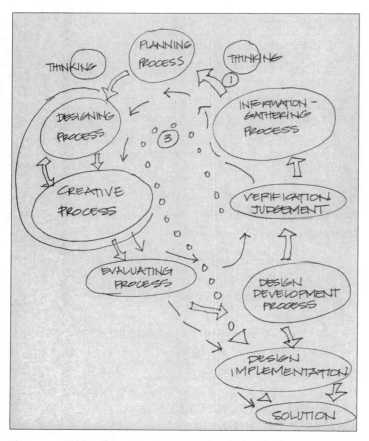

Figure 3.1 • Moving from one stage to another during the design process

STEP 1   Research.

Document the problem.

Analyze the project parameters (building constraints, spatial allocations, psycho-social needs).

Study the particulars of the project (may include project particulars, case study analysis).

Perform on-site surveys and client/user personnel interviews (when and if appropriate).

STEP 2   Analyze the research.

Establish the design criteria and design program/brief.

Create analytic and bubble diagrams.

STEP 3   Block planning of spaces and develop three-dimensional sketches or two-dimensional models.

Decide the conceptual approach.

Evaluate the design approach.

STEP 4   Design concept evolution (three-dimensional development, color and material concept, lighting concept).

Develop a more detailed concept.

Explore multiple possibilities for design development.

Walk through and develop interior space from user scale and spatial perspectives.

Design development and evaluation.

STEP 5   Evaluate the concept/define final concept.

Finalize production for presentation (modeled views and plans, elevations, design details, three-dimensional perspectives, fitment and furnishings, materials, furnishings, fixtures and equipment choices).

Offer presentation for critique.

(Karlen, 1993; Vaikla-Poldma, 1999; Laseau, 2001)

In this series of steps, the creative and conceptual processes are less evident. You, as the student, need to learn how to incorporate this type of thinking along the way. Examples of projects using this type of first-level process include:

- Residential planning (kitchens, workspaces, living spaces)
- Office design (simple offices, corporate interiors)
- Small-scale interiors
- Homes
- Cafés and small bars
- Retail stores less than 5,000 square feet or 500 square meters

- Boutique-type stores
- Lofts and residences

On the next pages are a couple of student case studies that illustrate first-level design projects.

Let's move on to understanding the nature of more complex design project problems. I refer to these as second-level interior design problems.

Second-Level Design Problems: Complex Design Programs

The idea of second-level design problems suggests that the problems have a second layer of complexity. This layer can be identified as one of several aspects of the design problem:

- larger scale
- multiple contexts (integrating several design types, multiple cultural, social, or other issues)
- complexity inherent in the type of project itself
- level of detail required for custom fittings
- complexity in user needs requiring a developed design program from the outset

These complex issues and contexts are numerous, and we will examine them as we go along.

What Is a Complex Project or Complex Design Program?

Generally, a complex design program is one where there are multiple players or stakeholders, where the spaces are medium or larger scale, or where the nature of the project itself is complicated. The design project parameters are broader, the scale of the project is generally larger, and there are more people involved at the different stages of the project.

Examples of complex projects include:

- medium and large-scale corporate office design
- hospitality, including hotels, restaurants, and bars
- recreational design
- institutions such as homes for the elderly, hospital environments, special-needs environments
- Specialty, multi- or interdisciplinary environments
- technologically based environments

In this chapter we will focus on the early stages of the pre-process and design process as they relate to relatively simple interior design problems and programs. We will learn how to organize research, collect relevant information, and prepare analytic elements that will help us sift through the information that we have collected. This will be a building block toward subsequent chapters where we will explore more complex design programs and case study projects.

ESTABLISHING THE PROJECT PARAMETERS (PRE-PROCESS)

When we do projects for our clients, we can use the design process as our mental guide, to keep us thinking about all the things we need to know. The project begins with the first client meeting.

Meeting the Client for the First Time

Our first contact with a client is the meeting where we get to know one another. Whether in the design studio where we are given a project as a student, or in the field when we meet a client for the first time; either way, we are now in the first stage of the pre-design process. We are trying to fact-find, to learn about the project. To be able to put together a program or understand the project, we need to first understand the nature of how the design will be created. At the first meeting with the client, depending on the scope, size, and nature of the job, you may be given a design brief, a program of needs, or nothing at all.

Asking Questions at the Outset of the Project

In school, we learn to become investigators. What are the questions that we have to ask? To be able to understand the design problem in its earliest stages, it is a good idea to look at the problem itself and attempt to decode it.

The following case study (3.1) is an example of a small-scale project. Let's read it and then examine the ways we can go about creating a design program from the project requirements.

When you meet a client or receive a project description in a design studio, your first job is to find

LIVING IN 350 CUBIC FEET

What would it be like to live in 350 cubic feet? Students were asked to create a living space for a young artist starting out. The following sketches show the initial diagram development, the final idea, and the solution in rough sketch form. One student considered the small space dynamics, what could possibly be placed in such a confined environment, and how an artist would want to live. The location was in a run-down area of town where tenement houses are mixed in with higher-priced condominiums and row houses.

The project problem: To design a place for an emerging artist in 350 square feet (60 m3) of space.

Constraints: The 350 cubic feet means that the entire space had to be a volume of 350 feet cubed. In essence, the height x length x width = 350 feet cubed total.

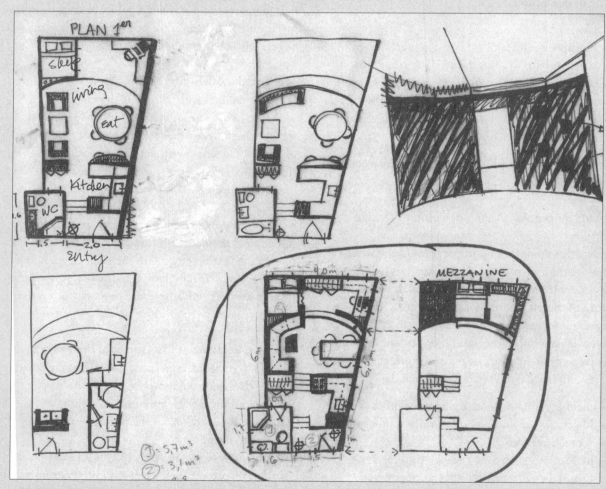

Figure B • Sketch analysis

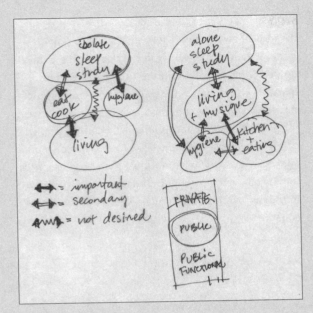

Figure A • Bubble diagram

Client needs: Provide the artist-in-residence with an interesting space that fits within the space parameters; consider what it means to create a convivial and functional small space. Figures A through C show the sketch development by a first-year design student and what she considered.

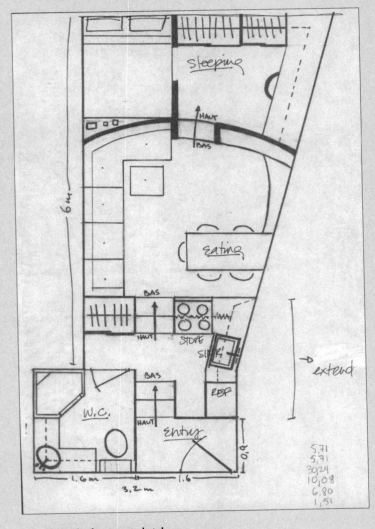

Figure C • Final concept sketches

STUDENT'S CONCEPT FOR A GOURMET STORE/CATERING SERVICE/RESTAURANT

(Third-year concept development)

In this design project, a student develops an evidence-based analysis of a real client situated in an older part of the city. She researches the client needs, evaluates the street access of the gourmet food store, analyzes what the store should present both as a retail store and as a caterer/restaurant, and determines how best to support these requirements.

The student proposes a new and innovative way to eat, situated within a fresh, bright, simple, and sophisticated space, with a concept revolving around the idea of gastronomic delight. The space provides a flexible, multi-activity environment consisting of take-out, catering services, counter eating and espresso bar, in-house dining, and retail sales of gourmet products made on site and imported. The dining concept reflects the traditional cultural idea locally of family eating together around the large table. The concept allows for this type of community gathering, essential to the culture of the neighborhood, while catering to the more intimate and private needs of the urban consumer.

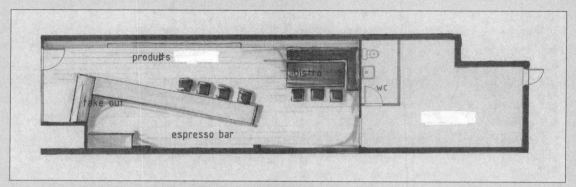

Figure A • Rough sketches of proposed gourmet store/restaurant

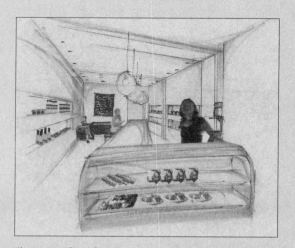

Figure B • Plan, elevations, and perspective of final concept

out the needs of the client and the users of the space. We generally interview our clients one-on-one to determine their needs. It is important to meet the client in his/her environment, whether at home or at work. This initial meeting is vital, as both the designer and client get to know one another and feel out whether or not they will be compatible and interested in working together. The work environment might be an office, a bar, or restaurant. The place to meet depends on the client, the project, and the ways in which the interior designer is going to be involved in the project.

After this is done, a design brief is drafted and the groundwork for the design program is developed.

Interviewing Clients

Determining client wants and needs is like being a detective. You must ask the right questions to understand what they need and how they work and play. When you first meet a client, you must almost "step into their head." You want to be able to interpret what they say and what they mean. As a student, your goal is to understand the parameters of the project in much the same way.

There are four major components in the earliest stages of information gathering for an interior design project:

1. Interviews with the client—finding out their needs
2. Case studies and precedents—finding out what is "out there" in the world
3. Documentation of the parameters of the problem—documenting everything pertinent to the project

4. Development of the design program—defining needs, assessing functions, documenting psychological and social needs, desires and vision for the project

The next case study (3.4) will provide some insight into students who met with a real client.

Defining the Client's Need as the Primary Function of a Design Program

The primary function of collecting information and using it to develop a design is to understand the client's vision for the project. Ultimately, you are hired as an interior designer to respond to the client's vision, goals, dreams, needs, and budget issues. In 2003, Satish Rao, an architect, laid out the basic steps for the development of a successful design program for architects and designers. I include this here as the definition of "design program" because it is simple and reflects the issues inherent with understanding client needs. "Programming transforms the client's goals into a statement of needs and design parameters. In case you haven't done it before, here are the basic steps," according to Rao:

- Determine client's vision and goals for the project: What they want to achieve and why.
- Interview client groups, including users, to gather and categorize data, occupancy parameters, space guidelines, site data. Be a facilitator; don't impose your preferences. Filter out data not relevant to design.
- If necessary, do background research on the client's operation and building type.
- Understand and analyze the processes: people, goods, information, services, circulation. Identify the required activities, spaces, equipment, furnishings.
- Distinguish between needs and wants; prioritize needs based on congruence with goals, beneficial returns, and costs. Determine phasing.
- Compile a set of requirements, both numerical and qualitative, for each indoor and outdoor space.

Case Study 3.3

Understanding the Meaning of House and Home (Resident Kitchen Renovation)

Project context: The interior designer meets a client for the first time. She assesses what the client's home looks like, and interviews the client. She has been invited to stay for dinner because the client would like the designer to understand her particular needs.

Client needs: The client wants to renovate the kitchen and, in the process, make the ground floor of her two-level town house practical and functional around the new kitchen. She sends pictures of her home to the designer (Figures A and B), and they meet over dinner at her home.

Figure B • Jackie's kitchen—before

Figure A • Jackie's kitchen—before

The First Meeting between Client and Designer for the Design of a Hair Salon

The interior designer is approached by the potential client—a hairstylist who wants to open a new hair salon. The building is under renovation, and the potential client has to meet the designer to see what is required. In this initial meeting, the designer and client go over the client's requirements. The client shows the designer what his current salon looks like, and brings the designer to see the new space. After the designer has seen the space, the questions begin:

- What agreement is there with the landlord in terms of what will be provided in the new space?
- What are the specific activities done in the salon during the course of a day? Do they do makeup and spa treatments, or specifically just hairstyling?
- What provisions should be made for hair coloring? For hair washing?
- What are the primary services that the salon will provide?
- What image does the stylist want to project?
- How is the space divided between the stylist and the other tenants on the same floor?
- What is the landlord's concept for the floor?

The designer asks the client if he has a list of requirements or a program. He does not, so the designer asks him to create one. These are the first steps. If the client is happy with the designer's suggestions and portfolio of current work, the designer will get the list of requirements and draw up a letter of agreement outlining the scope of work.

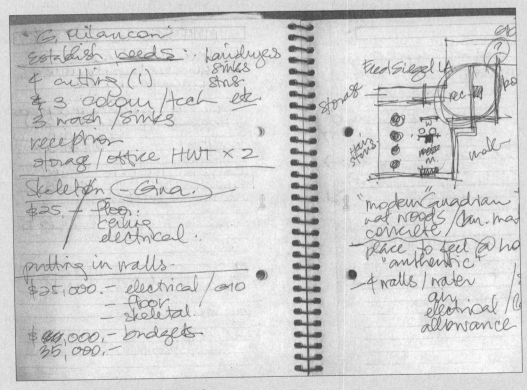

Figure A • Notes from initial client meeting

- Write a clear and concise statement of the problem and design goals. Address image and character, function, relationships, ambiance, and costs. (retrieved from 10.03 Architectural Record)

This is an overview of the general programming requirements that a designer or architect would need to address. As a student, you may look at some or all of these, depending on the problem at hand. As a designer or architect, you must address these needs concisely and objectively to be able to respond adequately to the design problem. We can add to this list of basic steps considerations that we make as interior designers:

- Understand your client and user: who they are, what activities will be done, what spaces and volumes are required, and what volumes of equipment or space are needed, such as:
  - What specific intimate needs must be addressed in terms of activity?
  - What are the territorial or social aspects of the activities that need to be identified?
  - What three-dimensional space do client needs take up?
  - What are the allocations of space required for each activity?
- Are there special needs? If so, how should these be addressed?
- What other needs might there be related to the activities and the capacity of the users to adequately fulfill their tasks? For example, what might be psychological needs and how are these related to the social needs (psychosocial needs)?

At this stage of the pre-design process, we are like investigators, trying to figure out what is exactly involved in the project. We are learning how to ask questions appropriate to the design issue/project or problem at hand. Let's examine an interior designer meeting a client for the first time in this next case study.

In this next student case study (3.5), students in the first year of a baccalaureate program research a project that involves three different clients living together in a working-class urban environment. In this case they cannot interview the clients, as this is a scenario created for the studio. What to do? The students must learn the cultural and social contexts of the project; the neighborhood and its flavor can help them to understand their "client." The students create the "client description" by studying the physical and social context within which the project is situated. The case study story in its preliminary stages follows.

As we have seen from the case studies, different projects require different approaches to collecting information to understand different users in their particular contexts.

PROGRAMMING AND BRIEFS: AN INTRODUCTION TO TYPES AND METHODS

The two most common ways to organize your information gathering are the design program and the design brief. Both of these documents are the foundation for your design. The client may have prepared a design brief or the designer and the client might develop one together. We will look at the design program here and develop first ideas about the design brief and design criteria. We will continue to develop these ideas in more detail and complexity in Chapter 4.

No design can proceed without a comprehensive program or brief. These are simultaneous in that we define a brief for a client and collect information that becomes our design program. Usually an interior designer drafts up a program based on the research that she/he has done.

The first and most important source of information is the client. Client-driven sources are in summary:

- client meetings, client interviews
- user interviews
- observations, video and photos of the space, the users in their activities
- case studies of similar designs

The key to a successful design project is communication between the interior designers and the user, establishing a successful comprehensive program and an appropriate design brief.

The Difference between the Design Program and the Design Brief

The design brief is a synthesis of the research and the document that defines the scope of work for the project. It is simple and contains very specific information such as:

- the spaces to be affected/designed/changed/reused
- the contents of the space to be intervened (stairs, circulation, lighting, furnishings, equipment, etc.)
- the scale of the design (spatial allocations)
- what is required for interior furnishings, fitments, and equipment (FF&E)

The design program is much more extensive than the design brief, and contains all the factors, elements, and research/analysis collected for a project. It is usually the basis for the design brief that is presented to the client. Depending on the type and size of the project, the design program is also presented to the client after it is finalized, either as part of a larger design team or within a specific mandate hired by the client or other consultants such as architects or project managers.

A Checklist for a Simple Design Program

When first beginning a design project, the amount of information collected can be very simple or mind-staggering in its scope. Here is a checklist for information you might collect for a simple design program.

1. Documenting the Activities
   - principal activities
   - secondary and tertiary activities (form: schematics and written words, narratives and interview notes)
   - the nature of the activities (passive, active, how, individual, collective)
   - functions within the space (activities or tasks needed, desired, or required)
2. Documenting the needs (user needs)
   - for each user within the space, individual and collective needs
   - psychological needs, social needs, perceptual needs
   - ergonomic and anthropometric needs, human factors and scale
3. Volumetric needs
   - furniture or equipment requirements, storage requirements
   - inventory of furniture or equipment to be used (new or existing)
   - other equipment required (lighting, mechanical, electrical, task-related)
4. Practical/functional needs
   - code requirements (fire, zoning, local authorities)
   - natural and artificial lighting needs or requirements
   - physical and physiological requirements
5. Specific project contexts
   - the individual and collective space needs as required (written and visual)
   - the possible functional schematic relationships (visual sketches)
   - the "macro" contexts that should be considered as they relate to the building (historic, contextual, or other)
   - the "micro" contexts that should be considered (human-object relationships, interior height, length and width and the impact of this on our perceptions)
   - other contexts relevant to the project (similar case studies, other examples of best practices)
6. Existing building conditions—documentation of building information
   - photos of the space, the building interior and exterior
   - measurements taken on the site of the actual space itself: the plan, the width and height, the length and breadth, the windows and existing walls, doors, and other characteristics, existing stairs, ceilings, open or closed ceilings
   - the "base building" characteristics, including elements that cannot be removed — slab floors and ceiling, columns, fixed elements such as window openings in period-style buildings, load-bearing walls
   - elements that can be removed: false ceilings, non-load-bearing walls, decorations, lighting,

Living in St. Henri

The project: To design living spaces for three different client types, all living under one roof within one town-house complex. There are three different client/users, and the client descriptions vary from student to student. Some examples are:

- Three generations living together (mother, daughter, granddaughter)
- Parents with a young child
- Three students living together
- Single mothers with teenagers and younger children

**Figure A •
Neighborhood
exterior view**

Neighbourhood views
St. Henri
Montreal,
Canada
2005
Photos:
P.M. Savoie

Project constraints include:

- Three floors of a row house with historical context
- A working-class neighborhood and near a large urban center
- Three people with different needs living together (generation, gender, social, and cultural differences)

Part of the project context is to read the text of Gabrielle Roy, a popular local author, who puts into context the spirit of the urban surrounding and the working-class roots of the community within which the student will design.

Establishing the context (research needed to do the project) includes:

- Understanding similar urban project typologies (historic urban development, existing North American social housing case studies)
- Understanding the client/user by defining who the clients are and how they live

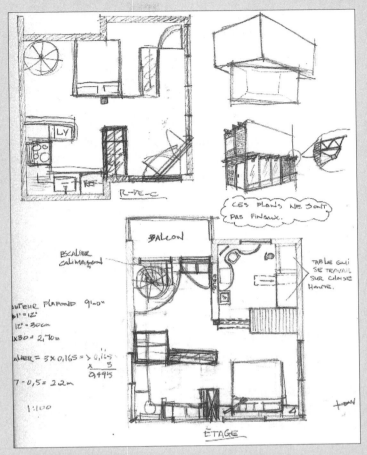

Figure C • Pierre-Marc's design concept initial thinking

Collecting research for the project

This phase includes asking and answering different questions:

- What are the activities and needs of each user in the space?
- What are the practical and ergonomic considerations related to these needs, for example, human scale (counter height and reach in the kitchen or bathroom, storage needs in the laundry area, etc.)?
- What are the physical, anthropometric needs (height reach for storage and cabinetry, kitchen reach from worktop to stove)?
- What are the family or individual social needs?
- What are the family or individual personal needs, desires, or wants?

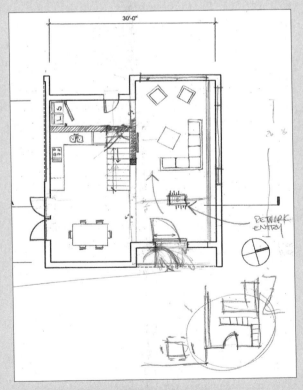

Figure B • Pierre-Marc's plans for the space

plumbing, heating, ventilation and cooling systems, "false" design elements

- plans and sections, exterior and interior elevations or details of the building or space
- case studies or precedents of similar projects done locally and abroad

7. Existing client space and/or premises
   - visual documentation of the volume of things to be reused
   - visual documentation of how people live and/or work in their environment: existing ways they do things, what works and what does not
   - photos and inventory of objects to be reused, replaced, or reconfigured
   - client ideas about the space and its potential: ideas, sketches, plans they may have drawn up by hand

Documenting the existing client needs and space helps you as the designer to understand the client's idea of what he needs. The visual documentation should include all the information that will help you break down these needs and compare them to the space itself.

INFORMATION GATHERING DURING THE DESIGN PROCESS

A design program is the final version of the research and analysis process. It encompasses both the tangible aspects of the design, such as client needs, as well as some of the intangible elements, such as client desires. For example, Case Study 3.3 shows how the design program develops from a series of client interviews, case study investigations, and research done with and apart from the client. The design program evolves from both the information gathered and an analysis of what the client needs as a user and as a home owner. Following an initial meeting, the interior designer lists out the requirements and develops a preliminary design program. Let's revisit Case Study 3.3 to see how this process evolves (3.6). The client understands her space well and can also see when it is presented in this format.

Through this example of a kitchen renovation, we have seen how we might go about researching a design problem. Now let us look at the different tools we can use to document the research and analyze the needs of the user.

COLLECTING INFORMATION FOR THE DESIGN PROJECT: RESEARCH AND ANALYSIS TOOLS AND METHODS

Let's review the different research collection and analysis tools we have studied to date in a little more detail. We'll begin with the simpler ones in this chapter and then move on to the more complex examples in the next chapter.

Interviews

Interviews are done with the client, the owner, and the different users of the space. They can be very systematic or informal. It is important to understand that these interviews happen over the course of several meetings. The number of meetings depends on the designer, the client needs, the project contexts, and the type and nature of the information to be collected.

Think about the goals of the interview. These can include:

- Understand the desires and needs of the user and the client. The client and user might be one and

> **BUILDING BLOCK** • *When we meet a client, and in particular one that is at home, there are certain things that we do not need to know. We have to be mindful and respectful of people and their privacy, and their personal lives are not of interest to us. We also do not need to know about their personal things, nor do we judge whether or not they are neat and tidy people. In terms of the interior space, we are not interested in the structure of the building unless this impacts on our design. However, any exterior influences such as windows or views, and circulation in or around the space, are important, as this may impact on our design approach.*

THE KITCHEN REVISITED

We return here to the kitchen from Case Study 3.3, building further on the understanding of the client interview and the experiences of the designer and the user/client.

The interview: This is where you write down everything you can about the client. I visited the client at her home in the middle of winter. I examined her kitchen and the surrounding environment: the hallway, the dining area, and the front living room that doubles as the music studio where she teaches piano. The kitchen is her haven, where she enjoys cooking and preparing meals for her and her son.

To be able to understand what the client needs, you have to see it, to experience it.

At her invitation, I watched her prepare a casual meal for us. I followed her moves to capture how she uses her kitchen, and we chatted as she prepared a meal from scratch. She showed me the storage issues, the ambiance of the kitchen moving from day into evening, and indicated how she likes to gaze out the window opposite her current sink location. The kitchen is bright but disorganized. She is not happy with the feeling and would like it to be warmer, more colorful, yet organized for her many kitchen tasks. The kitchen is the hub of her home, the place where she feels good.

Make a full list first; then split this into a list of requirements by priority.

What the client tells you: This client is sensitive to many fragrances and all toxic glues and adhesives. Right off the mark, I must consider material choices in these terms. Natural woods, no plastic laminates. Must have healthy and eco-materials in the space.

Questions to ask: Ask the client to describe to you what she does and how; let them talk and write everything down if possible. For example, this client needs working counters at least 24 inches wide on each side of the sink. From the interviews and obser-

vations, it is clear that she needs at least 15 feet of working counter (she currently has about 5 feet).

She needs to have adjustable drawers that pull out; she is small in size and requires easy access to utensils.

The client visit reveals many things about her particular needs. She enjoys healthy cooking, and wants a countertop work area that is convenient and with a lot of workspace, where she can make homemade bread and food from scratch. Appliances need to be available but hidden from view when not in use, and she uses cookbooks regularly.

She also points out functional problems on the ground floor. The existing hallway leading to the kitchen is carpeted, unpractical because she has students walking through and the maintenance is time consuming. She wants a visual flow from the hallway to the kitchen and through to the dining space, and from there to the living room where the grand piano is in full view.

We have dinner and talk about the things she loves that reflect her sense of self. She shows me precious objects from trips overseas and from family, objects that are currently stored away but that she would like to display in the kitchen. She loves Mediterranean bright colors, deep, rich terra-cotta, and natural tones. She also talks about her budget and its limits. This is important because the kitchen will have to be custom made, appreciably more expensive than one ordered from a kitchen manufacturer. Repairs to the house have to be done as well, and this adds to her overall costs. She needs good and varied lighting for the different cooking tasks, especially in the winter months because it gets dark as early as 5:00 P.M.

The next day we visit healthy material and kitchen stores and identify certain materials as preferable to others:

- flooring—bamboo, natural wood, natural slate and tiles

continued on the next page

continued from the previous page

- kitchen cabinets—natural wood only
- countertops—natural materials such as tile, wood, or granite
- walls—chemical-free paints

We also review the kitchen design and different choices for the colors, materials, and ambiance. We look at alternative kitchen types and styles, and she shows me what she likes as well as what she does not. After the research is collected, the client's requirements need to be analyzed.

Analysis of kitchen functional needs (counter area and work flow) includes:

- more counter surface for working; hidden storage for the appliances within easy access of kitchen work counter
- work flow goes from (hot foods) fridge → sink → worktop → oven → serving counter → table
Or
- (cold foods) fridge → sink → worktop → table

After analysis, the designer documents Jackie's work flow in the kitchen:

- Refrigerator → counter, work → sink, wash → return counter, work → prepare → microwave prep → counter, prep → oven, bake → table, serve → cleanup to sink, dishwasher

Kitchen activities and areas the client requires are places for:

- bread baking, making natural juices and soups, making homemade jams, yogurt, and natural foods
- eating with friends, family, or alone, reading recipes, and organizing bills and projects
- growing herbs, canning and freezing organic-grown foods

Analysis of spatial allocations:

- the need for things in specific places: bread baking, storage of things within easy reach due to her size; placement of things where she can capitalize on the outside view (sink near the window)
- areas for overlapping functions (juice making, bread making, preparing hot or cold foods; quick meal preparations)
- hidden storage for the appliances, yet within easy reach

Aesthetic and user needs analysis:

- wants all appliances stored away (does not like visual clutter)
- likes bright colors and Mediterranean influences
- likes her books and objects to be in view (but not too many; mainly treasured items from travels and gifts)
- wants visual access to the birds in her backyard; wants warm and high-quality lighting; likes warmer tones and colors, likes Mediterranean tile look
- must have nontoxic materials and finishes due to allergic reactions to fumes and chemicals (no plastic laminates, synthetic materials, toxic glues, or composite materials)

Functional and building needs:

- leak in wall behind sink needs to be corrected
- new appliances and kitchen layout as per her specific work needs; functional for her specifically, yet general enough for resale value
- all new floors for the kitchen, entrance hall, and living/dining areas (extent of which to be determined once the prices come in)
- all new materials and finishes in the kitchen

Building architectural criteria:

- reuse existing structure; window sizes remain the same
- consider the hall and dining room surroundings in the overall approach to the space
- lighting poor and needs updating; becomes support for the tasks and must be flexible to change with the various work flow needs

- electrical up to date but need to verify if adequate for appliance needs
- new appliances; sink area can be moved

Preliminary evolving design criteria:

- consider the Mediterranean feeling evoked by Jackie's objects
- chemical-free environment a must
- functional and dynamic working kitchen required; easy access to appliances hidden when not in use; organized work counter and easy access to all amenities
- new lighting required; new wall and floor finishes; all-natural materials (granite, ceramic tile, bamboo or wood for floor; chemical-free paint)
- accent with color and neutral tones in hard surfaces (floor, countertop)
- kitchen cabinets must be made out of natural materials only (e.g., solid wood)
- leave hall and dining room as is, consider sight lines from each, and tile through hallway from kitchen for durability and maintenance
- kitchen counter: granite/hard work surface; possibly removable butcher block for bread (storage of same)
- vertical storage next to fridge; requires side-by-side fridge for easier storage and access

Client-specific requirements:

- natural products due to allergic reactions to synthetic materials
- work counter requirements (for organic cooking)
- specific storage requirements, entertaining needs

Intangible design criteria and client desires:

- keep the sunlight and bright feeling currently in the space; capitalize on it with the placement of work counter
- better functioning space for the small size
- better storage and access for the appliances
- light and airy; lively colors with client objects as inspiration

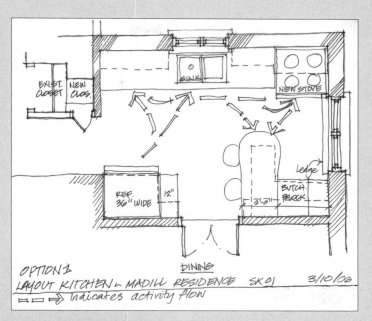

Figure A • Functional layout plan

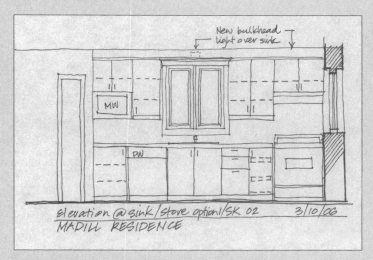

Figure B • Sketch elevations of two ideas

The overall concept begins to take shape as the design brief is created:

The concept is one of a kitchen with warmth and with all-natural, nontoxic materials to create a healthy environment. The concept that the designer develops is for a healthy and warm space, where all the materials, glues, construction, and choices are made

continued on the next page

Figure C

continued from the previous page

with the client's allergies and concerns in mind. The Mediterranean warmth that she desires is reflected in the color and material choices. The layout reflects her needs for flexibility through the placement of counters, fixtures, and storage spaces.

Specific requirements in terms of spatial allocation (becomes the scope of work):

- renovation of entire space: kitchen only (includes new finishes, cabinets, lighting, flooring)
- additional spaces to be done: hallway, dining space, and living room flooring only

Figure D • New kitchen after renovation

the same, or they might be completely different people.

- Understand the budget requirements and the client's idea of costs versus your knowledge of how much things cost in a design project. Are these poles apart, or is the client aware of project construction costs?
- Ask useful questions. For example, if the design is for a restaurant, specific questions can include:
  – What type of food?
  – How many people do you want to serve?
  – What turnover of meals do you need to have in a day?
  – Will you serve lunch?

Try to document everything the client says—ask for details on the size, the budget, and the scope of work that the client has in mind. Be prepared to tell the client some truths about his expectations. This is a delicate issue, especially if the designer is interviewing in competition with other designers.

In Case Study 3.6 we saw an example of an interview where the designer talks to the client, and simultaneously assesses and questions what she sees. The designer interviews the client, observes the client in the milieu where the design will take place, and uses conversation to generate feedback. A two-way dialogue develops that is built on trust and conversations that occur between the designer and client/user of the space. The designer understands the client, the budgetary requirements, and special requirements that demand particular attention.

Observation

Depending on the design situation, you may be able to observe people in their settings. You may also be asked to do so in a project where interviews alone are insufficient. This can occur in institutional and recreational design and in situations where people (the users) may not be able to speak for themselves. Observations can be done through the course of a day and during various activities within the same space. It is important to systematically plan out the observation time period, document the people observed, and get permission when the observations are of people

who may not have a say. These are ethical aspects that must be considered by the interior designer.

Things you should be doing as you learn about the client needs:

- Try to temporarily situate yourself in the client's shoes. Who are they? Are they the user of the space?
- Understand what people do in their different daily activities or functions.
- Try to understand what they are doing, why they need to do this a particular way, or if they are doing it as well as they could.
- Observe if they are comfortable, if they are having trouble, if the space and the equipment that they are using is suitable, and what they might be missing

Documentation

Documentation can take on many forms, including notes from interviews, observation, or recording the space and its characteristics. As we have seen, documentation can be done in many ways, including:

- Field notes such as written comments, interview notes, observations of the space in both written and visual sketch form
- Full documentation of the space itself through drawn plans and elevations, photos, videos, and written notes explaining the features of the space
- Photos of the surrounding environment, the exterior, and views from the space itself; detailed pictures of the characteristics of the space, particularly if these are to be conserved in a renovation
- Collected documents from the user (lists, object descriptions, equipment lists, notes, or program documents)

Full documentation is important because this is our way of understanding the space, its characteristics, and the people who use it. How this is done varies from firm to designer. Everyone develops their own systematic way of documenting a space, its occupants, and their activities.

Visually Recording and Measuring the Space

An important part of getting to know the project is to understand the space within which the new design will occur. The space may be an existing one, or a new one not yet built. Usually we record the space with a camera and by taking measurements. We want to thoroughly document the space visually as well as note its particular spatial characteristics.

Regardless of the form the space takes, it is vital to understand and record certain elements.

- Record flooring, ceiling, and wall types, window types and finishes.
- Document sections of the space to show the scale and dimensions.
- Plan the layout of the space with all the existing elements included. These may include the materials and finishes, the electrical outlets, the ceiling details and the existing elements within the ceiling or above any temporary or non-structural elements.
- Log the structure and the construction type.
- Record exterior views and sight lines.

DEVELOPING VISUAL ANALYTIC TOOLS IN DETAIL

After you have documented and recorded the space and user information, the next step is to organize the information into groupings, analyze it, break it down, and reconstruct it again. Why? As you decode the research, as you break it down, you can see patterns, different ways to understand the design problem. Here you enter into both an analytic and creative phase because your analysis hopefully helps you to see the problem in a new or different way. We will begin our exploration of analysis tools and methods by looking at them in two streams: verbal analytic tools and visual analytic tools.

Verbal/Narrative Analytic Tools

Verbal and narrative tools are tools based on the written word, on what has been said by people involved in the design project. This analysis can be gleaned from interview notes, conversations you have recorded, and observations that you have documented. The following are some different verbal and narrative tools that you can use.

Lists

Scenario: You have had numerous conversations and documented reams of research. Your head is spinning from all this information.

Tool: Make a series of lists. It is a good idea to begin with lists of the themes or groupings of information. Some possible topics include:

- client needs
- functional needs
- building characteristics
- project-specific contexts
- psychological contexts
- cultural issues
- physical needs of the user, including ergonomic requirements, anthropometric needs, age-related specific requirements, health-related specific requirements
- building needs summary—physical characteristics, human comfort issues

There are many ways to create lists. Figure 3.2 shows an example of lists for simple program development.

Charting Needs

Scenario: You have lists and conversations, notes and interviews. You are faced with too much information.

Tool: Creating charts is another good way to organize the information you have collected. You can chart the project information from the lists that you have made.

Charting Space Requirements

Scenario: You have made lists and charts, but you have no sense of the volumes that you need for the spaces you want to create.

Tool: Another important aspect of analyzing the research is to determine the space requirements for the design. No matter what the space, you need to know how much volume the activities will take

Departmental Staff Requirements (accounts for 20% growth over 3 years)
CURRENT 12 MONTH FORECAST 3 YEAR FORECAST
ALLOCATE SPACE (no desks etc. yet) FOR
STAFF TO SUPPORT 120 IA Teams
ID Type Operations IT [T+A+S] Marketing Operations IT [T+A+S]
Marketing Operations IT [T+A+S] Marketing
1 Full Office **2 03 [01+01+01] 1 2 03 [01+01+01] 1 2 03 [01+01+01] 1**
2 Call Center
Desks
7 04 [00+04+00] 0 7 06 [00+06+00] 0 9 08 [00+08+00] 0
3 Full
workstations
14 14 [08+05+01] 1 14 22 [13+08+01] 2 15 29 [16+12+01] 4
4
Department
sub Total
(*total of ID 2,*
3,4 below)
23 21 [09+10+02] 2 23 31 [14+15+02] 3 26 40 [17+21+02] 5
TOTAL 46 57 71
Departmental Storage Requirements (accounts for 20% growth over 3
years)
CURRENT 12 MONTH FORECAST ALLOCATE SPACE (no desks etc. yet) FOR
STAFF TO SUPPORT 120 IA Teams
ID Type Operations IT [T+A+S] Marketing Operations IT [T+A+S]
Marketing Operations IT [T+A+S] Marketing
5 File Cabinets **44 05 [00+02+03] 3 50 06 [00+02+04] 3 60 06 [00+02+04]**
3
Shared Resources Requirements
ID Type Quantity
1 Guest Office & Ben's Office 1
2 Meeting Room (Large), minimum 12 people 1
3 Meeting Room (Small), minimum 4 people 2
4 Kitchen 1
5 Lab Environment Benches (for teams in IT) 2
6 Lunch Room 1
7 Washroom 0
8 Consultant/temps work area 6

Figure 3.2 • Client list of requirements

Organizational list
Description of activities

Multicultural bar-restaurant and exhibition space
Sylvie Bélanger
Final project Cultural Complex, 2003

User type	Activities	Public/private	Needs
Manager	. management of the complex . event organizer	private	- office space with computer, telephone and blackberry - meeting space
Clients/visitors	. view art . meet with the artists . meet friends . be entertained . drink, eat . conversation, exchange . listen to music . meet clients . read . relax . dance . put clothes into coat check . go to restroom	private	- eating space - meeting spaces - viewing spaces for events - exhibition space for art display - restroom - entertainment views
Employees Offices	. work . complex management . event organization . telephone . meetings with potential clients . publicity and advertising . meetings with suppliers	public	- adequate work spaces for personnel - management and accouting services and support - marketing equipment and support services
Service personnel	. serve clients . organize spaces . seat clients . take orders . receive payment from clients . prepare food service/ drinks	public	- specific services locations within complex - storage for wine, beer, linens, glasses and service cutlery, dishes - bar service area for multi-use spaces - cash area
Support Services	. clean-up . daily maintenance . set up tables, chairs and event related accessories and equipment	Private/	- storage - clean-up and dirty storage zones
Event producers Artists	Create art/ interactive events	public	- exhibition area with interactive support - staging area with audience viewing - theatrical lighting and communication set-up - support for security and control - artists studio spaces - changing rooms and exercise studio spaces - back room kitchen and personal hygiene spaces
Producteurs	Produce events	public	
Comédiens	Comedy shows, revues	public	
Acrobates	Event productions	public	
Artistes exposants	Events, art exhibits, interactive shows and events; music shows, videos and cultural events	Public/ public	

up, independent of the rooms or physical spaces that might be designed. The SPACE requirements are different from the ROOM requirements. These can be listed in a list format, or charted and grouped, depending on the project.

Narrative and Stories

Scenario: You are visiting your clients and have been documenting the space. You need to get a sense of what they want. They were not clear when they first met with you. You need to get at what they want, and both clients—in this case a husband and wife—give you contradictory information when they speak to you.

Tool: Another great way to understand client or user concerns and needs is through the documentation of specific stories or conversations that you have with them. This is particularly useful if you get conflicting information from different users.

After compiling the lists, you can go back to the information and look for stories or conversations that represent the essence of what people want in their space. This will help you to determine the attributes of the space (see analysis methods in the next section). Case Study 3.3 is an excellent example of the intimate development of a design using narrative and conversation as the primary means to develop the project and evolve it from an idea toward a reality, using what people say and working together to develop design ideas.

Visual/Schematic Analytic Tools

The next step is to understand the research, the lists, and the conversations by analyzing the information with visual tools. Analysis means developing a connection between the meanings that you have uncovered in the client's words and the realities of the space requirements, the building contexts, and the user needs.

An important and often missed step is to develop visual interrelationships between user needs and user activities. This is a stepping-stone toward defining the space requirements. You may have determined certain spatial allocations earlier on—here you want to

make sure that these are realistic with your particular client and project requirements, through the development of schematic visual tools.

The following examples show you how to analyze your research using both words and visual schematic diagrams to see connections in the research. Using Case Study 3.3 and a few more student examples, let's look at the different ways that we can analyze a problem.

Listing Attributes in Schematic Form

One important way to stimulate the analysis process and your creative thinking is by forcing connections (Hanks & Parry, 1991, p. 66). This means using the lists you have created to make connections and understand the contexts of the problem.

Hanks and Parry suggest that the way to do this is as follows:

1. Clearly state your problem.
2. List all the attributes of your problem
3. Consider attributes for which you have a solution, even if it is for another application.
4. Make links—force connections between the attributes of your problem and the solutions you noted in Step 3. In Figure 3.4, we see how this might occur, using Case Study 3.3. as an example.

Developing a Visual Metaphor

A metaphor is another way to analyze the design problem. This is both an analytic method as well as a creative technique. When used for analysis purposes, the metaphor is a way to understand the design issue by comparing it to something else entirely. We borrow from what we know, and create ideas and concepts based on metaphors that we develop from images and words. When I was in my final year, I used the metaphor to develop a final design concept. Here is my story.

> While working on the design for a space station, I tried to understand the research through a series of analytic methods. As I was creating the needs charts, I thought about the need for survival and how a space station would be sustainable

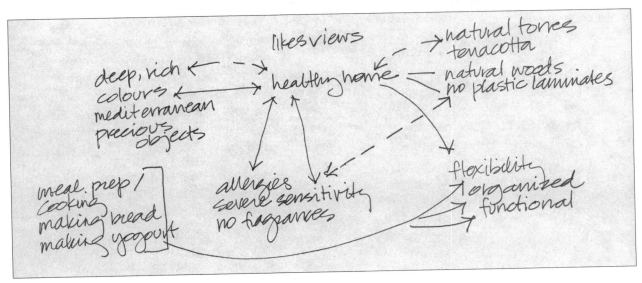

Figure 3.4 • Case Study 3.3—making connections

even in the event of a nuclear attack. Survival from nuclear attack and the depletion of natural resources was of great concern in the seventies and eighties. (Note: This was before the current sustainable design movement.) I compared the space station to a tree, with the Earth as its roots, feeding the space station like a series of branches, each one growing with the connection.

A metaphor is an orderly way to compare the analysis you are doing to something that is a symbol of the analysis. The space station that I designed was a very technical project about human survival in space. The metaphor of the tree was used to suggest that as with trees, human survival would be sustainable if the space station evolved from the Earth and could eventually survive on its own.

Mapping Inner Space as a Means to Develop Concepts of Themes

During the analysis process, your mind begins to create mental images of the various concepts. You can map these as a series of drawn images, both real and schematic.

This is called mind mapping. You can map on paper the images that you see in your head, be they cartoons, mental images, metaphors, or concepts.

Nancy Margulies talks about this technique in her book *Mapping Inner Space*. She suggests that visual and mind mapping are means for "generating and organizing any idea. Using a central image, key words, colors, codes, and symbols, the process is both fun and fast" (2002, p. 10).

A visual map has a central idea with radiating images or symbols that are connected with arrows, lines, or squiggles. This is a great way to break out of thinking only in words, although you can incorporate words with the images that you generate.

Figure 3.5 shows an example of a mental visual map that we might use in interior design. Each of us can develop our own visual mapping techniques. We will explore this method further in Chapter 6.

Matrix Analysis

The matrix analysis is a method that has been used for many years by interior designers. It is a means to organize activities and functions to determine space allocations and relationships. The matrix diagram is a functional organization of a space or activities, as a means to prioritize the different things going on and help the designer to organize the information that has been collected.

The matrix analysis should be used whenever there are multiple activities, and also multiple

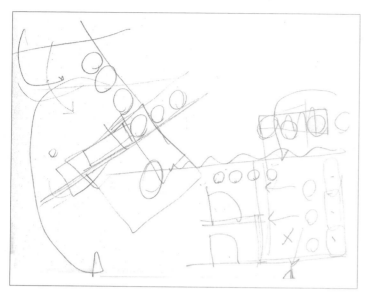

Figure 3.5 • Example of a visual map

functions and client needs. It allows the designer to make sense of the collected data and to organize it into priorities. When a matrix has useful information in its analysis, schematic drawings can then be generated. The matrix can be a way to begin to link the written word (information collected) with visual schematic sketches. Figure 3.6 shows an example of a simple matrix analysis.

Figure 3.6 shows how the matrix is organized to connect every idea to another in order to see what emerges. Hanks and Parry suggest that what emerges is "forcing connections between items that may not be considered otherwise" (1990, p. 68).

Let's return to Case Study 3.3 and try out the matrix analysis using the information that we have collected. We established several things with the lists that we compiled, and develop the design criteria for the client as follows:

- She likes to look out her window when she prepares food and bakes bread.
- She likes to spread out and work on the counter, close to the fridge, sink, and stove.
- She needs to put away her cooking utensils when they are not in use.
- She does not want to have her sink interfere with her view.

- She needs to prepare fresh, organic foods and homemade bread, yogurt, and meals.
- She wants to see her Mediterranean objects and gifts from travels abroad.
- She wants to move easily from refrigerator to sink to worktop right to the stove.
- She need for things to be in easy reach for her small frame.

This is not the only way to analyze; quite possibly the matrix unlocks a new or different way to "see" the data that you have collected in a different way. It is an organizational tool (see Figure 3.7).

Visual Information Screening and Key Word Development

We acquire new knowledge as we gather information. In the analytic phase, we need to learn how to sift through this information to decide what is useful and what is not. As Hanks and Parry (1991) suggest, "The more information you have to work with, the more connections you have the potential of making."

How do we sift through this information? How do we know what to keep and what to discard? We have to be careful not to collect *too* much; otherwise, we can get bogged down by the overcollection of information. This is where you can ask some questions. Each piece of information can be questioned as follows:

- Is this information absolutely vital to my understanding of the problem?
- Does this information help me to better understand the issue at hand?

You can screen information by creating a more complex matrix analysis, and linking this to visual schematic diagrams.

Generating Planning Schematics and Bubble Diagrams

An important part of working through collected research is to analyze using schematics and diagrams of all kinds. Schematic plans and bubble diagrams of spaces are pre-design ways of seeing the project before you get into the actual design. Depending on the scope of the project, these diagrams are meant to be a fast means of visualizing the space before you get too far into detailed planning.

Schematic plans can be done as block plans or layouts, where the spaces are "blocked out" within a space in the approximate sizes that are needed. (Karlen 1993, Rengel 2003) You can create quick block plans using hand-drawn or virtual schematic layouts and trying out different ways to place spaces within the larger building context. Bubble diagrams are a type of schematic. Let's look at these next.

About Bubble Diagrams

For example, interior designers have used bubble diagrams as a first means to organize the schematic spatial needs they have generated either as lists, charts, or schematics. These bubble diagrams are developed systematically from the analyzed information that has been gathered. Specifically, an interior designer tries to see with bubble diagrams how spaces, activities, or client desires might be assessed before they become real walls and rooms.

The bubble diagram is a schematic diagram that you can create before the space is finalized or rooms become fixed (Figure 3.9). It is a way to envision the space and to work out the functional aspects through a series of possible layouts. One well-done bubble diagram can help lay the groundwork for several possible layout options later on.

The bubble diagram:

- organizes information about the space, its needs, and the activities and functions/desires that flow from these
- helps you to see the activities as visual representations of the functions and the needs
- keeps the functional aspects loose and free, unconstrained by the space

Some designers use these diagrams and some do not. This is up to you. If you are able to plan out the space and sculpt it without first organizing it in schematic form, then do so.

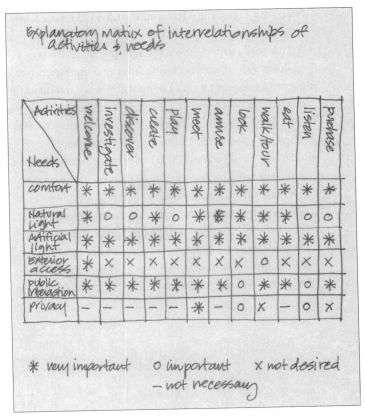

Figure 3.6 • Example of a simple matrix analysis

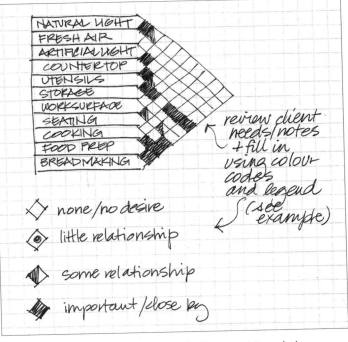

Figure 3.7 • Case Study 3.3—Example of a simple matrix analysis

Mapping Dynamic Movement and Experiences in Space

An essential aspect of designing interior space is understanding, and planning for, the dynamic movement of the human body in space. We are in constant movement when we walk around and use our spaces. Circulation sketches, flow diagrams, and kinesthetic maps are used often to track these movements. For example, Paul Laseau (2001) uses the kinesthetic map as a technique (among others) to show how people circulate around and within a space. If we consider Case Study 3.6, one important element to study was how the client moved within her space and did her kitchen activities. She moves around her kitchen in a particular way while performing varied tasks, and when she moves around dynamically, she has what is known as a kinesthetic experience. Paul Laseau discusses this type of movement:

> Circulation is one of the most under-considered functions inherent in a building program. Many of the experiences of a house, its impact on people, take place as they move through and between spaces. These are referred to as kinaesthetic experiences; they are dynamic experiences unlike sitting or standing in one space. (p. 90)

In interior design, mapping out the circulation, or dynamic movement of people, is as important as understanding static functions such as sleeping. When you create a list of activities, you can do several things to understand the movements that they generate.

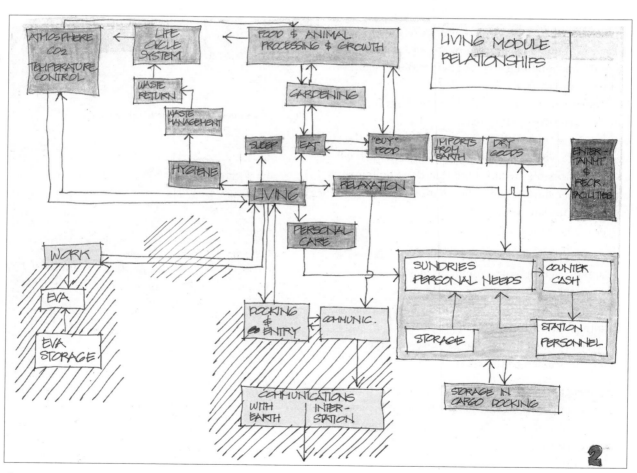

Figure 3.8 • Example of space station matrix analysis

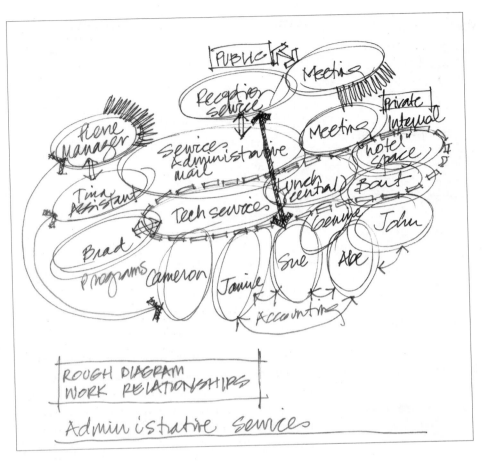

Figure 3.9 • Example of a bubble diagram

- Prioritize the movements. This can be done by looking at who moves how, mapping it on a plan, and then looking at the number of movements.
- Look at the main circulation points. How are people moving in and around the space? Where are there crowded places? Where is there congestion, and how could this be alleviated?

Figure 3.10 shows how we might create a kinesthetic map.

MATCHING THE RESEARCH AND ANALYSIS TO THE CLIENTS AND THEIR NEEDS (IT IS NEVER BLACK AND WHITE)

The purpose of interviews and meetings with clients is to lay the groundwork for the design itself. The interior designer is responsible for a thorough investigation of user and client needs, established within the clients' budget expectations and within an aesthetic that hopefully innovates or adds value to the designed space. Problems arise when interior designers fail to understand the complexity of a problem, do not take the time to meet and speak with the client, or fall into a project without doing the necessary research.

Sometimes clients think that they know what they need, but upon investigation, the designer sees the client needs differently. The interior designer looks at the problem in ways that the client may not have considered, or grasps the budgetary implications differently. Clients may not always know what their needs are, or may have unrealistic expectations for the work to be done relative to the costs involved.

This is why it is so important to study the various types of design programs and the different ways of establishing project needs. An integral component of this research and analysis is the intent of client and designer in the process. Let's examine this aspect of the design process next.

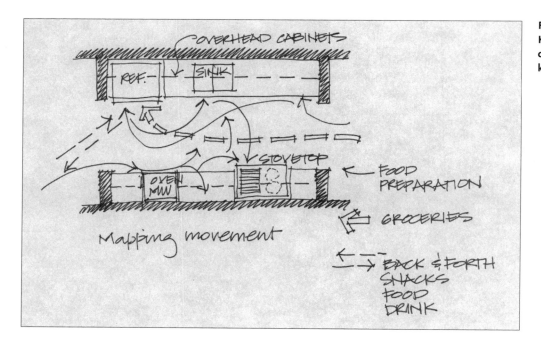

Figure 3.10 •
**Kinesthetic map of
client work flow in the
kitchen: Case Study 3.6**

Design Intentions

As interior designers, we make certain choices deliberately. We may choose to have:

- an aesthetic approach
- a creative approach
- a functional approach
- a philosophical approach

Each time we create or conceive a design, we bring
with us preconceived notions about aesthetics, philosophy, and our own creative sense. This is our design
intent, and much of what is designed has an intention
or a purpose. Remember, the dictionary says that to
design is to have an *"aim, purpose, plan, intent, objective, object, goal, end, target, hope, desire, wish, dream,
aspiration, ambition."*

This concept of *intention* is difficult to grasp
because we all have our own personal design intentions. They are the reason why we go into interior
design in the first place. On one hand, we may want
to improve the interior environment, or we have a
better way to envision space. We may have a desire to
help people better their lives through design. These
are altruistic aesthetic design intentions. On the

other hand, we may strive to be the star designer who
creates concepts that will appear on the pages of a
magazine, or we may only want to create interiors for
the wealthy. We may see our vision of a space as more
important than that of the client or user. These are
also design intentions, whether of an aesthetic nature
or of a more altruistic nature.

About Prejudice

As soon as you embark on a design project, you bring
certain assumptions or prejudices with you. This is
human nature. We all have certain prejudices that
we carry with us at all times, whether we realize it
or not. These are value assumptions, and they are
fundamental to who we are as human beings. (Vaikla-
Poldma, 2003) For example, if I have never worked in
my life, my values, concepts, and assumptions about
work will be quite different from someone who has
worked from the age of 12 to earn money to support
a family. If I am a single working mother, my life
experiences will differ from those of a married stay-
at-home mother of four. As an interior designer, I
must become aware of these value differences and the
way that my own assumptions carry into my design
decisions.

Introduction to Aesthetic, Philosophical, or Creative Approaches

Design approaches can be aesthetic, philosophical, or creative. They can be functional, cultural, or humanist, and they can be intellectual or emotional as well. Understanding that these are design intentions is a first step; understanding that these approaches are integrated into how we understand design problems is crucial. We use what we know to develop our design ideas and, whether male or female, young or old, we bring with us our background, our cultural identity, and many other elements that shape how we see and do our designs.

Here we will take a very introductory look at what design intentions are by examining a few types of design approaches. We will introduce these intentions and approaches with four examples: aesthetic, philosophical, functional, and creative.

Aesthetic Approaches

A client hires a designer because they have a certain style. The client wants you to help them create a homey feeling, or a modern and timeless sense of space. Each of these requirements relates to how we understand the aesthetic of a space, the more artful way that we make the space "fit" a feeling.

An aesthetic approach means that we give more emphasis to the look and feel of form and space as an aesthetic experience, and give this priority over function and need. When we design aesthetically, we choose to define our design by the look, the form, and the response of the person using the space. Aesthetic intentions are grounded in what we consider to be beautiful or visually pleasing. We use design elements as an aesthetic "language" to give the interior cohesion, and to give the user an aesthetic experience.

Aesthetic approaches as intentions are framed within our understanding of spaces and how we attach meaning through aesthetic components of interior space. We may want to change the way people live by showing them how they might live better, live differently, or accomplish their daily tasks using objects other than what they are used to. We create spaces using aesthetic intentions, which allow for better living through the design decisions we make.

We do so by designing spaces with form, color, light, and material.

Philosophical Approaches

A philosophical approach might be a deliberate desire to change the way that people do things because we want to create a better environment for them. This reflects the philosopher Ludwig Wittgenstein's (1997) pragmatic philosophical approach. Wittgenstein believed that life could be more aesthetic. Here Richard Shusterman (1997) presents Wittgenstein's ideas:

> Wittgenstein wanted to communicate a model of how to live philosophically:
> What help is it . . . to solve philosophical problems, if (one) cannot settle the chief, most important thing—how to live a good and happy life? (Mo 506–507). "Live well" is the supreme philosophical commandment. . . . (p. 21)

Shusterman interprets Wittgenstein's pursuit of better living through aesthetic thought and process:

> Today's moral scepticism . . . has revitalized the aesthetic model, the idea that life should be practiced as an art. . . .
> . . . art, which looks at the world with a happy eye, has beauty as its end. (N75,86, in Shusterman, pp. 25)

Wittgenstein is a philosopher who suggests that this approach is, in fact, an aesthetic necessity: to be able to live better through the concrete pursuit of better living through aesthetic means. A philosophical approach to designing means that we approach the design problem knowing that it is grounded, in part, in ethical decision making. We understand that our intentions are going to affect how people "see" and use a space, and how they respond to it. This means that, as a designer, I want the design to help people live better, and this then becomes my personal philosophical "stance" or intention. Who we are and how we live becomes a philosophically grounded construct that affects how we design for others as clients and as human beings with cultural, social, and gender-biased

Figure 3.11 • Developing an aesthetic approach

Figure 3.12 • A design concept reflecting a philosophical approach

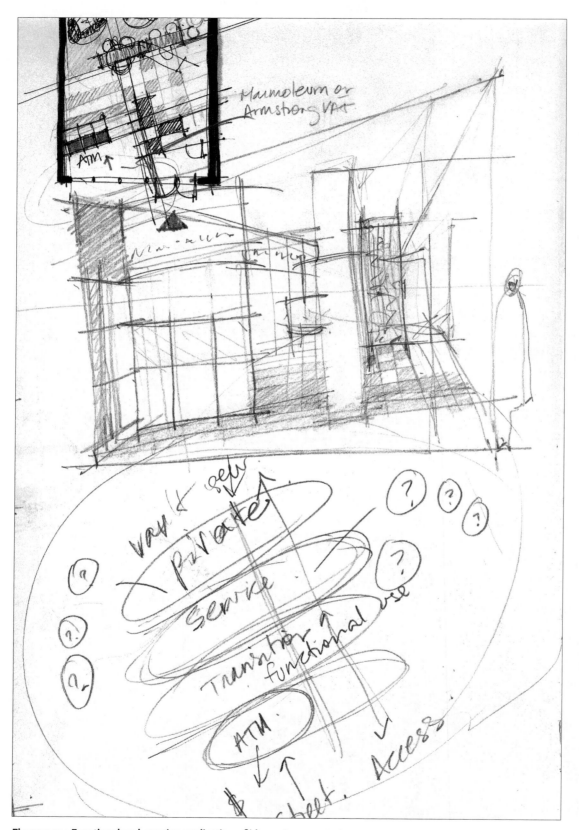

Figure 3.13 • Functional and creative application of ideas, store concept

philosophies (Shusterman, 1997; Csikszentmihalyi & Rochberg-Halton, 1981).

This concept of philosophical intentions will be explored further in Chapters 8 and 9.

Functional Approaches

A functional approach, on the other hand, is when we respond specifically to user needs and program requirements as our design intentions. We satisfy the practical needs of the client, and we have a space where people say, "I can work well here."

The intention of a functional approach is the implementation of a design program as defined by the client. The space must "work" in that people should be able to fulfill their activities easily and without difficulty. This means being productive at work, able to prepare meals easily at home, or eat comfortably in a restaurant.

A functional intention may be present with or without aesthetic or philosophical intentions, although usually it works in concert with both. Function does imply the notion of "fit," that an appropriately designed space suits the needs of the user, for example.

Creative Approaches

The creative approach is one where we apply creative thinking intentionally. Creativity is a difficult concept, due to the many ways we understand creativity in society. People's ideas about creativity are very broad. One way of understanding creativity is that the designer "creates" the design out of his head, from a lonely artistic sense of what the design "should" be. This is a traditional and very common understanding of the "creative approach." The assumption is that to be "creative" means to have an inherent creative ability that you are born with.

An alternative approach to creativity is when we can develop a creative intention and approach that is as much skill as talent. Design approaches and intentions can be considered creative when they:

- innovate
- problem-solve
- provide new perspectives

- help us see things a new way
- apply aesthetic, functional, and philosophical responses
- reorganize things differently
- rattle our sense of what design is

Creative intentions cannot be contrived or created rationally. They occur "despite oneself" during the design process. We will consider creative approaches and thinking in greater detail in Chapter 6. We can now move into examining more complex projects and design programs/briefs for larger projects.

BIBLIOGRAPHY

Ching, F. D. K. (1979). *Architecture: Form, space and order.* New York: Van Nostrand Reinhold Company.

Ching, F. D. K. (1987). *Interior design illustrated.* New York: Van Nostrand Reinhold.

Ching, F. D. K. (2003). *Architectural Drawing.* New York: John Wiley & Sons.

Cooper, D. (Ed.). (1992). *A companion to aesthetics.* Cambridge, UK: Blackwell Publishers Ltd.

Csikszentmihalyi, M., & Rochberg-Halton, E. (1981). *The meaning of things: Domestic symbols and the self.* Cambridge, UK: Cambridge University Press.

Danko, S., Meneely, J., & Portillo, M. (2008). Humanizing design through narrative inquiry. *Journal of Interior Design Education and Research, 31*(2), pp. 10–28.

Franz, J. (2000). An interpretive—Contextual framework for research in and through design: The development of a philosophically methodological and substantially consistent framework. In D. Durling, & K. Friedman (Eds.). *Foundations for the Future: Doctoral Education in Design: Proceedings of the Conference held 8-12 July in La Clusaz, France.* Staffordshire, UK: Staffordshire University Press.

Guerin, D., & Martin C. (2001). *The interior design profession's body of knowledge; Its definition and documentation.* Original Report prepared for the Association of Registered Interior Designers of Ontario (ARIDO). Toronto: ARIDO.

Hanks, K., & Parry, J. (1991). *Wake Up Your Creative Genius.* Menlo Park, CA: Crisp Publications.

Karlen, M. (1993). *Space Planning Basics.* New York: Van Nostrand Reinhold.

Laseau, P. (2001).*Graphic thinking for architects and designers.* New York: John Wiley & Sons.

Malnar, J.M., and Vodvarka F. (1992). *The Interior Dimension: A Theoretical Approach to Enclosed Space.* New York: Van Nostrand Reinhold.

Margulies, N. (2002). *Mapping inner space: Learning and teaching visual mapping* (2nd ed.). Tucson, AZ: Zephyr Press.

Massey, A. (1990). *Interior design of the 20th century* (1st ed.). New York: Thomas and Hudson.

Miller, S. F. (1995). *Design process: A primer for architectural and interior designers.* New York: Van Nostrand Reinhold.

Nelson, E., & Stolterman, E. (2003). *The Design Way: Intentional Change in an Unpredictable World.* Englewood Cliffs, NJ: Technology Publications, 2003.

Pena, W. (1977). *Problem-seeking: An Architectural Programming Planner.* Houston, TX: CBI Publishing.

Pena, W. M., Parshall, S. A., & HOK Group. (2001). *Problem-seeking: An architectural programming planner* (4th ed.). New York: John Wiley & Sons.

Pile, J. F. (1995). *Interior design.* New York: Harry N. Abrams.

Poldma, T. (2005). *Considering Wittgenstein's legacy for design and architecture: self-reflection and aesthetic meaning.* Paper presented at the Wittgenstein, Art & Architecture Conference, CCA, Montreal.

Poldma, T. (2007). *Living in complexity: First-year design studio experiences.* Paper presented at the IDEC 2007 International Conference: Design and Social Justice, Austin, TX.

Rao, S. (2003). Practice matters: Programming regains importance in tough times. *Architectural Record, (10)*3.

Rengel, R. (2003). *Shaping interior space.* New York: Fairchild Publications.

Rodemann, P. A. (1999). *Patterns in interior environments: Perception, psychology and practice.* New York: John Wiley & Sons.

Shusterman, R. (1997). *Practicing philosophy: pragmatism and the philosophical life.* New York: Routledge.

Sloan Allen, P., Stimpson, M., & Jones, L. (2000). *Beginnings of interior environments* (8th ed.). Upper Saddle River, NJ: Prentice Hall.

Soanes, C., Waite, M., & Hawker, S. (Eds.). (2001). *Oxford dictionary, thesaurus and wordpower guide.* Oxford, UK: Oxford University Press.

Vaikla-Poldma, T. (1999). *Gender, design and education: The politics of voice.* Montreal: McGill University, Author.

Vaikla-Poldma, T. (2003). *An investigation of learning and teaching processes in an interior design class: An interpretive and contextual inquiry.* Unpublished doctoral thesis. Montreal: McGill University, Author.

Wang, D. (2006). A form of affection: Sense of place and social structure in the Chinese courtyard eesidence. *Journal of Interior Design Education and Research, 31*(2), pp. 28–39.

Chapter Four

SCENARIOS, DESIGN BRIEFS, AND USERS

Objective

In Chapter 3 we introduced concepts about the interior design process that include the client, the user, and how to create the design program and design brief for a particular interior design project. We discussed how to research and collect information for a simpler and smaller project, and how to analyze the project as a design problem from various perspectives. You were introduced to the basic steps of programming and how to collect the information required for a design project.

In this chapter we explore these ideas in greater depth, for larger and more complex projects. We will see what constitutes the design program from a broader perspective, and how we develop design thinking from information that we collect. We will also explore first ideas about planning out the space and how you can get into a design project in its earliest stages.

As projects get larger and more involved, we have a tendency to forget that we are designing for people, for a "human user." Larger projects bring with them more complex needs, requiring a higher level of development in the design program. We will look at these larger, second-level design program problems and examine what we need to know as we analyze design projects involving multiple players and contexts.

CREATING THE COMPLEX DESIGN PROGRAM: CONCEPTS AND ISSUES

Let's begin by reviewing the steps of the design process, and then applying this in larger, more complex design projects and problems.

Review of the Concepts: The Design Process Steps

If we remember from Chapters 2 and 3, the design process unfolds in three steps: the pre-process, the design process, and the post-design process. A brief review of five stages within these processes is as follows:

1. Information-gathering process (research and analysis)
2. Planning process
3. Designing process
4. Creative process
5. Evaluation process/thinking process

The process flows from one aspect to another, and sometimes certain steps overlap or return later on.

Let's look at these and complex design program formulation in a little more detail.

Contextual Issues in Design Program Development

As interior design projects grow in size and scope, so do the research requirements, analysis methods, and the subsequent design interventions proposed. Each aspect of the project becomes a little more complicated. One moment we are working on the intimate needs of a person in her home; the next we might be organizing the ways that people work together to achieve a corporation's goals. In yet another moment we might look at well-being in a recreational environment such as a spa or hotel, or design restaurants, relaxation spaces, and boutiques.

In these types of projects, we are no longer intimately involved with a single client or user the way we might have been with a smaller design project. The more stakeholders (users, clients, consultants, specialists) we have within a project, the more layers we have of different requirements, specific design considerations, and more complex interrelationships between the designer, users, spaces, and designs. We create designs to satisfy the needs of both users and stakeholders, and although we need to meet with clients to understand their needs, in more complex projects we do not necessarily know whose values we are designing for: the user who needs the space a certain way, the client who needs the user to perform a certain task, or someone else altogether.

Complex Design Brief/Program

When we consider multiple users, needs, requirements, and diverse spatial contexts, we enter into complex design projects and briefs. Developing a more complex design project means understanding:

- the type of project with its general contexts (user, occupancy, circulation, movement, spatial, and other contexts)
- multiple-user types and requirements (age, gender, type, scale, cultural, or social contexts)
- multiple space and activity requirements (type, volume, need, responses)

- specific and varied contexts and issues relative to the project (user, contexts, needs, responses)

The complex interior design program usually includes a client-driven design brief, multiple or more complex interior spaces, and additional people involved as consultants or actors within the project. Larger projects require the expertise of architects and engineers or other consultants who are specialized in their particular field. Usually you become a team player who is integrated into the project at some point, and not always at the outset of the project.

Users and Environmental Design Types

Interior designers work within the broader world of the built environment. We may work on many different types of interior spaces and projects, depending on our interests, our expertise, and our knowledge. Our contemporary society is constantly changing and developing new needs, both local and global. Projects are increasing in size and scope, and are constantly evolving to accommodate more complex needs in work and leisure. This adds to the complexity of design projects, and this is why it is vital that we learn how to organize information for projects with complex contexts, multiple uses, or different user groups.

In a nutshell, environmental design encompasses the following different types of interiors:

- Residential design: small-scale individual, multiple housing, assisted housing
- Food service design: including restaurant and café design, bars and nightclubs, cafeterias and coffee shops, specialty food spaces
- Recreational design: including sports complex and spa spaces, arts and cultural centers, museums and galleries
- Merchandising and retail design: including boutiques, chain and box stores, branding and graphic image
- Government and institutional design: including government offices, schools, hospitals, assisted-care institutions, student residences and spaces
- Hospitality design: including hotels and diverse accommodation spaces, spas, specialty recreation spaces

- Transportation design: including train, plane, and cruise ship interiors
- Specialized design types: including exhibition design, interaction design, technology-based environments, specialized or mixed environments not fitting a particular type (adapted from Davidson & Leung, *Interior Design*, 2006)

There are many other types and mutations of these types, as we mix and combine different types and uses with changing tastes and times.

What differs in each design type and environment are several key concepts. These include:

- human scale and perception
- space as a place, or as a dimension
- the view that we have of the space, as different stakeholders or users
- human perception and reactions to and within spaces, as both inhabitants and as passersby
- the way we use forms, materials, and finishes to sculpt interior space to support certain activities
- how we develop details to understand how the space should be framed, set up, or understood as the backdrop for a particular activity
- how we develop intimate responses for people through the choice and use of color, form, light, and material

The interior designer becomes the interpreter of these requirements, advocating for the client, the user, and their vision of a project. We essentially become negotiators and collaborators among clients, users, other stakeholders, and the various consultants involved in getting the project built.

Client Driven versus Needs Driven

When we develop programs for a client (or clients), it is not the same as creating a program for the user, in the more intimate way that we explored user needs in Chapter 3. We might develop a research program for a particular client, and this may have nothing at all to do with the well-being of the user. Ideally, creating a client-driven program should include designing for

the user and their well-being simultaneously, but this is not always the case, nor is it always possible.

There are times when we do not necessarily respond to a design brief. Sometimes we collect information for clients who are users, or clients who may become users, or for users who are not yet defined. This would be research-driven program development. When we do research for a future use, the end result may (or may not) be a designed space, or it may be research done to determine potential uses for a space (scenarios).

The Client as a Person and as a User of Interior Space

One thing that complicates research for a given project is how we approach the people involved to conduct our research. In Chapter 3 you saw a relatively simple approach:

- We speak to the *people* who want change within an existing space or a concept for a new space.
- We understand and document the users' *needs* (usually one and the same person).
- We understand the various *contexts* related to the project, such as the building, the space, the idea or concept for the project, the parameters, the constraints, and the desires.
- We interpret these needs by developing a design program, from which we define the design brief that we then present back to the client, and as a *response* to what we have identified as needs and contexts.

In essence, we understand the design problem by understanding four basic concepts:

person → needs → contexts → response

The last element, *response*, is our response to the first three elements: the person, their needs, and all of the contexts surrounding the project at hand.

In complex projects, this direct link becomes complicated by the layers of people we must deal with. We might speak to one person about the program, and yet observe others at work. Often the user is not one and the same. We collect our information from the different perspectives of different people including users, people who control the budgets, and the stakeholders in the space. Let's look at these next.

Complex Users: The Client, the User, and the Stakeholder

In more complex projects, clients can be the user, an investor who will never see the space, or can be both the stakeholder and user. You will find that clients want to create new designs for many reasons, whether it is to make more money and be more productive, or to live better and improve their environment. Table 4.1 charts some examples of different types of stakeholders, users, and clients:

As you can see from this chart, there are many different combinations of users, stakeholders, and project sizes. These are loose groupings and offer only a sampling of various projects and their sizes.

DEVELOPING THE COMPLEX DESIGN PROGRAM

Another important aspect of developing a complex design program is to understand the variety and complexity of the project context itself. You need to do the following:

- Gather the data that you will need for the design of the complex interior.
- Organize this data so that it is useful for your design.
- Use the data and assess its usefulness while doing the design.

We essentially must collect information to be able to create a design program. Then we must use this program to develop a cohesive set of needs and design parameters that become the client **project needs** statement. This includes organizing the information (data) that we collect in terms of:

1. Developing the design program
   a. Define the clients' needs as the primary function of a design program.

b. Develop the components of the design program itself.
   c. Research the specific contexts of the design project.
2. **Developing the design criteria for the program**
   a. Analyze and summarize the components, contexts, and needs in more concise terms and concepts that can be linked to the spatial development of the design.
   b. Develop the concise terms and concepts into design criteria, a set of ideas, concepts, lists, and schematics that explore the potential design ideas that are emerging, based on research, analysis, and intuitive development.

After we have deciphered the clients' needs, we can begin to develop the design program by systematically moving into the research and information-gathering processes. Let's look at the various tasks we might do within this process. We need to define the clients' needs as the primary function of the design program, and the components of the design program itself. To be able to define and develop these components, we go back to the processes that we use. The first one is the information-gathering process.

Information Gathering (Research and Analysis)

After you have met the client and understood their basic needs and desires for a project, you have to switch into a new gear to develop the program. In complex program development, the level of research is deeper. We will look at each different concept next.

Preliminary Description of the User/Client as a Person

When assessing project needs in the early stages of the project, we learn most of what we need to know from our clients, the people who hire us. We must understand at the outset that they may not be the end user, so our questions are framed with this in mind. We must ask these questions when we first meet a client:

1. Who is the client?
   - Age, sex, life status, and so on
   - Cultural background

Table 4.1 • Project/Client/User/Stakeholder Roles

Project scope	Client	User	Stakeholders
Small			
Residence	Husband/wife	Family/children	Family
Three generations	Mother/daughter/family	Granddaughter	Family
Parents	Single mother	Parents and daughter	On her own
Kitchen renovation	Owner/single mother and child	Same	Same
Home renovation	Husband and wife	Husband and wife	All extended family
Hair salon	Owner	Hairstylist, shampooist, manicurist	Owner/hairstylist/administrative assistant, support staff
Retail shop or boutique	Owner/manager	Manager/service staff, buyer/shopper/browser	Owner/manager
Design office	Owner/designer	Owner/designers	Owner/designer
Café (0–50 people)	Owner/manager	Servers, patrons (inside, takeout)	Owner
Medium			
Office (persons) • Financial • Corporate • Institutional	Employees Clients	Employees, clients, visitors	Corporation
Home for the elderly (condominium)	Management	Owner	Both
Restaurant/café (50–150 people)	Owner, chef	Patrons, service, owners	Owner, chef
School cafeteria (100–150 people)	School administration	Students, teachers	All
Large			
Hospital	Managers	Nurses, doctors, patients, family	Administrators, government, doctors, employees
Hotel	Owner of chain, hotel manager	Tourists, businesspeople, visitors	Owner, developer, employees
Shopping mall	Development company, landlord	Landlord, tenant, consumers, tourists	Developer/investor
Restaurant (150 people +)	Owner	Patrons, tourists	Employees, owner, chef
Other types of interiors (Small but complex needs)			
Exhibition, trade show	Company	Visitors, tourists, businesspeople	Company, exhibition hall, cities
Transportation interior			
Train/cruise ship Jet or airliner	Owner/carrier	Tourists, businesspeople	Employees, carrier, cities/ports

Small (0–1000 sf); Medium (1000–5000 sf); larger (5000+ sf)

- Religious background
- Relevance of each for the project
- Each person's role in the space; the role of the client

2. Who is the user?
   - Is the user the client?
   - Who is the client?
   - Who is the proprietor of the space?
   - Who are other people using the space?

3. Client profile
   - Personal characteristics
   - Tastes, wants, desires
   - Practical or functional needs

Activities and Needs of the Client and the User

Next we must determine the activities and the needs of the client/user. Not only will people perform activities within the space, they will have perceptions and ideas about what they require and what they want to do. We need to watch people in action, speak to them to see what they do, understand why and how, and then decipher who does what and how within the space. We do this by identifying their needs and activities.

These are as follows:

1. Primary needs
   - What are the principal needs that the user or client requires for this space?
   - Individual or collective
   - Type
     - economic level
     - ages, gender
     - how related to the client profile

2. Secondary needs
   - What are the desired or secondary needs?
   - What would the client like to see but perhaps is not necessary?
   - What are required functions but not primary in nature?

3. Tertiary needs
   - What are other needs that might be useful or an added benefit?
   - What are support functions that are necessarily primary or secondary?
   - What needs might be served?

Activities

Fundamental to designing interior space is the relationship between people, the contexts of their needs, and how these are perpetuated through their daily activities. Possible things to look for when charting activities are listed as follows:

1. The nature of the activities
   - Passive/active
   - Noisy/tranquil
   - Private/public
   - Requires equipment, utensils, support materials
   - Requires certain aids (lighting, window or daylight, proper ergonomic support)
   - Requires virtual communication capacities

2. The hierarchy of these activities
   - What are primary, secondary, and tertiary?
   - How are these activities interrelated?
   - Understand the movement of one activity to another.
   - Develop conceptual schematic diagrams between the needs, the activities, and the desires on the part of the client, independent of (and in preparation for) the design.

After you have identified the activities, an important exercise is to analyze the interrelationships of the needs and activities. You can make a list of these concepts and organize them into a simple diagram, and we have already seen some examples in Chapter 3. We will explore more examples later in this chapter.

Territorial Needs

Related to the activities of people are certain territorial needs that we like to explore as interior designers. Theorists believe that people operate best when they have a "territorial space" around them (Sommer, 1969), and that designers can help change patterns of behavior through design interventions. Territorial needs may include:

- personal space requirements for each activity; personal preference or way of doing things (color and style, subjective vision of how he or she would like something)

- desire—how the user might like to see the space from a layman's perspective
- particular interest linked to activities
- personal needs as expressed with the distances between certain spaces (Sommer, 1969)

There is an infinite amount of literature on this subject. Behavioral and social needs are defined by different authors and different types of knowledge, such as environmental behavior, sociology, gender studies, and anthropology. What is important here is to research the specific ways that people require personal space in a given design, and how you can research best practices on how this might be achieved.

Personal Space and Spatial Human Boundaries

Robert Sommer (1969), in his seminal book *Personal Space*, shows us how to situate personal space as a place of invisible boundaries that we create as a means of keeping our personal and psychological comfort. As he suggests, the best way to understand personal boundaries is to test them with real people:

> The best way to learn the location of invisible boundaries is to keep walking until somebody complains. Personal space refers to an area with invisible boundaries surrounding a person's body into which intruders may not come. Like the porcupines in Schopenhauer's fable, people like to be close enough to obtain warmth and comradeship but far enough away to avoid pricking one another. Personal space is not necessarily spherical in shape. . . . It has been likened to a snail shell, a soap bubble, an aura, and "breathing room." There are major differences between cultures in the distances that people maintain—Englishmen keep further apart than Frenchmen or South Americans. (p. 26)

People need their invisible boundaries as much as they need the contact of others when they want it. Designers cannot force distances and relationships to change because basic human instincts will always prevail. The trick is to understand human behavior because a designer is to support certain ways of being

and help move other ways of being into new and perhaps exciting and appropriate realms. As with the office design examples we have seen thus far, we cannot change how people work, but through design we might help them to work better, more productively, or with more comfort.

There are many ways to understand space, and each one comes from a particular point of view. As we saw with the concept of invisible boundaries (Sommer, 1969), each culture and person has their own tolerance level for how closely people interact with them. This influences our design decision making. As designers who are concerned with the complexity of the interior environment, we need to understand the theories and then adapt them to our understanding of the user and client. Observe people, what they do and how, and try to find a design solution appropriate to their needs. We cannot "know" what territorial needs people have; we can only assume and judge based on the research that we do, and through the tools and means we have identified thus far.

On another level, you, as the interior designer, must learn the various points of view, and use your own judgment to understand how these relate to how you see and study people. As we saw with Jackie in Chapter 3, an intimate view of interior space is important when dealing with a client who is also the user. This approach would not be appropriate for an office design, where there may be 300 people to place within a space. Each context brings with it a different approach, both to the information gathering and the needs analysis.

Social Spatial Requirements

Social spatial requirements include the idea of space as creating intimacy, accessibility, adaptability, or flexibility, and the nature of space as socially constructed (Poldma, 1999; Vaikla-Poldma, 2003). Space is by its very nature socially constructed, in that we create spaces that replicate the social values of a particular society and enhance (or diminish) certain behaviors within that space. (Sommer, 1969; Poldma, 1999).

Social spatial requirements include:

- social distances between people for certain types of activities
- placement of furniture for optimal social contact
- spatial territorial requirements, whether practical, psychological, physical, or social (people need certain distances for conversation, eating, working, etc.)

Social spatial concepts include understanding:

- how spatial and human factors interact as social aspects of the project
- how actual spatial parameters can influence people, their movements, and subsequent social interactions
- the socially constructed nature of space as place, a political or social entity, as promoting or inhibiting certain activities over others, or excluding certain people

Each project has specific spatial and territorial needs. Frank D. K. Ching, in his book *Interior Design Illustrated* (1995), outlines spatial and territorial needs through a series of sketches and diagrams that show us how to organize people and their activities. In *Anatomy for Interior Designers*, Henry Dreyfuss (1969) demonstrates how people organize their lives with designed space. Concepts such as intimacy, flexibility, and spatial proximity (Sommer, 1969) are theories used to understand and explain optimal distance for conversation and discussion between groups of people. These are important considerations you should make as you analyze people's activities and needs.

In Figures 4.1 and 4.2, we see how distances are optimal for different types of activities. For example, if two people are dining in a restaurant, the distance between them is intimate and should be no more than one yard. If the same two people are having a conversation in a living room, they can be farther apart.

Figure 4.1 • Conversational distances between people

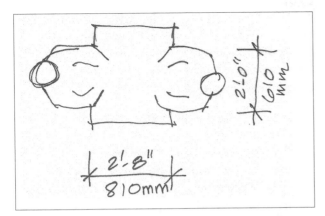

Figure 4.2 • Two people talking across a dinner table (adapted from Ching 1995)

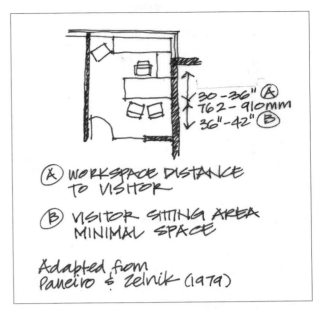

Figure 4.3 • Optimal space between two people in an office

Figure 4.4 • Round table and two chairs

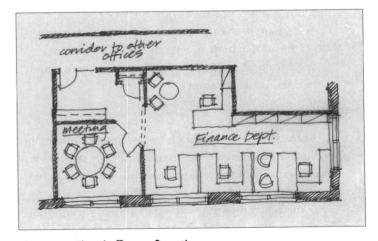

Figure 4.5 • Closed office configuration

However, if the distance between their two chairs is farther than two meters, the intimacy is broken, and the conversation changes to one that others can hear and join in. Distances are fundamental aspects of spatial design that we must consider to help affect certain types of activities.

On another level, a space and its characteristics can also determine how people will interact socially with one another. A space can be ordered to move people in a certain way, create intimate zones, or encourage public interactions. In Figures 4.3 and 4.4 we see two space layouts for an executive office. In Figure 4.3 we see a desk separating the visitor from the executive. This is a power relationship, as the desk provides a physical barrier. In Figure 4.4 we see a round table and three chairs. Here the executive is at the same "power level" as he joins the visitors equally around the table. In still another configuration, a closed office provides privacy in Figure 4.4. While in an open office, the same desk and chairs are no longer "private," and are part of the noise and activity of the office, in the following Figure 4.6.

Finally, spaces are socially constructed through their design. A space can be denied to some and not others, such as a bar or social club for men only (Poldma, 1999; Vaikla-Poldma, 2003). Social clubs, for example, are places that keep certain people out. In the Victorian era, smoking rooms were common in wealthier homes; these were male sanctuaries after formal dinners, where women and children were

Figure 4.6 • Open office configuration

forbidden (Ardener, 1981; Spain, 1992). In the open and closed offices shown in Figures 4.3 and 4.4, the "closed" implies power relationships with the people outside the closed environment.

Many cultures have social or religious rituals that are aided or controlled by spatial parameters (Spain, 1992). Spaces can also be used to define political boundaries, cultural atmospheres, and specific milieus.

Human Physical and Comfort Requirements

There are certain physical and physiological distances that are preferred and used for optimal human anthropological and ergonomic needs. These differ from the social and psychological contact elements we have just noted in that they are based on the physical characteristics of people. Henry Dreyfuss (1966), Julius Paneiro, and many others (Paneiro & Zelnik, 1979) have developed several important references on the human body in interior space. We will look specifically at anthropological and ergonomic issues in interior space design next.

Anthropometrics

Anthropometric theories have developed throughout history in an attempt to understand body size and its relationship to the physical environment, usually in terms of aesthetic proportions. The study of anthropometrics is the study of human dimension and the differences in individuals and groups, and optimal distances for various types of activities (Paneiro &

Zelnik, 1979, p. 23). In their book *Human Dimension and Interior Space*, Paneiro and Zelnik outline the theory of anthropometry and discuss how people have studied the human proportion and dimension for centuries. As they state,

> The fascination of philosophers, artists, theoreticians, and architects with human size dates back many centuries . . . (however) humanity's basic concern with the human figure historically has been more aesthetic than metrological, more involved with proportion than the absolute measurements and function. (pp. 17–18)

They cite Vitruvious, the Golden Section, and Le Corbusier's Modulor as examples of these proportional systems (p. 17–18). These are man-made "systems" in that they attempt to put into mathematical proportion the human body and its relationship to the surrounding environment.

There are many ways to consider variable human dimensions and the optimal distance for the multitude of activities that are performed in interior spaces. These include (and are not limited to):

- understanding the range and limits of children, full-grown adult males and females, and people at different ages
- anthropometrics of seating
- sketches and distances for various activities (as in dining or working on a computer for living spaces, working in offices, shopping in stores, eating and drinking in restaurants, needing care in a hospital, enjoying leisure time, participating in public or audiovisual spaces)

If we consider the entire population fairly, we must use a universal design approach. A universal approach considers the entire population's needs, including:

- physically challenged people's requirements
- special needs of people who have mild or severe disabilities (hearing impaired, visually impaired, blind, deaf)
- needs of people with disorders who respond to cues in space such as lighting or loud noises (autism spectrum disorder [ASD])

We will examine this idea of universal approaches further in Chapter 9.

Ergonomics

Ergonomics is human engineering, as it relates to specific human/machine interfaces such as operator/computer interactions. This applied science considers factors such as distance from eye to task, hand to computer keyboard, and other measurable distances and factors that affect productivity. Originally developed for the workplace when the computer first came into use, this field has evolved into Human Computer Interaction (HCI) and other design research dedicated to developing interactive interfaces between people and computers.

The intention here is to introduce you to basic ergonomic concepts. The ergonomic "fit" of a person to various tables, chairs, workspaces, and tools is the "good fit" between one's body and the objects that they are using. If we place a laptop on a standard traditional coffee table, the user must bend over too far and is not comfortable. We have not properly designed the space and its objects considering the ergonomic needs of the person using the laptop. We see in Figure 4.7 what happens if we use our equipment in ways that make us struggle.

However, if we design a retractable arm to reach our laptop user on the couch, we are designing with his comfort in mind (some might say too comfortable!), as we see here in Figure 4.8.

Approaches Situated in Context

A very important part of doing research for any project is getting to know the different contexts of the project and how this will affect your decision making. By context we mean the actual scope of work and the specific issues of the design situation that give it its particular characteristics. Although we can use the above-mentioned design elements and principles, we must do so understanding the contexts specific to the problem at hand and understanding universal principles of design (Lidwell, Holden, and Butler, 2003). Let's examine a couple of case studies (4.1) and their contexts.

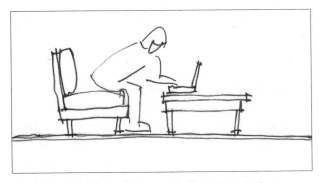

Figure 4.7 • Person bending over a coffee table to look at a laptop

Figure 4.8 • Person with laptop on a retractable arm and comfortable on the couch

This is a very simple introduction to the idea of contexts. Let's add the idea of values to contexts next.

The Context of Values

When we design thinking about the context, we enter in a murky idea of values and how our values and those of others affect our design decision making. What are the values that people attach to the services and objects of a space? How are values important in the design process?

A value is something we hold to be true and important. When we study people, we need to understand **their** values as part of the contexts of a particular project.

Value is defined in the dictionary as:

Noun 1. cost, worth; market price, monetary value, face value. . . . 2. usefulness, advantage, benefit, gain, profit, good, help, helpfulness, avail, importance, significance. . . . 3. ethics, moral

Research on Children

Project: A therapeutic playroom in a hospital

We revisit the case study of students who were asked to design a playroom for children between the ages of 6 to 10 in a hospital. When they were asked, they were stumped at first. They knew nothing about children in a hospital environment. They began by doing research on issues of health, staying in a hospital environment, and what children would like to do if they were in a fantasy situation. Students tried to understand the context of being a small person in a hostile environment, away from family and friends and familiar things, and dealing with a horrific personal situation. Students visited hospitals and tried to understand what it is like to be in this situation. In Figure A we see their concept and how they understood the scale of the child and the sense of playfulness needed in the design to lift the children from their daily difficulties.

Figure B • Therapeutic playroom project concept by Faye and Émilie

In this second concept shown in Figure B, another student considers what it means to need a familiar, homelike cocoon as a play space, to feel safe and to feel good in an environment that is often somewhat clinical.

Each student developed a concept sensitized to the critical issues of being ill in a hospital environment. The project was also situated in a specific type of constructed building, adding another context to the project.

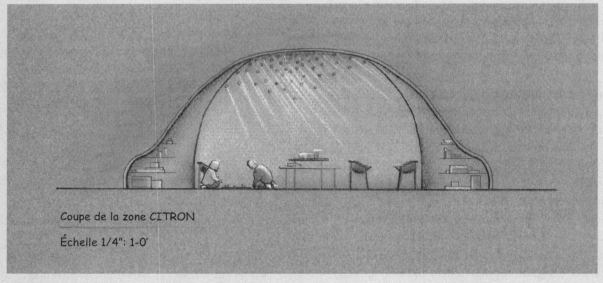

Coupe de la zone CITRON

Échelle 1/4": 1-0'

Figure A • Playroom concept by Raphaelle

code, morals, standards, code of behavior. . . .
verb 1. evaluate, assess, apprise, prize, put/set a
high price . . . . 2. have a high opinion of, hold in
high regard, rate highly, esteem, set (great) store
by, appreciate, respect; prize, cherish, treasure.
(p. 1433)

We all hold several values as true, and two of
these are "material" and "immaterial." Here we mean
that we value the material things that are the physical
elements of the places we inhabit, whereas immaterial
aspects are ideas, concepts, and beliefs embedded in
our value systems within a particular society. Some
examples of different values we might consider when
understanding the design problem are as follows:

- the context of the site (location, social status,
  cultural location)
- material context (local qualities, ecological concerns, sustainable concerns)
- cultural concerns (creating a design for a person
  in a different cultural milieu or location)
- objective contexts (size, shape, constraint, belief,
  need)
- subjective context (desire, desire perceived as
  need, ideal desire)
- philosophical values attached to an object or type
  of environment

For example, designing a sustainable interior environment means designing with a value system that re-
spects finite resources, and is evidenced by our choice
of materials and objects. We might choose materials
such as bamboo and not the finite resources of exotic
trees. Why? Because bamboo is a renewable resource.
While in an open office, the same desk and chairs are
no longer "private" and are part of the noise and activity of the office (see Figure 4.6). Not only do we make
a choice for sustainability, but we make a sound fundamental design decision that will hopefully influence
the people we are designing for. Thus, we become
ambassadors for sustainable decision making. The
seeds of sustainability begin with small yet important choices that affect our interior environment

(McDonough & Braumgart, 2002; Winchip, 2007).
We will consider the issue of integrating sustainable
thinking further in Chapter 9.

Let's look at Case Study 4.2 in the context of
values as they relate back to the user within the space,
and how these values are transmitted to the designer
and then into the design approach itself.

Affective Contexts

Another idea related to values is the ways that we see
how design affects our mental states. These affective
aspects include such elements as how we feel about a
certain look or space, or what we value in terms of a
look or feel. Clients and users always have ideas about
how a space should look or feel. We can reframe their
thinking by respecting these values, but we can also
jar their preconceived ideas by introducing new ways
of thinking about a space or its use.

Affective aspects are those aspects of the design
that support user activities with the look and feel of
the interior space. This means thinking in terms of
specific contexts relative to a theme and the possible
spatial qualities that we can create to support these
contexts. In this instance, program requirements
include specific considerations such as:

- the quality of the ambiance desired
- the feel and look of materials as supporting a
  particular desired feeling
- the type of experience that you want to create for
  the user
- the use of lighting, materials, and forms as catalysts for a particular user response or as support
  mechanisms for particular activities within the
  space

Let's return to compiling information for a complex
design program. Let's walk through some examples of
information gathering for a more complex problem.
We will use the example of an office design for an
investment advisor partnership as our guide.

How do we go about finding these things out? We
will explore various information-gathering tools next.

Revisiting the Concept of Home

When we first looked at the kitchen remodeling case for Chapter 3, we analyzed how the client functioned in the kitchen. We also tried to understand her needs from an ethical and values-based context. Several contexts emerge:

- her need for allergy-free products in both construction and material selection
- her desire for a "sense" of coziness, home, and comfort through the display of objects and kitchen function
- her desire for a sense of the kitchen as center of the home through its layout and concept
- her need to recycle, reuse, and lower consumption and waste

The client's needs stem from that desire we all have, as human beings, for the idea of home. Home can be where we work, play, or retreat from our hectic lives. Her needs also stem from the real, physical aspects of her health and her own sense of ecological behavior. She composts, makes bread and yogurt, and tries to live her life by protecting the environment whenever possible. Her kitchen and home should be a functional and aesthetical reflection of her values.

Information-Gathering Tools

In this next section we develop more complex versions of verbal and visual data collection methods.

Complex Verbal/Analytic Methods

When we get into more complex design problems, larger budgets, and multiple stakeholders, we also enter into a different way of collecting information.

Direct Interviews with Clients

In complex projects, direct interviews are more difficult to conduct because the client and user become different people, often in a hierarchical relationship to one another. For example, whereas your client might be the president of a company, the end user may be a secretary working within a small department. More often, the client might be the president of the company or a personnel officer and in this role they have specific goals for their company in terms of profit and productivity. Their goals and needs may differ from the goals and needs of those working within the spaces, depending on the nature of the corporate structure.

In other project types, such as restaurants and recreational spaces, the goals vary, and this depends on the use and objective of the concept envisioned. Restaurants profit by how many meals can be seated in the course of a day or evening, whereas retail stores profit from purchases made by consumers. Hotels cater to a return or tourist clientele, but many make more money from business and corporate clients. Each environmental type requires a different approach. Direct interviews with the clients help to establish the vision and goals of the people who make the investment, or have a direct stake in the success of the business.

In Case Study 4.3 we can sift out of our large list the following elements that the client could help us with:

- What are the goals for the space (look, feel, function, need)?
- What are the objectives of the company?
- What is the corporate structure and how do people work together within the office?
- What are the staff and employee projections?
- Who are the current and future employees?
- What do the different employees do and what equipment and spaces do they need?
- What are the current and future space requirements?
- Who needs to be next to whom? What are the space adjacencies?
- What is the corporate image?

The designer then "translates" these broad questions into direct questions they can ask the client during an interview. The client can be a business manager, managing partner, president, vice-president

Designing for the Work Environment, Part 1

Gathering Information for an Office Project

In this corporate interior design project, the client requires very specific spaces for investment advisors who work in teams. The following information is part of what is collected to understand how the company functions, and how the company sees the space supporting the corporate goals and needs.

- What are the goals for the space (look, feel, function, need)
- What are the objectives and corporate structure?
- How do people work in the office?
- What are the staff and employee projections: current, future employees?
- What do the different employees do? What equipment, spaces?
- What are the current, future space requirements?
- Who needs to be next to whom? What are the space adjacencies?
- What is the corporate image?
- What are the furniture requirements? For example, if an engineer works with computer data but needs to see the maps he works with, he would

need a printer close by to print the maps and a wall surface to pin them up on.
- What are the information technology (IT) system needs and how do these interface with the advisors, the technical support personnel, the administrative personnel?
- What are the equipment requirements?
- What furniture types are needed for each job type, such as custom or systems, traditional or modern?
- What are the cost comparisons of one type of furniture compared to another?
- What are the code requirements for the office building space?
- What are the characteristics of the space that will be leased? How does this integrate into the overall office building?
- What are the building parameters in terms of a "green, sustainable" building versus a traditional building? What specific requirements are there for interfaces such as alarm systems, sprinklers, lighting, and HVAC (heating, ventilation, and air-conditioning) and base building systems? How will these affect the personal environmental comfort of employees?

of operations, and so on, and the designer might ask questions such as:

- What is your corporate structure?
- What functions does each person do?
- Who needs to speak to whom?

The client assumes that you only want to know about the space itself. You will have to ask questions to understand the functions as much as the space. You want to get a sense of the corporate structure and then evaluate how this does (or does not) coincide with the way knowledge is produced within the space.

Direct Interviews with Users

Direct interviews with users are interviews done with the people "on the ground," usually the people who will receive the design intervention in one form or another. From the busboy in a restaurant to the clerk in the office, these people are the backbone of the corporation, and you need to see and understand how they work. User interviews are generally of two types:

- open-ended interviews as conversations
- closed interviews with specific questions

Depending on the way the project is organized, interviews can be conducted within a meeting or two, or in several steps. Using Case Study 4.4, let's examine how we might go about getting information from the user.

Sometimes there are conflicts between the information that you collect from the client and the user interviews. Conflicts can arise when the client wants you to execute the design independent of the users within the space. A responsible and ethical designer will bring both sides together and work through these conflicts with the client, demonstrating how to best marry corporate requirements with optimum design practices for employee well-being and productivity. This requires expertise and experience, and knowledge of what the client is willing to tolerate.

Observations of Users: Interviews with Clients

Sometimes the client does not want the designer to interview the staff for a variety of reasons. However, for a design to be appropriated by the person who will use it, it is the designer's responsibility to try to convince the client to have some access to them, even if it is to observe their work habits and see the workstations that they occupy, to determine whether this coincides with the client's conception of what they do. The corporate manager's view of these things will not be the same as the users. What is a "good workspace" for them?

When we cannot speak directly with users, we can observe how they work while collecting the building data. We can observe who they work with, their daily movements, and what they have within their workspaces. It is imperative that we look at the activities independent of the client and see for ourselves if the client's perception of daily user activities is true. This is not always easy to do, especially if the client wants the design to be a certain way.

Information Gathering as a Means to Develop Pre-Lease Spaces

Sometimes in retail, merchandising, or work environments, clients look to the interior designer to help them reorganize the space before other interior designers are hired. For example, if developers are building shopping malls, office buildings, or multiple-space complexes, they can use interior designers who work with architects to plan out pre-lease spaces. Let's look at two case studies that illustrate this.

In Case Study 4.5, we will look at how interior designers can be pivotal in developing pre-leasing designs to help plan out spaces before physical lines and walls are actually drawn, in the development of future retail spaces for an interior mall.

Figure 4.9a and b show but one way of doing many such sketches, whether created by hand or in AutoCAD, that explore potential options and help lease spaces to potential tenants.

Planning Spaces with the Future in Mind

In work environments, the corporate client often has a specific set of needs based on the performance of the people who produce a profit for the company. A well-planned office space integrates planning of both present and future needs, and hopefully from both client and user perspectives. Sometimes the client may expand quickly and needs the guidance of the designer to help match the emergent corporate needs with an appropriate space design that plans for needs six months, one year, or several years into the future.

In Case Study 4.6, we will look at this type of complex issue, and how the designer might help the client consider different options.

Current Case Studies and Precedents

A necessary component of information gathering is the research of case studies and precedents. We introduced this concept in Chapter 3 when we looked at understanding precedents for a particular design type or style. We can use case studies and precedents to help us situate the design with others of the same type, or to get a better sense of what is being done elsewhere in the realm of a particular design.

If we continue with Case Study 4.4, we can investigate ideas for the corporate client office space by studying a design from a magazine or through an Internet search. When we analyze a case study, we may want to dissect it to understand it and incorporate it into own design thinking. We might ask ourselves questions such as:

INVESTMENT ADVISORS CORPORATE INTERIOR, PART II

As we continue with the corporate office design information gathering, the interior designer has access to the client and all the users as necessary. After the initial interview with the client, the designer decides to interview various employees at all levels as a means of verifying the information given by the client. The designer uses each interview as a building block for the next one by asking the following questions:

- What is your name and job description?
- What do you do?
- How do you work?
- What specific projects do you work on and how?
- What technical or information support do you need?
- What storage requirements do you have, either virtual or physical?
- What do you need?
- Where do you keep your personal belongings?
- Who do you work with closely? Daily? Weekly? Occasionally?

- What support equipment do you need? Access to? Close to?
- Do you meet with the public? Or do you have internal clients?
- Do you participate in informal meetings? Are these formal meetings? Do they include luncheons in house?

The designer allows the people being interviewed to speak freely, documenting everything said. This helps us to "step into" their shoes temporarily, to understand what they need. For example, they may tell you things such as:

- They want a good workspace.
- They want a large work surface to do what they need to do.
- They need storage for their files and archives; they work paperless and have no storage needs (yet you see piles of paper on their desk?!).
- They need a place for their computer; they prefer a laptop to a desk model; they need a printer nearby; they have no need for printing or peripherals.

- What is the size of the office, and the number of employees?
- What is the corporate structure?
- How is the design created? What are the goals for the company?
- How are these goals and needs translated into the design of the space?
- What aesthetic elements are used to express the corporate image?
- How did the designer respond to the design brief?
- What does the final design look like?
- Do we like it or dislike it?

Case studies offer both a perspective of what is done and a perspective of what constitutes good and poor design practices.

Analyzing the Program Requirements for a Space

Finally, information gathering for a project means collecting the relevant information and understanding the problem in context. With this in mind, we will now examine two examples of complex design programs through various verbal and visual formats that illustrate differing contexts.

Developing Complex Analytic Tools

In Chapter 3 various analytic tools were introduced for simpler design problems with few users or smaller spaces. Here we will develop more complex analysis tools for larger and more involved projects. These are starting points for your own further analytic development and exploration.

CONFEDERATION COURT MALL, CHARLOTTETOWN, CANADA

Tanya O'Brien is the vice-president and general manager of Confederation Court Mall in Charlottetown, a capital city in the province of Prince Edward Island in Canada. This is an interior mall that is surrounded by historic buildings that open out to the street. With company president, Michael Arnold, Tanya develops lease agreements for spaces in the complex that has more than 650,000 square feet of leasable space linking several buildings, with 400,000 square feet dedicated to the mall interior. Mike and Tanya work with the interior designer to develop potential lease layouts of spaces for potential tenants on an ongoing basis. Architects, project managers, and other consultants become involved when the project becomes larger and more complex. Leasing agents are also hired to secure the appropriate stores for the projected new space.

Figure 4.11 shows but one example of many such sketches done, whether in hand or in AutoCAD, to explore potential options and to help lease spaces to potential tenants.

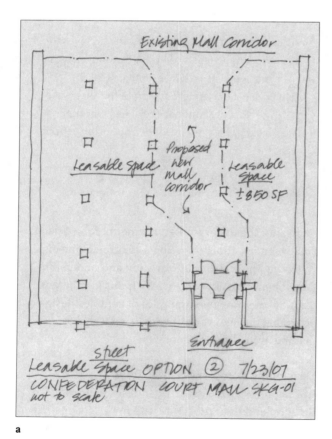

a

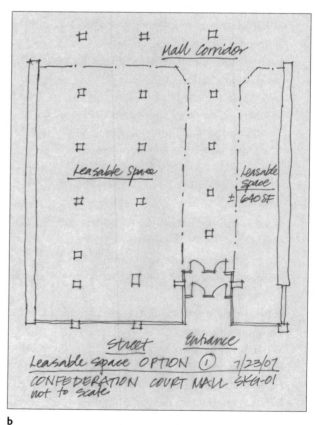

b

Figure 4.9 • Two examples of the pre-lease space concept, by a developer, for a potential tenant

WORK ENVIRONMENTS (COMPLEX PROGRAM NEEDS)

Project: Organizing growing departments for a corporate client

Here we see a couple of plans and a first conceptual devlopment of a corporate office department for a branch office. This is a relatively simple set of requirements for an office of this size.

After potential layouts are produced and discussed, and this first stage is finalized, the detailed design and concept are developed. Table A shows the client needs and requirements.

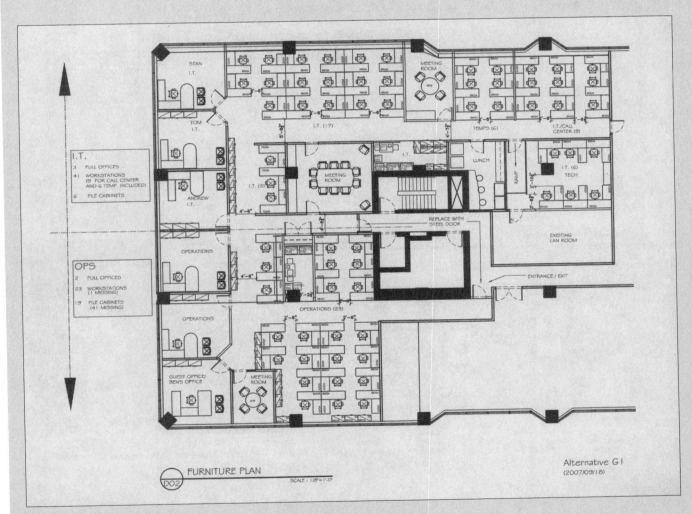

Figure A • Plan of space—option 1

continued on the next page

continued from the previous page

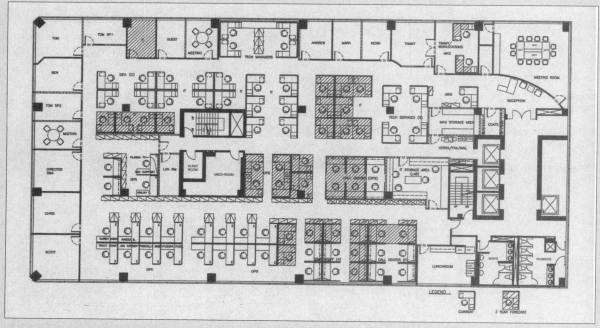

Figure B • Plan of space—option 2

Figure C • Concept for the space—three-dimensional sketch

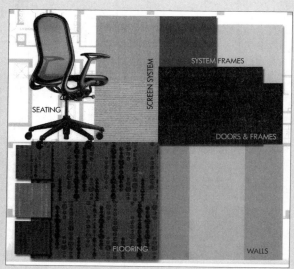

Figure D • Material board for the concept and systems furniture

Table A • List of client needs

Departmental Staff Requirements (accounts for 20% growth over 3 years)

| ID | Type | Current | | | 12-Month Forecast | | | 3-Year Forecast
Allocate Space (no desks, etc. yet)
For Staff to Support 120 IA Teams | | |
		Operations	IT	Marketing	Operations	IT	Marketing	Operations	IT	Marketing
1	Full Office	2	3	1	2	3	1	2	3	1
2	Call Center Desks	7	4	0	7	6	0	9	8	0
3	Full workstations	14	14	1	14	22	2	15	29	4
4	Department subtotal (total of ID 2, 3,4 below)	23	21	2	23	31	3	26	40	5
	TOTAL	46			57			71		

Departmental Storage Requirements (accounts for 20% growth over 3 years)

| ID | Type | Current | | | 12-Month Forecast | | | 3-Year Forecast
Allocate Space (no desks, etc. yet)
For Staff to Support 120 IA Teams | | |
		Operations	IT	Marketing	Operations	IT	Marketing	Operations	IT	Marketing
5	File Cabinets	44	5	3	50	6	3	60	6	3

Shared Resources Requirements

ID	Type	Quantity
1	Guest Office & Staff Office	1
2	Meeting Room (Large), minimum 12 people	1
3	Meeting Room (Small), minimum 4 people	2
4	Kitchen	1
5	Lab Environment Benches (for teams in IT)	2
6	Lunchroom	1
7	Washroom	0
8	Consultant/Temps Work Area	6

Expectation

1. IT indicates the quantities within the IT department.
2. Layout priority: Fit the people in first. Then worry about filing cabinets, etc.
3. Must be able to fit 46 FT staff now, and in 12 months be able to fit 57 FT staff, and in the future be able to accommodate 71 FT staff.
4. Office door must be secure and use steel instead of the existing wooden at entrance with appropriate door locks.
5. New carpets in existing IT area (needs to be replaced due to wear and tear).
6. A lab environment (equivalent of 2–3 workstations of space on a bench). 2 Lab stations requested (1 staging area and 1 workstation lab).

Operations Notes

1. OPS team should be in close working proximity. They often have to have group talks to work out solutions to more complex problems.
2. Operations is a CAGE function—all documentation must be locked and inaccessible to any retail or nonauthorized staff.
3. Sound/noise may be a constraint with repeated phone calls—barriers of sorts to avoid disturbing neighbors may be required (food for thought).
4. Two admin assistants (classified as 1 OPS and 1 IT full workstations) should sit near front door so they can manage the front door and courier administration but should also be near.

Marketing Notes

1. Marketing staff would like to have privacy walls on their desks due to the confidential nature of some projects.
2. Marketing has to store some marketing items at various points throughout the year and should have some storage area available.
3. Prefer to have an office closer to retail side as there is frequent interaction with coworker.
4. Marketing director wants to have support staff workstations closer to her office.
5. Quantities stay the same, 2 workstations.
6. The marketing director will need new desk with credenza with filing cabinets.
7. Marketing will also need a dedicated color printer.

IT Notes

1. n/a

Organizational Lists

Organizational lists are summary lists of the information collected, organized by different themes, aspects of the project, or other contexts. These can include the various client, building, and project contexts, organized for efficient information retrieval.

Inventory Lists

Inventory lists are generated by listing all the existing furniture, equipment, and objects that exist within a space and might be reused for the future design. If a future design moves people from one location to another, or is a renovation of an existing space, inventory lists become very useful. Inventory lists are also used to create new furniture requirements, and are a means of communicating needs to different stakeholders, such as furniture suppliers or IT personnel who are interested in wiring the space for communication and IT systems. An inventory is often created in office design, when equipment and objects are placed for the various personnel.

Visual/Schematic Analytic Tools

Establishing relationships by means of schematic analysis is a good way to develop an understanding of user needs and requirements, and spatial ways of seeing functional relationships. You were introduced to matrix analysis and bubble or schematic diagrams in Chapter 3. Let's look at more complex examples of each.

Schematic Diagrams

Schematic diagrams are a great way to organize the interrelationships that you see emerging between different and dynamic elements of a design, the organization of people, or the spaces themselves. Schematics can develop more elaborate organizational elements of a company, its required activities, or how workspaces might interact with one another. Schematics can help make the bridge between the research as written word and the plan itself, which is a visual drawing.

Matrix Analysis

Tables 4.4 and 4.5 show matrix analyses that are examples of more developed analytic processes for more complex projects.

Bubble Diagrams as Complex Schematics

As noted in Chapter 3, bubble diagrams are a great way to visualize lists of information quickly by selecting interesting key words out of the information collected. We can assign priorities, group spaces, and visualize user functions and/or relationships together without being confined by the space itself. We can then use the diagram as one way to plan out the space. Let's explore some different examples of bubble diagrams for more complex projects.

Bubble Diagram of User Activities and Spatial Roles

If we look at an office design, for example, our priority is not spatial relationships but rather elements such as:

- the interrelationships of different workers and the organizational needs and priorities
- the proximity of people relative to their immediate coworkers
- the adjacencies required for different tasks (workers)

For example, it might be important to see these interrelationships within departments, and then create schematics for the interrelationships of departments to one another within the larger company. In our example of Case Study 4.6, using a bubble diagram, we can explore what activities occur within a department and then in relationship to other departments, as we see in Figures 4.10 and 4.11.

Spatial Proximity Diagrams

The most common bubble diagrams are the ones used to develop spatial proximity (Karlen, 1995; Laseau, 2001). Figure 4.12 is a student example of these types of bubble diagrams.

Charting the Research and Analysis to Develop Design Criteria

Here we examine how a student investigates the factors and requirements for a multisensory interactive science center for children and teenagers. The table shows the different aspects of the project through a list of spatial requirements, whereas the figure shows the analysis diagrams she generates of spatial interrelationships.

As you can see, the student begins with a list of requirements, and then thinks about how these requirements translate into a spatial organization that she represents as a schematic layout.

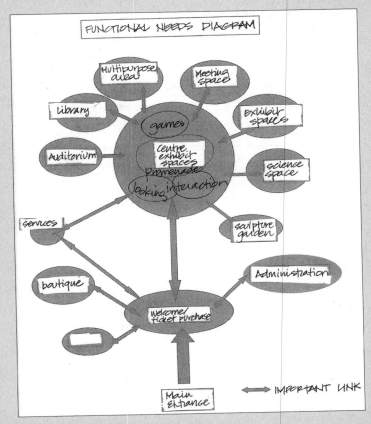

Figure A • Analytic diagrams generated

Table A • Student list of requirements for a space

Activities	Welcome	Investigate	Discover	Create	Play	Meet	Amiss	Look	Walk/tour	Eat	Listen	Purchase
Needs												
Comfort	*	*	*	*	*	*	*	*	*	*	*	*
Natural light	*	o	o	*	o	*	*	*	*	*	o	o
Artificial light	*	*	*	*	*	*	*	*	*	*	*	*
Exterior access	*	x	x	x	x	x	x	x	o	x	x	x
Public interaction	*	*	*	*	*	*	*	o	*	*	o	*
Privacy	–	–	–	–	–	*	–	o	x	–	o	*

* Very important
o Important
x Not desired
– Not necessary

Table 4.2 • Example of an organizational list

Description of activities
Multicultural bar-restaurant and exhibition space

User type	Activities	Public/private	Needs
Manager	• management of the complex • event organizer	private	• office space with computer, telephone, and BlackBerry • meeting space
Clients/visitors	• view art • meet with the artists • meet friends • be entertained • drink, eat • conversation, exchange • listen to music • meet clients • read • relax • dance • put clothes into coat check • go to restroom	private	• eating space • meeting spaces • viewing spaces for events • exhibition space for art display • restroom • entertainment views
Employees/offices	• work • complex management • event organization • telephone • meetings with potential clients • publicity and advertising • meetings with suppliers	public	• adequate workspaces for personnel • management and accounting services and support • marketing equipment and support services
Service personnel	• serve clients • organize spaces • seat clients • take orders • receive payment from clients • prepare food service/drinks	public	• specific service locations within complex • storage for wine, beer, linens, glasses and service cutlery, dishes • bar service area for multi-use spaces
Support services	• cleanup • daily maintenance • set up tables, chairs, and event-related accessories and equipment	private/public	• cash area • storage • cleanup and dirty storage zones
Event producers			
Artists	Create art/interactive events	public	• exhibition area with interactive support
Producers	Produce events	public	• staging area with audience viewing
Comedians	Comedy shows, revues	public	• theatrical lighting and communication setup
Acrobats	Event productions	public	• support for security and control
Artists	Events, art exhibits, interactive shows and events; music shows, videos, and cultural events	public	• artists' studio spaces • changing rooms and exercise studio spaces • back room kitchen and personal hygiene spaces

Table 4.3 • Example of an inventory list for a project

Room	Item	Descr./Manuf./Size	Quantity/Finish/Remarks
IA—	Investment	Advisor typical office requirement	
RP301	Table	24" ou 36/??" round	2/mahogany
	Guest chair	??	4
	Desk chair	??	1
RP302	Desk chair	Krug "Me" MTH1 M2 1 2 B	1/fabric Maharam, col.003 Bisque
	File cab.	18" x 36" (4 drawers)	3
RP303	Conf. table	204" x 42"	1/mahogany
	Conf. chair	??	14
RP304	—	—	
RP305	—	—	
RP306	Desk	36" x 72"	1/mahogany
	Side return	18" x 36"	1/mahogany—all cabling
	Desk chair	Krug "Me" MTH1 M2 1 2 B	1/fabric Maharam, col.003 Bisque
	File cab.	18" x 36" (4 drawers)	5
RP306A	Desk/ped.	Krug/36" x 72"	1/mahogany
	1A link top	Krug/24" x 36"	1/mahogany
	1A credenza	Krug/24" x 72"	1/mahogany
	Over shelf	16" x 72"	1/mahogany (against wall)
	Desk chair	Krug Cadence High back Sw. Tilt	1/graphite leather fabric
	Guest chair	Krug Cadence armchair	2/Maharam 004 Jasper
	File cab.	18" x 36" (4 drawers)	2
RP307	Desk	36" x 72"	2/mahogany
	Side return	18" x 36"	2/mahogany—all cabling
	Desk chair	Krug "Me" MTH1 M2 1 2 B	2/fabric Maharam, col.003 Bisque
	File cab.	18" x 36" (4 drawers)	3
RP307A (1A) 1A credenza	Desk/ped.	Krug/36" x 72"	1/mahogany
	1A link top	Krug/24" x 36"	1/mahogany
	Krug/24" x 72"	1/mahogany	
	Over shelf	16" x 72"	1/mahogany (against wall)
	Desk chair	Krug Cadence High back Sw. Tilt	1/graphite leather fabric
	Guest chair	Krug Cadence armchair	2/Maharam 004 Jasper
	File cab.	18" x 36" (4 drawers)	2
RP308	Desk	36" x 72"	2/mahogany
	Side return	18" x 36"	2/mahogany—all cabling
	Desk chair	Krug "Me" MTH1 M2 1 2 B	2/fabric Maharam, col.003 Bisque
	File cab.	18" x 36" (4 drawers)	3
RP308A (1A) 1A credenza	Desk/ped.	Krug/36" x 72"	1/mahogany
	1A link top	Krug/24" x 36"	1/mahogany
	Krug/24" x 72"	1/mahogany	
	Over shelf	16" x 72"	1/mahogany (against wall)
	Desk chair	Krug Cadence High back Sw. Tilt	1/graphite leather fabric
	Guest chair	Krug Cadence armchair	2/Maharam 004 Jasper
	File cab.	18" x 36" (4 drawers)	2

continued on the next page

continued from the previous page

Room	Item	Descr./Manuf./Size	Quantity/Finish/Remarks
RP309	Desk	36" x 72"	2/mahogany
	Side return	18" x 36"	2/mahogany—all cabling
	Desk chair	Krug "Me" MTH1 M2 1 2 B	2/fabric Maharam, col.003 Bisque
	Overbin	??	2
	File cab.	18" x 36" (4 drawers)	5
RP309A	Desk/ped.	Krug/36" x 72"	1/mahogany
(1A)	1A link top	Krug/24" x 36"	1/mahogany
1A credenza	Krug/24" x 72"	1/mahogany	
	Over shelf	16" x 72"	1/mahogany (against wall)
	Desk chair	Krug Cadence High back Sw. Tilt	1/graphite leather fabric
	Guest chair	Krug Cadence armchair	4/Maharam 004 Jasper
	File cab.	18" x 36" (4 drawers)	2
	Conf. table	36" round Krug	1/mahogany
RP310	Desk	36" x 72"	3/mahogany
	Side return	18" x 36"	3/mahogany—all cabling
	Desk chair	Krug "Me" MTH1 M2 1 2 B	3/fabric Maharam, col.003 Bisque

Bubble Diagram for Three-dimensional Relationships

Sometimes bubble diagrams can be useful when organizing activities and spatial adjacencies as vertical relationships (three-dimensional thinking), in addition to horizontal relationships (two-dimensional thinking), as we see here in Figure 4.13.

Use these diagrams to get to know your project needs intimately. Use them as a student because you are not yet familiar with how to "see" the organizational aspects of the space. As you gain experience in "seeing" these relationships, you will no longer need these diagrams.

Early Brainstorming Techniques

At this stage of the project, you are engrossed in the research and may have a few ideas popping up. This is a great moment to temporarily step away from the research and brainstorm. Usually this means jotting down ideas floating around in your head, or just getting into the project in a different way.

During the information-gathering and analysis phases of your work, you will be itching to try things out in the space. Here are some ways to explore and brainstorm during this analytic phase.

Go and See a Movie

When possible, find a movie that visually represents the concept you are researching. For example, if I am designing a modernist space reflecting a minimalist look from the sixties, Alfred Hitchcock's *North by Northwest* gives a great sense of space with an interior that reflects the mood I may want to achieve. Great inspirations can come from understanding movies and settings that reflect the mood we might be trying to create.

Daydream

While you are engrossed in the research and analysis, take time to look away and daydream. Think about the ideal in terms of no constraints, and see where your mind wanders. When you come up with something interesting, sketch out what you see in your mind's eye.

Envision the Idea of Using a Three-dimensional Model of the Existing Space

If possible, build a three-dimensional model of the existing space in a scale that enables you to see inside. Although this is a representation of the space, putting it into model form early on helps to see the space from a perspective that differs from lists and diagrams. You

Table 4.4 • Student example 1 of a complex matrix analysis

	Main entrance	Other entrance	Hall/reception	Cloakroom	Restrooms	Café	Atrium	Renting space/after-hours	Chapel	Restaurant	Exhibition area	Kitchen	Office space	Storage area	Dressing room	Staff room
Main entrance	—	□	□	□	x	□	x	□	□	□	□	x	□	x	x	x
Secondary entrance	□	—	□	□	x	□	x	□	□	□	□	x	□	□	x	x
Hall/reception	□	□	—	□	x	□	x	□	□	□	□	x	□	x	x	x
Cloakroom	□	□	□	—	□	□	x	□	□	□	□	□	□	□	□	x
Restrooms	x	x	x	□	—	□	□	□	□	□	□	□	□	□	□	□
Café	□	□	□	□	□	—	□	□	□	□	□	□	□	□	□	□
Atrium	x	x	x	□	□	□	—	□	□	□	□	□	□	□	□	□
Rental space/after-hours bar	x	□	□	□	□	□	□	—	□	□	□	□	□	□	□	□
Restaurant/stage	□	□	□	□	□	□	□	□	—	□	□	□	□	□	□	□
Restaurant	□	□	□	□	□	□	□	□	□	—	□	□	□	□	□	□
Exhibition area	□	□	□	□	□	□	□	□	□	□	—	x	□	□	□	□
Kitchen	x	□	x	x	□	□	□	□	□	□	□	—	□	□	□	□
Office spaces	□	□	□	□	□	□	□	□	□	□	□	x	—	□	□	□
Storage areas	x	□	x	x	□	□	□	□	□	□	□	□	□	—	□	□
Dressing rooms	x	x	x	x	□	□	□	□	□	□	□	x	□	□	—	□
Staff room	x	x	x	x	□	□	□	□	□	□	□	□	□	□	□	—

Legend

□ Major adjacency

□ Minor adjacency

□ Not closely related

x Undesirable

Table 4.5 • Student example 2 of a complex matrix analysis

A SUMMARY OF BASIC RELATIONSHIPS

FUNCTIONAL RELATIONS – A SUMMARY / FEB. 11, 1982

do not need to have a design concept at this point. Sometimes seeing the interior space from a bird's-eye view built as a physical model helps you to "see" the space differently.

You can also develop a virtual model using one of many available programs. Walk-throughs of a space are a great way to understand circulation paths, the ways that we see the space as we navigate it, and the views that we might have. Without modeling out the space in one form or another, you cannot envision the three-dimensional sense of the space.

Generating Perspective Sketches from Models
When you develop a physical model, you can create different views of the space. In the student example of the interactive science center, we see how she works up the interior in AutoCAD and in three-dimensional views from hand-drawn sketches as she looks at her paper model (Figure 4.14). She then takes these rough, hand-drawn sketches that she visualizes from her head, and maps out the views in virtual modes. In Figures 4.14, 4.15, and 4.16 we see how the student

moves from the model she created into hand-drawn first tentative sketches and then immediately into computer-generated views of the space.

Another way is to envision the space virtually from the outset, and model in virtual spaces. However, understand that virtual spaces will become real in human, physical terms later on.

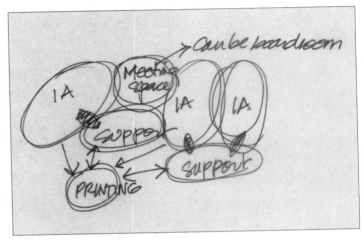

Figure 4.10 • Bubble diagram of people within a department

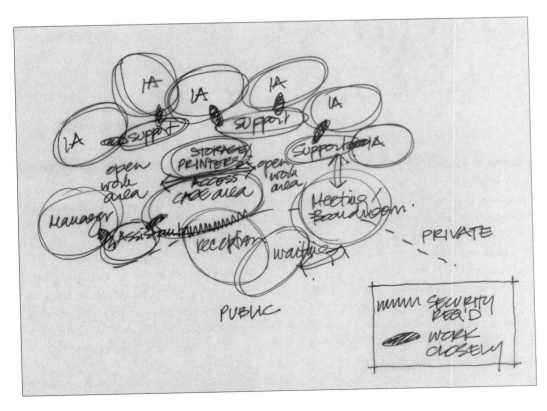

Figure 4.11 • Bubble diagram example

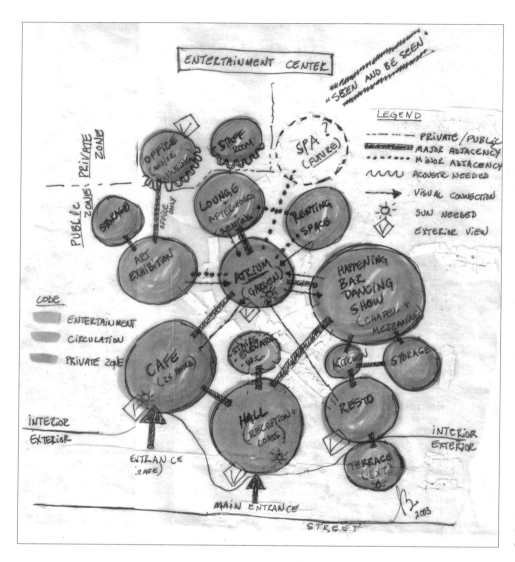

Figure 4.12 • Student example of bubble diagram

Trying to Capture Spaces and Ideas in 360 Degrees as a Catalyst for Design Thinking

Another technique for understanding the space is to videotape it, or to photograph the space in sequence, or create ideas about it in 360 degrees. For example, you can photograph the entire interior you are working on in sequence, and you can then print out the photos and put them in the 360-degree version of the interior in sequence onto your wall so that you can see it from all of the different angles.

We see in Figure 4.20 how a student explores ideas in a circular montage as a reflection of her daydreamed ideas.

Using these various visual analytic and brainstorming techniques as a catalyst to further investigation of the problem is critical to getting the creative juices flowing. One problem we have as interior designers is that we tend to get wrapped up in the details of research, and we do not let our creative juices flow. Or we get our creative juices flowing and the ideas are not grounded in the realities or contexts of the project. The exercises and examples we have discussed here are meant to help you "deconstruct" the existing space and "see" it as it is or might be.

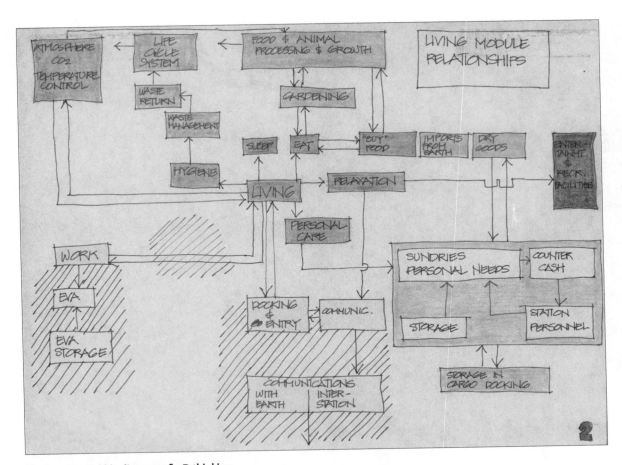

Figure 4.13 • Bubble diagram of 3-D thinking

Figure 4.14 • Student sketch of interior view

Figure 4.15 • Debra's model for the space as she gets into design

Using Quick Creativity Exercises to Foster Project Thinking

Let's complete our discussion of the early planning process with some techniques to jump-start creative thinking by infusing artistic methods into the design processes. Art is a great way to encourage the creative mind.

Creating art has many purposes. It can be used to understand how:

- design principles and elements represent things in space
- aesthetic elements such as form are created
- to integrate aesthetic ideas into design problems

Two artful techniques that are useful to explore at this stage are sculptural form development and collage. Let's examine each here in a little more detail.

Sculptural Form Development

Using art to express design principles is a fundamental aspect of design. For example, sometimes sculpture may be used as the catalyst for a particular concept in design. In this first-year project, simple design elements such as form and plane are used to understand the concrete walls and floors of a warehouse space. The form and shape of an interior environment can be created using artistic elements and properties (Figure 4.17).

Collage

Imagine this scenario: You are working on a project for a new themed restaurant, but despite collecting a large amount of information, you have absolutely no idea how to go about creating the design. You have begun to plan the space, but you are not inspired.

A great way to conceptualize this information is to create a collage.

Collage comes from the French word *coller*, which means "to stick" (Davis & Butler-Kisber, 2000). It is an art form that glues together various items such as magazine pages and found everyday things such as materials, string, buttons, clippings, and other items that you might otherwise throw away. A collage of images is a wonderful way to understand and give visual meaning to ideas that you have floating around in your head, but that you may have difficulty pinning down with design sketches.

How to Make a Collage

With a collage, you can express ideas that you may not be able to do with the written word. For example, your research is complete and you are now at the stage where you need to generate some ideas about the plan. Before you do this, go to magazines and look for images that represent:

- feelings about the space
- ideas about what the intent might be for the project
- people who look like the client
- people who look like the people you are designing for (the restaurant dinner couple, the hotel guest, the mom, dad, and kids at home)

Figure 4.16 • Perspective view of the final design proposal

- images whose nature illustrates how you feel about the subject (sun = happiness, sea = introspection, green grass = clean and fresh, and so on)

Cut up the pictures and glue them in an overlapping fashion onto a board. The size depends on you. I like to use small 2.5 × 3.5-inch cards and A4 (letter) formats. For a design studio collage on a particular theme, you might use a larger 18 × 24 or 24 × 36 format to express many issues within a particular project.

Here are some examples of student collages and the contexts of the projects they were designed for. For example, in first year, your goal is to understand the different issues that surround a project. As you develop different ideas about your user (client), use collage to express ideas about the design that you may not yet be able to do through other communication tools such as drawing. Until you can master drawing a perspective or an interior, you can make a collage to reflect the feeling of what you are trying to create. This may be a concept board for your project, or it may be just a collage of thoughts and ideas that you

cannot say or draw but that you would like to express. Figure 4.18 shows the example of a collage made in the third year.

At the second-year level, you might consider using collage to express your ideas for a potential design in images. In Figure 4.19 we see an example of a therapy playroom concept collage.

Finally, at more advanced levels, you can use a collage as a means of exploring the multidimensional nature of a design problem. In Figure 4.20 we see how a student tries to create a 360-degree collage through a photo of the space to get a sense of being within the space and within her idea of arts technologies. She also places it around the head of the viewer and then turns it so that the viewer experiences her ideas through a multidimensional effect.

In another example, a student gets her fellow classmates to help build her collage, which ends up being constructed to reflect her idea of multiple constructed spaces for her concept of the arts technologies' multipurpose space that she is designing in her third-year project. In Figure 4.21 we see the succession of images as they build the collage together.

In summary, it is important to move from both the program development and research, analysis phase right into the brainstorming and project concept development. Sometimes there are clear steps, and sometimes you have to do it as you go along. The lines become blurred at times between the realities of the project and the ideal and conceptual things that can be developed.

In the last part of this chapter, we introduce the basis for the design of interior space and the experiences that people have within interior spaces.

THE BASIS OF INTERIOR DESIGN: HUMAN EXPERIENCES IN SPACE

In Chapter 3 we explored some basic concepts of space planning and establishing user needs. We also looked at the people using the space as clients or users with particular needs. Our next step is to transfer this knowledge into an understanding of the human user within the space itself, as a person with

Figure 4.17 • Debra's proposal in perspective

physical and physiological associations with the space
and other occupants. Each person using or occupying
a space has height, weight, and scale relative to the
objects they use, the surfaces on which they work, or
the counters against which they lean.

Two major and related components of designing
interior spaces are the form and shape of an interior
environment using artistic elements and properties.
Space and human scale are intertwined concepts,
in that our perception and capacity to see space is
influenced by our physical relationship to it, our relative height, weight, and proportion.

Designing interior spaces includes organizing
space around human activity, and creating the support environment in which it occurs. One of the most
important elements of designing interior spaces is to
realize that we are designing around dynamic people
engaged in activities. We are trying to help people
do these activities well, in comfort, and to their best
potential. "Design," as we saw at the beginning of the
book, means planning, ordering the environment for
a certain purpose. Designing interior space around
human activity implies helping to create order where
there may be either order or chaos.

Figure 4.18 • Example of a student collage

Human Scale in Interior Space

To be able to achieve these goals, we must understand how the human body reacts in space as we go about doing our daily activities. The dynamic activities and movements that people generate are influenced by the relationship among ourselves and other people, the interior space itself, and the objects within the space.

The human body navigates designed space, moving in and around things that are placed within it. Part of your role as the designer is to help guide people through spaces. As the user of the space, the moment you arrive at an interior, you are asked to open a door and step in. At this very moment you are

entering a world designed for you. The moment that we enter a space, we begin a relationship between our body, other people, furniture, and other objects within the space. If the space is large and unencumbered, we can place things as we like. However, many spaces are small, which requires the placement of objects, or multiple-use spaces that are flexible and changing.

Traditional Concepts about Space

In traditional terms, interior space is that which is bound by an architectural envelope. Interior space in this sense is enclosed space (Ching, 1987; Malnar & Vodvarka, 1992). This enclosed space has dimensional boundaries—height, width, and length—and the enclosed space has a structural system that holds it in place—wood or concrete beams, concrete, wood, or steel vertical posts, ceilings, and walls with windows. Dimensions might be long and narrow, square, rectangular, or organic in shape. The three-dimensional aspects of space include height—one, two, or three stories, one floor or many, or split level.

It was Le Corbusier who many years ago stated that a building is conceived from its interior when he said that:

> A plan proceeds from within to without. A building is like a soap bubble. The bubble is perfect and harmonious if the breath has been evenly distributed and regulated from the outside. The exterior is the result of the interior. (p. 167)

This statement suggests the primacy of the plan as the generator of the design of the building. As we plan as well, we decide on the movement of people and function of the space.

Stanley Abercrombie, in his seminal book *A Philosophy of Interior Design* (1990), discusses how we approach an interior space from the outside and move through each aspect of the interior. As interior designers, our role is to meld together the research and the needs of the users with the more ephemeral aspects of designed space.

In the next chapter we will explore different views of interior space from various perspectives and within different types of environmental design. We will also

Figure 4.19 • Example of a student collage

Figure 4.20 • Example of
a 360-degree collage

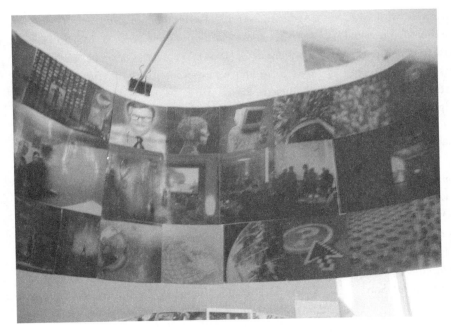

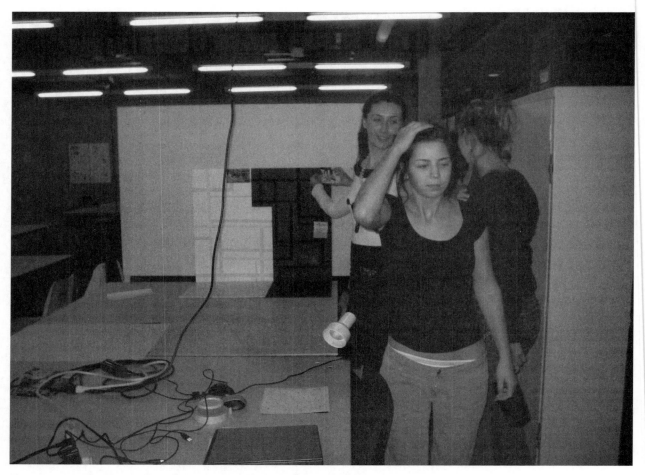

Figure 4.21 • Student interactive collage creation with the interaction of fellow students

move into the designing of the space itself while we revisit our case studies and explore them from visual design perspectives. We'll learn how to generate ideas on plan and in different dimensions, and how to juggle the known and unknown aspects of the design process while doing the actual designing.

BIBLIOGRAPHY

Abercrombie, S. (1990). *A philosophy of interior design*. New York: Harper & Row.

Amin, A., & Cohendet, P. (2004). *Architectures of knowledge: firms, capabilities and communities*. Oxford, UK: Oxford University Press.

Allen, J. (1988). *Designer's guide to Japanese patterns (original book concept by Takashi Kanato)*. San Francisco: Chronicle Books.

Ardener, S. (Ed.). (1981). *Women and space: Ground rules and social maps*. New York: St. Martin's Press.

Bachelard, G. (1964). *The poetics of space: The classic look at how we experience intimate places*. Boston: Beacon Press.

Baecker, D. (Ed.). (1999). *Problems of form*. Stanford, CA: Stanford University Press.

Ching, F. D. K. (1987). *Interior design illustrated*. New York: Van Nostrand Reinhold.

Ching, F. D. K. (1996). *Architecture: form, space and order* (2nd ed.). New York: John Wiley & Sons.

Davidson, J., & Leung, W. (2006 January 1). Top 100 interior design giants, *Interior Design Magazine*. Retrieved from http://www.interiordesign.net/ id_article/CA630962/id.

Davis, D. & Butler-Kisber, L. (1999). *Arts-based representation in qualitative research: Collage as a contextualizing analytic strategy.* Paper presented at the American Educational Research Association Annual Meeting, Montreal, QC. (April) Resources in Education, 34. 11, 135.

Devos, L. (1999). *La maison*, Éditions du Seuil.

Fourastié, J. et F. (1973). *Histoire du confort.* Presses universitaires de France.

Gallagher, W. (2007). *House thinking: A room-by-room look at how we live.* New York: Harper Perennial.

Goubert, J.P. (1988) *Du luxe au confort*, Éditions Belin.

Karlen, M. (1993). *Space planning basics.* New York: Van Nostrand Reinhold.

Kunstler, J. H. (1996). *Home from nowhere: Remaking our everyday world for the 21st century.* New York: Simon & Schuster.

Laseau, P. (2001).*Graphic thinking for architects and designers* (3rd ed.). New York: John Wiley & Sons.

Le Corbusier (1985). *Towards a new architecture,* trans. F. Etchells New York: Holt, Rinehart and Winston.

Le Goff, O. *L'invention du confort, naissance d'une forme sociale*, Presses universitaires de Lyon.

Lidwell, W., Holden, K., & Butler, J. (2003). *Universal principles of design.* Gloucester, MA: Rockport Publishers.

Malnar, J. M., & Vodvarka, F. (1992). *The interior dimension: A theoretical approach to enclosed space.* New York: John Wiley & Sons.

McDonough, W., &. Bruangart M. (2002). *Cradle to cradle: Remaking the way we make things.* New York: North Point Press.

Perrot, P. (1995). *Le luxe, une richesse entre faste et confort, XVIIIe–XIXe siècle*, Éditions du Seuil.

Poldma, T. (1999). *Gender, design and education : The Politics of voice.* Unpublished master's thesis. McGill: Author.

Rodemann, P. (1999). *Patterns in interior Environments: Perception, Psychology and Practice.* New York: John Wiley & Sons.

Rybczynski, W. (1989). *Le confort, cinq siècles d'habitation*, Éditions du Roseau.

Schirmbeck, E. (1986). *Idea, form and architecture: design principles.* New York: Van Nostrand Reinhold.

Schittich, C. (2007). *In detail. Housing for people of all ages*, Redaktion Detail, Munich.

Sèze, C. (1994). *Confort moderne, une nouvelle culture du bien-être.* Éditions Autrement.

Soanes, C. (Ed.). (2001). *The Oxford dictionary, thesaurus and wordpower guide.* Oxford, UK: Oxford University Press.

Sommer, R. (1969). *Personal space: The behavioral basis of design.* Englewood Cliffs, NJ: Prentice Hall.

Vigouroux, F. (1996). *L'âme des maisons.* Presses Universitaires de France.

Winchip, S. (2007). *Sustainable design for interior environments.* New York: Fairchild Books.

Wong, W. (1972). *Principles of two-dimensional Design.* New York: Van Nostrand Reinhold.

Wong, W. (1993). *Principles of form and design.* New York: Van Nostrand Reinhold.

Chapter Five

CONTEXTUALIZING INTERIOR DESIGN PROBLEMS

Objective

In this next stage of the design process, you begin to develop the final design in depth. We always want to explore different ways of shaping the interior space to suit both functional and aesthetic needs. After the program and research are done, and before any planning is finalized, we need to explore the space itself.

DEVELOPING CONCEPTS AND DESIGNS

It is now time to integrate the research, your knowledge of the various needs, and the different things that you have collected into the three-dimensional creation of the space. At this point, you need to:

- understand the space as a real place
- design the space considering the user with particular needs
- make choices in terms of space design, orientation, and space movement, guiding principles that will help you develop the space
- decide the ambiance and choose forms, materials, furnishings, lighting, and fixtures that will enhance your design ideas and respond to virtual and real needs such as flexibility, functional requirements, and specific user needs

To be able to do this, we will work through designing in terms of:

- creating design criteria
- understanding the space-related aspects of interiors
- understanding and moving from initial concepts into developed designs

You must think about the space itself in the context of the people who will experience it, the look and feel of the space, and its various volume-related aspects.

Understanding the Design Criteria as the Catalyst for the Design

As we saw in Chapters 3 and 4, the design criteria are a broad set of guidelines synthesized from collected information and analysis. They can take many forms, both written (verbal/narrative) and visual (schematic).

The design criteria are what you develop into a set of parameters to guide your design decision making, and evolve from the design program, the research and analysis you have done, helping you to begin the design development.

We have seen thus far how we can approach the design by understanding the space through either physical or virtual modeling. We work through the criteria, envision and design potential concepts for the space, and judge the ideas and their worth relative to the project program and design brief. This chapter explores how to go about designing and developing concepts.

Stepping Toward Unknown Territories of Designing

As we move through this chapter, we will see the deliberate weaving of ideas concerning planning and designing using the design process, thinking about the people who will use the spaces that we design, and the interior space itself. Our role as interior designer shifts into the designing phase of the process as we retreat from the public arena from which we have gathered the information that we need. We may work with others when designing, and this may occur in an office environment. But we are now in a more intro-spective part of the process, where we move from what we know and have researched into the unknown territory of designing where we explore the design in depth.

We review the process of planning, generating preliminary design ideas, and judging their appropriateness. We will introduce and develop concepts of interior space, and look at how we can set up the

> **BUILDING BLOCK** • *If you jump from the information collecting right into the design, and do not take the time to develop design criteria, your design thinking will not be complete. Being able to define design criteria means being able to prioritize the intentions and goals of a project, to decide what is important (and what is not), and to help give your design a framework.*

right mood to design. We will then move into creative techniques in Chapter 6, and look at how to develop detailed and final design solutions in Chapter 7.

CONTINUING THE DESIGN DEVELOPMENT

You are at an exciting stage of the design process. You have collected, analyzed, and developed a series of ideas, criteria, and data that will inform your designs. You may have tried out some preliminary ideas in two or three dimensions or modeled ideas virtually. Now you are about to shift gears and develop full concepts for your project. Let's look at what happens next.

First Elements and Steps in the Design

We will turn now to looking at various ways to design and develop ideas. These different techniques com-plement the ones you have just reviewed. Sometimes we move directly from analysis into planning, and sometimes we want to model the space and see it in its entirety before planning goes too far.

Planning Out the Space

Planning the space means organizing it in a bird's-eye-view type layout. We need to keep in mind that we are seeing the space very differently than when the user walks through it (Rengel, 2003). Planning means just that—ordering the space so that it has a logic, a systematic pattern of movement that brings a person from the outside in and then to his destination. We may plan the organization of a kitchen, as we saw in Case Study 3.6 in Chapter 3, or we may plan several floors of a large corporation. There are many ways to plan out a space, and each act of planning has its own particular approach and dimension (Karlen, 1999; Rengel, 2003).

There are many books dedicated to planning interior spaces. This book introduces some basic con-cepts, but it is impossible to explain all of the nuances of planning here because the scope is too broad. We will use the case studies from Chapters 3 and 4 to see how design programs become planned spaces and to illustrate what is possible in a general approach to planning. We will use various examples from the different environmental design types. We will then look at how we develop the space itself from generated ideas.

Using Needs Assessments

An important step, and one that is often overlooked in the design process, is making the link between the data and the human aspects of the design, and then using the collected data and research to actually begin the designing. What are the experiences of the user? How will these fit with the user as a person using the interior environment? How do we use this information, which is essentially logical, to design an interior space aesthetically?

One of the first ways to assess user needs is by understanding the relationships of the activities relative to the project context. This idea of linking data is a way of integrating the research and analysis that you have done. You have collected a lot of information, and hopefully at this point you have sifted through it and organized it into lists, charts, or diagrams.

For example, in office design for government institutions or large-scale corporations, concerns about user needs may include:

- staff and employee projections
- current space requirements
- future space requirements
- optimal adjacencies

We can use the information that we have by organizing it into visual representations that we can then apply into the plan. We saw examples of different methods in Chapter 4.

Linking User Needs with Spatial Parameters

At this point in the design process, it is important to understand the interrelationship between user needs and planning decisions, and how these relate to the spatial contexts and three-dimensional implications of the planning decisions. In this next case study, we examine how user needs and design ideas come together in the design of a food court for an interior shopping mall in a small-scale urban center.

Generating Preliminary Ideas

Throughout the research and analysis processes, and in these early planning stages, your mind is coming up with ideas and you are possibly modeling some of them already. The danger is letting the ideas go, or trying too hard to rationalize them.

Ideas Are Just That—Ideas!

Ideas need to fester, ferment, and develop through whatever means you have to develop them. You will have ideas at each phase of the design process. The key is to develop a way to document them, use them, and evaluate them!

Trying something in both two and three dimensions can be a great way to generate ideas within the space. You may want to see it in plan first and then try it in the volume of the space. Or you may want to model the three- or four-dimensional views first as a walk-through, and then go back and look at the plan.

Two-Dimensional Plan Development

When you first begin to plan out a space, you need to consider the possible configurations. You will have certain space requirements, and you will need to look at these in terms of the plan and what is possible. You might begin by block planning the space, or trying out bubble diagrams within the plan itself. In a larger project, we usually begin by planning the space, just to see if things fit and how. I strongly recommend that you plan quickly and then try to model or envision the space in three dimensions as soon as possible. Try not to plan too much without going into the other dimensions as well. Think about the three-dimensional impact of the design as you plan it out in two dimensions. This will be useful as you develop the final functional plan because after you have decided on the functional layout, you can then develop detailed design aspects in three dimensions.

Understanding the Space and Its Parameters Relative to the Design Program

By planning out the space in different ways, we can come to understand the space, its parameters, and the

Food Court, Confederation Court Mall

This project is a food court concept development. The food court is a part of a much larger complex that includes several thousand square feet of retail, office, and multipurpose spaces in an office and retail complex that amalgamates several historical buildings that surround a three-story interior shopping mall. The clients are the developer, Mike, and the vice-president of operations, Tanya. The designer has worked with them over the past 20 years to develop different projects. (We saw the example of the pre-lease earlier in the book.)

This particular project is the central food court and its periphery food service kiosks that cater to both morning and lunchtime business clients. The food court also attracts tourists and shoppers during opening hours. In this concept development, the client and designer work together as a team to develop both upgraded services and create new features for the eating areas. Initially built in the early seventies, this underused space had become dated and worn out by the late nineties.

The clients needed to attract both new customers, and create spaces for new and more inviting food tenants to increase foot traffic and add economic value to the mall. The challenge was to make the food

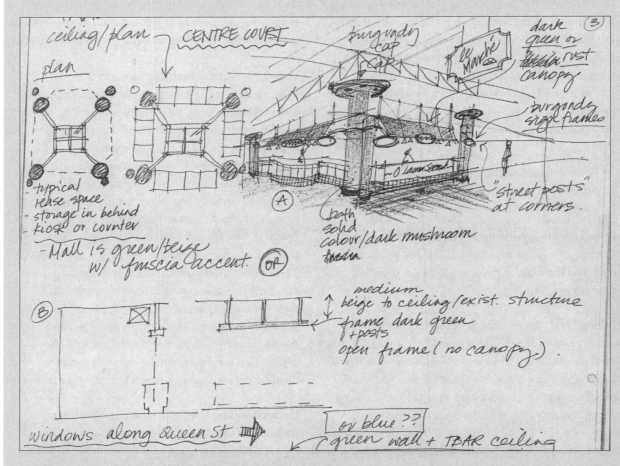

Figure A • Sketch of the food court—initial concept developed in 1998

court and surrounding stores welcoming, but not too comfortable so people could have a bite at lunch or meet for coffee, yet not linger too long so as to discourage loitering. The developers also want to create a temporary staging area, one that would not be used often but that would be available for different events such as fashion shows or organized public community events. Figure A shows the first developmental sketch in 1998.

In this initial sketch, the first color and design concept features are imagined, prior to any planning. This sketch was created, in effect, to "sell" a potential idea. Before any design concept could be developed, the clients (as developers) needed to know what such an undertaking might cost. Based on the initial ideas that were discussed, the designer prepared potential budget allocations to determine how much could be spent on the renovations and realize capital expenses. The designer presented three different budget scena-

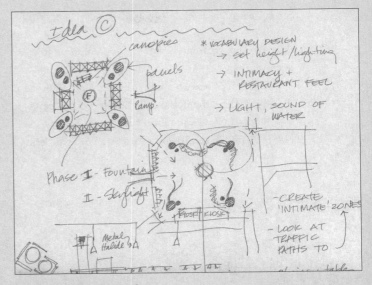

Figure B • Development plans

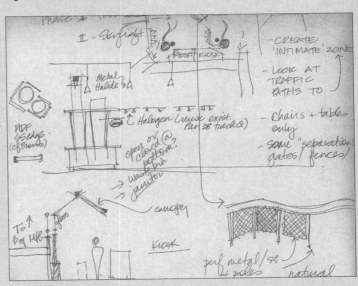

Figure C • Development sketches

rios for possible projects and the concept that each might entail, and how each one could be realized through construction, leasing, and fitments.

Based on budget calculations done by the designer with an initial targeted budget of $800,000, the choice was made to proceed in two phases: first spend $450,000 in 2000 to renovate the food court; then allocate funds to renovate the consignment

Figure D • Final concept perspectives

continued on the next page

continued from the previous page

space for approximately half the initial budget in a second phase.

The first phase was built in 2000. Figures B through E show the initial development of the concept.

Figure E shows the food court as it is today. Named "Talk of the Town," it attracts both tourists and businesspeople with the aim of creating a dynamic meeting place within the downtown core. In 2006 the clients renovated by adding a food service provider who updated the look and the food offered with a more contemporary offering. The design continues to support the changing needs of the mall, and the initial investment was well spent.

Figure E • Talk of the Town food court today

client's needs altogether. As a first try, you can either throw the bubble diagram you have created into the space, or block plan using the space allocations that you have developed.

Here are a few examples. First let's revisit the kitchen renovation we explored in Case Study 3.3 in Chapter 3. We can plan out the space in different ways, considering the client's various requirements. In Figure 5.1 we see a first layout idea with the sink under the window. Although it is a nice view, this layout obscures the direct access that the client was looking for. An alternative plan in Figure 5.2 shows an alternative layout.

A second, more complex example is an office design for a government agency. In this design, the initial planning consists of fitting together different departments in separate sections of two buildings and then linking them together through a longer, narrower building link. The interior designer needs to see, first in very rough schematic form, how people can sit side by side within the departments and then how the departments would fit into the two buildings. The designer then works out the space planning of each department locally, through block planning and workspace layouts.

Figure 5.3 represents some of several schematic diagrams done to see how different alternatives might fit. We see how we might first lay out the spaces using fairly rough schematic sketches, then work up a block plan to represent the approximate volumetric spaces that each person takes up relative to the other. There is no "wall" or fixed element designing at this point—we are primarily interested in seeing how people will work within their space and how they fit one next to another (Karlen, 1999).

As you sift through the research and develop your analysis, it is vital to test out initial ideas in the space almost immediately. The first way we do this is by planning out the space. Sometimes we block plan the space; sometimes it is good to try out the bubble or schematic diagram as it is within the plan to see what happens.

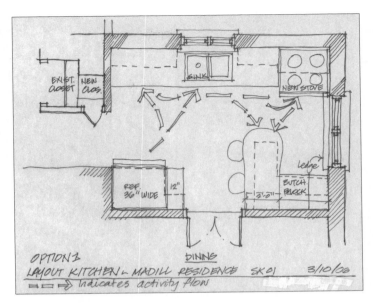

Figure 5.1 • Plan layout of kitchen—Idea 1

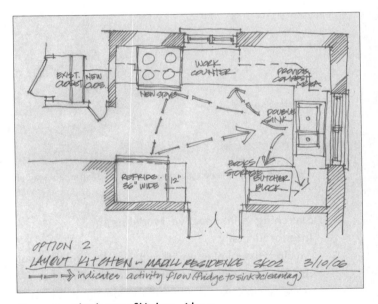

Figure 5.2 • Plan layout of kitchen—Idea 2

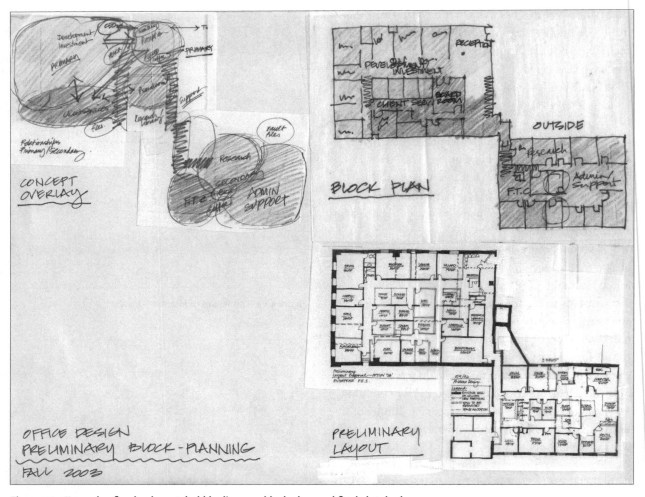

Figure 5.3 • Example of a plan layout, bubble diagram, block plan, and final sketch plan

Sketching in Perspective/Modeling the Interior Virtually

An alterative to planning is to design by modeling out the design concept volumetrically right off the bat, as we saw in Case Study 5.1 in the food court design exploration. The disadvantage to this approach is that you may not have as yet understood the planning needs entirely. You can then try and plan out the space to fit the concept, but this is harder to do. Planning tends to suffer when we approach the space as a purely three-dimensional place only. However, the space can be envisioned first in many projects where planning is less of a concern or priority.

In the next example we see a senior student's project in its very early design concept stages (Figure

5.4). She is trying to develop a flexible space that can change to suit the four needs identified by the client—an exhibition space, an artists' studio, a rave nightclub, and a meeting and conference center. She develops first ideas to see what is possible and then moves into the detailed development of her concept in a second iteration of her design. She models it virtually from the sketches that she has generated (Figure 5.5).

If we go further into the student's project, we see how in a second design concept stage she generates plans and sketches simultaneously. For example, if we look at how the student did her first conceptual sketches, we see how she tests her idea by planning it out and also trying her conceptual ideas immediately using bubble diagramming and sketching. For example, in Figure 5.6, we look at how she plans four different ways of laying out the space while creating organizational sketches, and then visualizing this in Figure 5.7 with quick sketches of views of the space in a holistic design conceptual approach.

Drawing from this inspiration, we can plan out a space in different ways to see if functions and needs are serviced by trying a few things:

1. Use form, plan, and shape to help define the space.
2. If you have a certain pattern, intention, or idea, you can use this as a starting point.
3. Try out different forms and elements of design to help create a plan, all the while respecting your functional and spatial bubble diagrams.
4. Always think about how the people will sit, feel, move, and orient themselves when you plan out what they will do.

Two- and Three-Dimensional Design Concepts

Another way to plan out the space is to use the structure of the building as a catalyst for planning. The building you design within has certain characteristics and form that are inherent in its design. Sometimes we want to use these forms; sometimes we want to introduce new forms that integrate with older ones.

Figure 5.5 • Modeled idea from computer and generated sketch

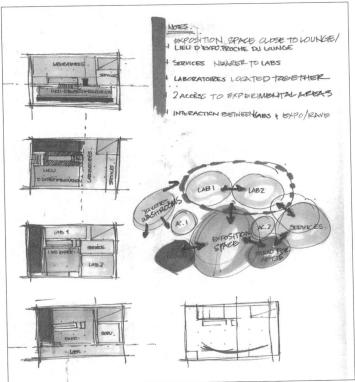

Figure 5.6 • Conceptual plans of an idea

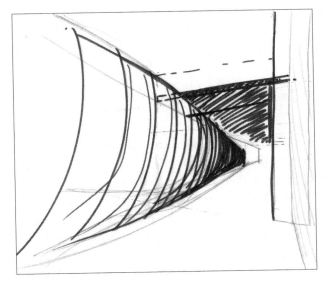

Figure 5.4 • Original rough sketch

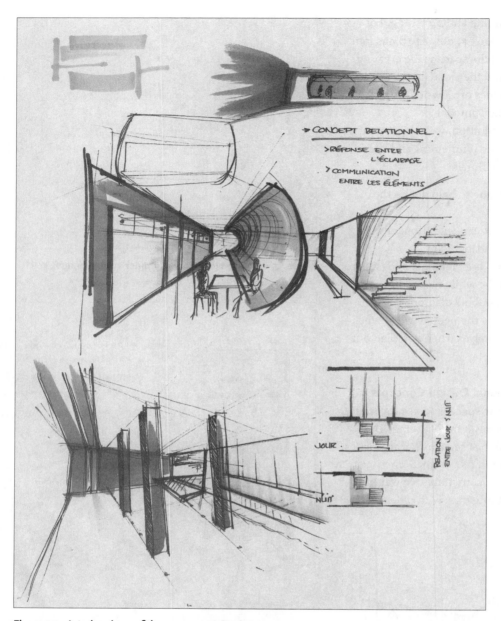

Figure 5.7 • Interior views of the same space/concept

You can begin your planning by first putting up the plan in a three-dimensional model made out of foam core or cardboard. This is a good way to see the scale of the space—add a cardboard cut-out of a person to understand the relative size of the person within the space. In Figure 5.8, we see how the same student tries out her ideas both in plan and in section.

We can see in this example how the designer takes the space, tries things out in somewhat sketchy form, and then develops a concept around a theme that she has developed.

Here in this next series of sketches, we see her idea begin to crystallize as she develops more detailed plan sketches and parallel perspective views. In Figures 5.9 and 5.10 we see how she develops her rough plans.

Alongside this initial planning and sketching, we can also develop sectional sketches. Each view is

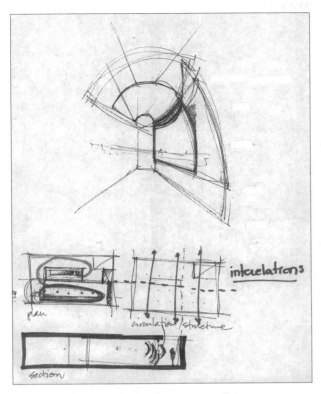

Figure 5.8 • Sketch of another idea with a section

two dimensional—what we can imagine in the space and then put down on paper—but an "unknown" idea put into plan can help with a "known" idea, such as a functional plan.

Iterations of the Ideas

Finally, there are multiple iterations of plans that are developed for designs where complex functional issues are involved. This next example presents different iterations of the schematic planning of the exhibition/rave/artist space. In Figures 5.11, 5.12, and 5.13, we see several different ideas for the same set of needs. The designer considers the people within their work environment and their relationship to their

> **BUILDING BLOCK •** *As you are planning a space for the first time, establish an understanding of it through a plan and section or model examination of the space. Use this to help you to draw up a plan with a geometric element or an organizing principle.*

work as well as their coworkers. Even at this early stage, she considers views toward natural light, comfort within the provided environmental system, and other factors that might influence well-being.

These are just three of many different plans schematized for this space in which people interact with others. This is really a vital early stage because we are not prescribing the place that people must work, yet we do not ignore how they will feel working within the space. We consider how they will sit, who they face, what temporal and territorial parameters they need, and how they will socially and personally interact within their workstation and with others.

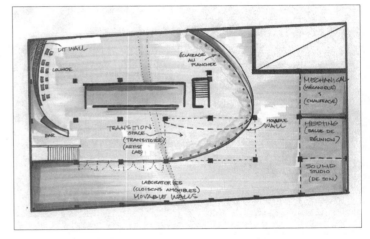

Figure 5.9 • First iteration of the design concept in plan

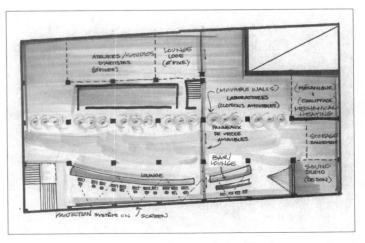

Figure 5.10 • Second iteration of the design concept in plan

Figure 5.11 • Perspective idea 1

Figure 5.12 • Perspective idea 2

Figure 5.13 • Perspective idea 3

Using Design Elements, Fundamentals, and Principles

Form, scale, color, light, and repetition can be useful catalysts for organizing spaces in plan (Wong, 1979; Rodemann, 1999). For example, we can take a simple design element such as a circle or a square, place it into the plan we have sketched, and see what this might do to help organize our designs.

Design elements that can be used specifically to develop first design plans include point, line, and plane. Two-dimensional planes are the result of lines and points—walls, floors, ceilings, and surfaces are planar in nature. Volume is another basic design element that has features that can be used as the focal element in the space (Laseau, 2001; Ching, 1995; Ching, 1996; Wong, 1993; Rengel, 2003).

Plans can evolve as organic circulation and movement-oriented places, as places with a focal element, or with shape, color, light, or other dynamic elements as the focal elements. As Roberto Rengel suggests (2003), shape is often the determinant in the plan.

For a plan to be dynamic and alive, planning must also consider lighting effects, color dynamics, and the ways that the forms and materials mediate the shapes that are introduced.

If we continue to look at the example of the student design of the artists' collective, we see how three and two dimensions are worked together with patterns and forms. The plans were developed in general blocked spaces that were easily defined. But then the development of the detail in three dimensions required "working the plan" to fit the design and retain the integrity of the original plan layout. In Figure 5.15 we see an example of the developing ideas and how the student begins to shape the space with her concept.

In another example of the same project, another student develops a different approach by sculpting the space into segments that are modulated within the space. She then puts these into the functional plan she has developed and brings the two ideas together.

Design principles include proportion, scale, balance, harmony, rhythm, and emphasis. These principles work with design elements to help organize

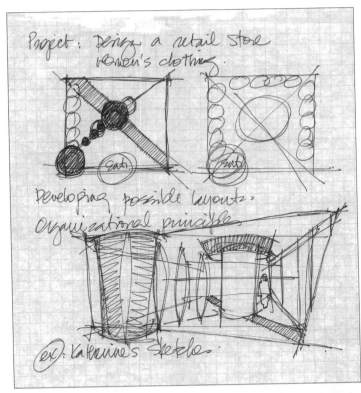

Figure 5.14 • Plan of circle, square, and triangle and how each might look in three dimensions

visual arrangements among interior design elements. Inspired by fine art and the Bauhaus movement, these forms help us to generate first ideas and form the elements that we want to integrate into our plans. Figure 5.18 shows some examples of each.

Patterns in Nature and Design

Patterns are organizational elements that are found in nature, and can be organized or organic, controlled or fluid. Patterns are useful because we can use them as a direct means to plan out a space in two dimensions, or to help organize a way of systematizing the

> **BUILDING BLOCK •** Work with design elements while simultaneously considering human use and function. When you plan, think about the users and their movements first and then sculpt the space using the elements and principles; finally, return to the function and make sure that the space "works" for the user.

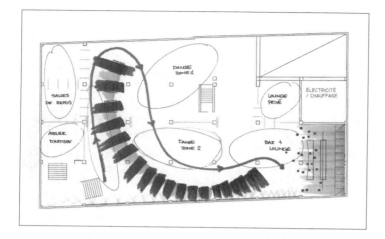

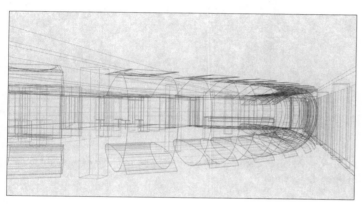

Figure 5.15 • Developing plan and sketches using geometric principles

design (Alexander, 1970; Allen, 1988). One way to use patterns at the beginning of the designing is as inspiration.

Another way to use patterns is to select them as applied materials. There are an infinite number of patterns to be found in fabrics, surface materials, wall coverings, and objects that, when combined a certain way, can facilitate our enjoyment of an interior space. Patterns inspire us, and we react to them perceptually. Learn to understand the perceptual nature of patterns and how you can use them as you plan. Patricia Rodemann develops the idea of patterns as psychologically useful and suggests that "pattern design is an expression and extension of ourselves" (p. 7).

Human Factors and Scale

Human factors such as scale are vital to good and thoughtful planning of a space. The age, gender, and physical perspective of a user are central to the proper design and function of a space. One of the first things to consider when planning interior space is the relationship of the human body to space and the issue of human scale. How are the people who will occupy the space going to move within it, negotiate their way through it, or arrive into the space and settle down to do an activity?

Let's return to the case study of the children's therapeutic playroom we saw in Chapter 2 to see how human scale becomes a fundamental aspect of the design (see Case Study 5.2).

EVALUATING PRELIMINARY DESIGN PLANS AND IDEAS

Evaluating ideas is an important first step of this first planning stage. When you first create ideas, you must evaluate them objectively. What does this mean?

We step back and look at our ideas to see what works and what does not work. We then take a break and look at each plan. A good idea is to print hard copies of things generated in virtual form. We can then write next to each plan both the positive aspects and the negative aspects of what has been designed. We need to judge which ideas to use and which ideas to discard. One of the reasons we do many iterations

Figure 5.16 • Color, light, and texture development in conceptual design

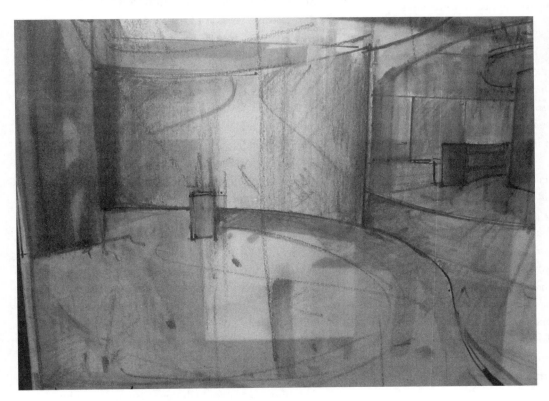

Figure 5.17 • Another development sketch by the same student

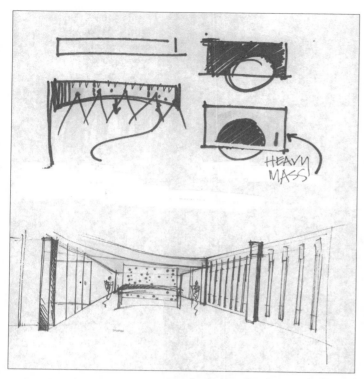

Figure 5.18 • Examples of principles and elements such as proportion, scale, balance, rhythm, and emphasis in student sketch ideas

---

of a plan or design within a space is because there are many possibilities. How do we know which idea is the best one?

Before you move too far into a design, it is essential at this point to step back and evaluate the design possibilities, plans, and/or concepts, either alone or with the client, to determine which design or layout has the most potential. In these early stages, it is also a good idea to see how all of these organizing methods allow us to see different ways to plan out the space in 2-D and early 3-D concepts. We can develop a design plan with several different approaches and then evaluate each one as having potential or not.

As we move further into designing, we explore the space in different dimensions. This is a way for us to understand the space, plan it out, and design it to work for the users and their needs. Let's look at some of these design process methods next.

Modeling

Modeling the idea is perhaps more important than planning the space. You want to "see" the three-dimensional version of the space as soon as you have an idea.

Traditional Modeling

One of the easiest ways to see your design ideas is to put them into the scale of the actual space using a model you make, either out of paper, cardboard, foam core, or plastic.

A physical model in a scale that you can see is a great way to understand the space you are designing. You can then photograph the model from different angles to see what happens if you change things that you have built.

Sketching the Idea

It is important to develop ways to map out your ideas. This is different from creatively generating ideas, which we will look at in Chapter 6. By mapping, I mean immediately putting onto paper your first thoughts as they happen.

You should always have paper, black markers, or a sketchbook with you, wherever you go, even by your bedside. Allow yourself time away from the de-

---

BUILDING BLOCK • *Develop your plan idea using some of the techniques suggested here. When you are done, put them into the order you produced them—identify each by date, and concept a, b, c, d, and so on. Print them out if they are drawn in the computer.*

Then step back and look at each one. Bring out your analysis and research, and identify next to each plan the positive and negative aspects of the plan. Write down at least two or three different things that work or don't work right next to each one.

Hopefully you will see that each one has interesting alternatives, and perhaps you can take an idea from one plan and move it to another, generating yet another plan option.

The more ideas you put down, the more you should judge them to see which ones comply most closely with the research and analysis that you have done.

CHILDREN'S THERAPEUTIC PLAYROOM

We have seen the sketches for this playroom in Chapter 2. Here we see how important the sensitivity to scale becomes. We see how the designer considers the perception and viewpoint of the child. A child is smaller than an adult, and their eye level is lower, so they will see the space as bigger and higher than an adult would. In Figures A and B we see how the child might "see" the space.

Figure A • **View from child's perspective**

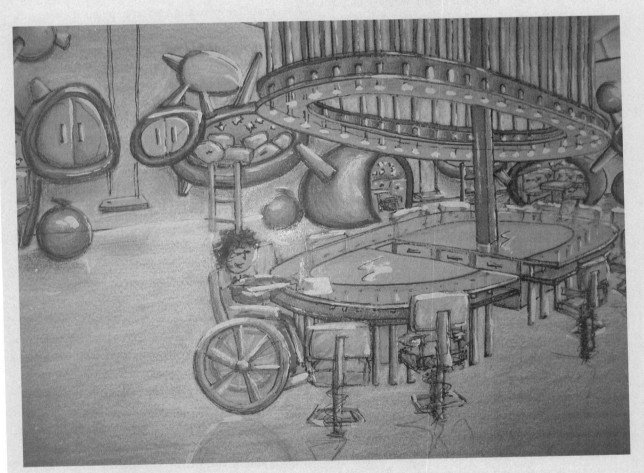

Figure B • **View from child's perspective**

signing—when we relax our brain, thoughts and ideas enter more freely and allow us to visualize our ideas.

Interior designers tend to be visual people—we "see" the idea, concept, or possibility. We can envision the space as we might design it before we have begun to design. With experiences, we hone this skill and develop it.

Virtual Modeling

Modeling the space virtually means setting it up in your computer with one of the many programs available on the market. It is important to get the design going in more than two-dimensional CAD format because the interior space is a three-dimensional being.

You can create different scenarios with programs such as Cinema 4 or SketchUp and see what the plan will look like in three-dimensional space. Although you can sketch up an idea quickly this way, it is risky to assume that this will be the final design. When we model out a design idea in three dimensions but do not plan out the space concurrently, we risk designing for visual effect rather than making the space actually work for the user and the context of the project. It is important to model up the idea in virtual form; then go back and develop a detailed plan from the modelled idea. Also use a sketch pad and sketch out ideas while you model on the computer. Do this because our ideas begin in our heads and need many forms of expression. As designers, our thinking is trained through the ways that we put ideas from our heads onto paper or into the computer.

We have already discussed some ways to generate design ideas in three-dimensional space. In summary, they are as follows:

- Try a plan one way; then turn it and try the same plan off-angle (Figure 5.19).
- Look at the interior from the view of a real built model. Build it with foam core or cardboard and paper, and take photos. Change your vantage point. When you take the photo, place yourself at an opening of the model and squint as if you are as small as the actual scale of the model, squinting your eyes so that you look into the space as if you were a small person, and then take a photo of what you see.
- Change your view of the space by changing its spatial organization; what happens if exactly the same plan and sketch are done using a different spatial organization, for instance? In Figure 5.21, we see this tried out with one plan superimposed upon another.

Let's now explore this aspect of the design process a little further.

Spatial Organization

We generally use four basic design principles to develop the plan into three dimensions.

1. Experience the space through circulation
2. Movement and sight lines
3. Forms and shapes in spaces
4. Color and light modulations of interior spaces

Circulation

Begin to plan and design the space as you arrive. You may be outside looking in, or inside moving from one space to another. What do you see? Move from one area to the next, and each time sketch it out. As you circulate within your designed space, see what you would want the user to see by creating an image of it. Video modeling is an excellent way to walk through a space and record what you visualize. You should develop several three-dimensional views of what you visualize in the space.

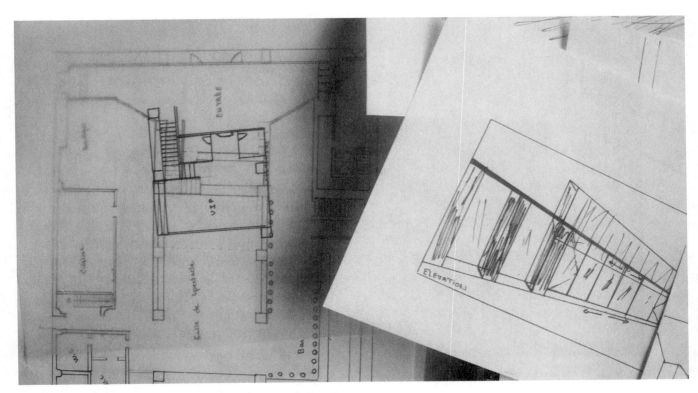

Figure 5.19 • Example of plan in two different ways—on and off angle

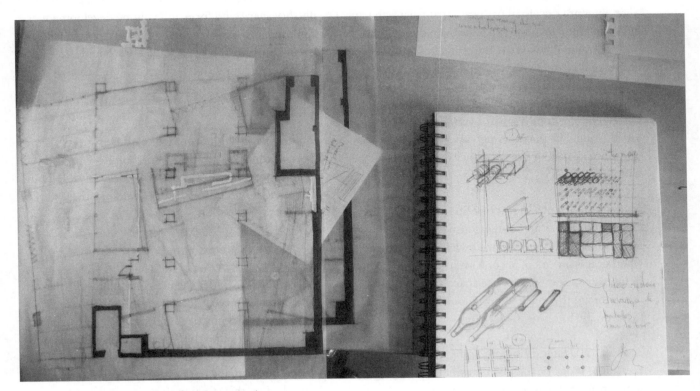

Figure 5.20 • Plans and sketches of ideas germinating

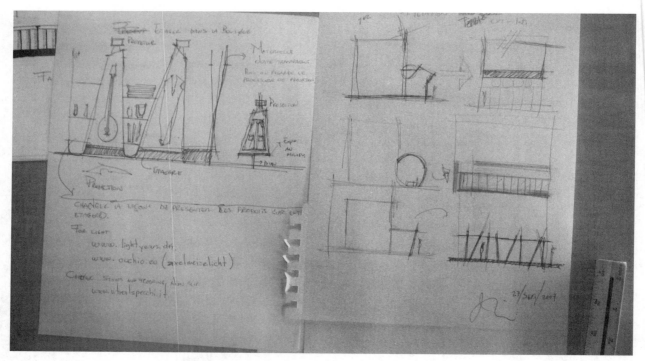

Figure 5.21 • Early ideas in detail developing

Movement and Sight Lines

Sight lines are the visual pathways that we use to navigate space, and gain a sense of horizon and stability. You cannot underestimate the impact of forms, shapes, color, and lighting on spaces as we move through them. This is the aesthetic aspect of designing that affects how humans feel about a space. The placement of a door, a wall, or various forms can greatly influence the everyday experience of the user. These are all part of the sight lines that we create within spaces.

Forms and Shapes in Interior Spaces

Forms and shapes are used extensively in many different areas of design to transform ideas into objects, whether it is a work of art or a sculpture or a product. In interior spaces, we can use space and form as mediators of the space. We will look at a few ways to accomplish this next.

Space as a Design Principle and Element

Years ago, Wong developed a way of understanding space from art forms in multiple dimensions. He used principles such as positive and negative space, flat and illusory space, and form and volume development as a grammar to explain what we see and design within space (Wong, 1972, pp. 89-93). For example, in Figure 5.23, we see how a simple form can be the catalyst for a space concept.

Integrating Design Processes and Design Development

We must remember that on a very basic level the fundamental design process is one that links these key elements:

Person ➔ context ➔ need ➔ response

The response includes the interior itself as the designed space. Recently I invited my colleague and internationally renowned interior designer Michael Joannidis to speak to third-year students about the design process and creativity. Here are some of the points that he made to the students just before they embarked on their final project.

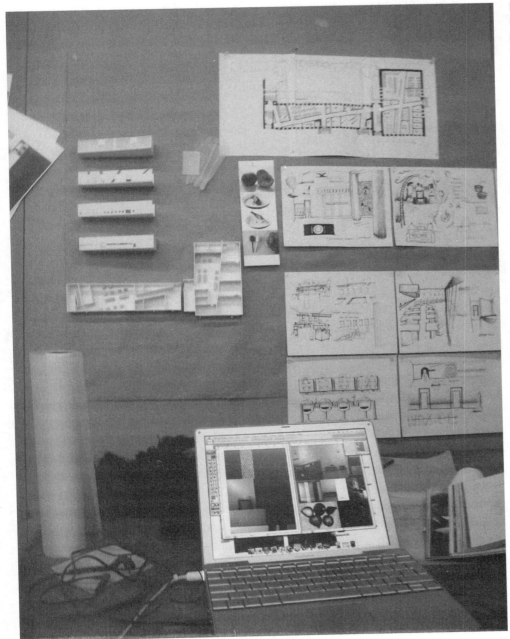

Designing interior space is about attitude as much as know-how. Investigate! The resources available to you now through virtual and electronic means are infinite. The problem is, we expect the answer at the click of a mouse and with this infinite amount of available information we are not learning how to *search* for what we actually need.

The idea that we come up with original ideas is a myth. Creative problem solving means using and trying things differently, as in how do *you* take what you know and create something different? *Read* the information next to the pictures in magazines. It is there for a reason, giving you insights into what the architect or interior desi-

Figure 5.23 • Using basic art forms as a means of exploring spaces

gner might be thinking. *Go out* and *look* at the projects when they are built and if you can get access to them. Develop a critical eye and mind. Do not accept everything that you see as beautiful or well done.

The interior designers' competitive edge consists of their knowledge of:

- intimate ways to respond to user needs
- materials, lighting types, and assembly techniques
- the usefulness and appropriateness of finishes
- how these all become part of the choices that the designer makes.

Think about the details. How do you make the idea *take shape*? Think about the context of your ideas. For example, how do people enter through a door into

a space? A heavy door, for example, needs two hands to open it. You design a heavy door, and you have changed the way that someone opens the door. You have created a sense of entrance.

Joannidis's words are important ones because they set the tone for how we as designers think. You, as the interior designer, control how people arrive and move through the space (Abercrombie, 1990). You want them to experience the interior in a certain way.

Movement through the Interior Space

We spoke about movement within a space earlier in this chapter. The way that someone sees a space for the first time has an impact on how they will respond to the space once inside. For example, if we think about dining out as an experience, we might conjure up images of the food, understand the goal of dining, and then we need to entice the senses, to enhance the dining experience, through the spatial experience.

Let's continue with Joannidis's ideas as he talks about the space as it is used and experienced:

The smallest gestures that you make affect how the user experiences the space. If you want to explore a concept, such as food, look into the science of food. Look at nature, at the world around you for inspiration when you create a plan.

You need to step away and try thinking about the space from different vantage points: around, inside, and outside. For example, if we are designing a stairwell, how do we think about what is underneath? We can make choices and each one affects our sense of the space and how we walk toward, around, inside, outside. . . . What can we do with this?

Open
   Closed
      Opaque
         Safe
            Seat
               Looking
                  Experience
                     Around?

You want to captivate the person who experiences the space. Designing interior space means creating an environment considering all the angles. The entrance to the space, the parking, walking, arriving, what are the first things that you do when you approach the space itself?

We go through the space thinking about how people move, and this happens very quickly:

PERCEPTION → VIEW → MOVEMENT → EXPERIENCE → ACTIVITY → RESPONSE → NEW PERCEPTION

We must understand a space as a place we bring people toward and then into, making them part of the space in an intimate way. We arrive at the space, and are moved into and around it, deliberately or spontaneously.

Seeing the Design and the World around You

You can find many sources of inspiration in the world around you. Examples include:

- nature
- the world itself
- diverse cultures
- travel (Even if you do not have the means to go around the world, you can travel into the next neighborhood, the next city, or venture out into the countryside.)

In the next part of Joannidis's talk, he considers his sources of inspiration:

Developing the idea into the concept means using the creative process—bringing the creative juices into play. Imagine yourself going through the space, how to treat the circulation, the finishes, the look, and the feel. How will I feel, as myself as the person? Draw on your own personal experiences. For example, what do you hate? For example, I hate blinds in hotel windows . . . so what can I do? I can make the facade the blind and control it from the inside out. It performs the function that the hotel patron needs for controlling light and privacy, and it is an aesthetic deci-

sion for the building face as well, designed from the inside out.

Using Color, Light, and Materials to Create Forms and Spaces

As we see with Joannidis's narrative and our exploration of interior space concepts, we begin to contextualize vague spatial ideas with details such as the form and its interrelationships with sound, touch and feel, or visual sensory responses. We become interested in the ways that color and light modulate interior space. Light can modulate space quickly when strategically placed with materials and forms. The use of lighting can be very explicit or very subtle, depending on the intent of the project concept. Light can also play with the space and its various negative and positive forms, creating subtleties as a way of either modulating the space or helping to create variety.

At this stage, we can already develop the lighting concept and our approach to materials and color choices, alongside preliminary custom-designed or architectural features we might be considering for the interior space. Color and light are major design elements that complement the development of the form and spatial characteristics. Both color and light work with form to elicit certain psychological and social responses. They are tied subjectively to our taste and feelings about certain colors and how they are in a space, or objectively to our responses to psychological or physiological aspects of certain colors and light effects (Birren, 1976; Mahke, 1996; Gordon, 2003).

When we suggested that we develop form and space using design principles such as balance or symmetry, we can include light and color as elements that modulate forms and spaces as well. Light can modulate spaces by adding higher or lower contrasts, playing with forms and materials. This allows the interior to create spatial relationships that excite, calm, or support activities within the space.

When we design with light and color, we attempt to solve the functional problems associated with comfort, and the ability to do certain tasks within the space, while creating subjective responses that excite, calm, or relax us (Gordon, 2003; Mahke, 1996). To be able to work these two ideas together, we must systematically think about the movement and pattern we create through our color and lighting design choices. This means that we select finishes and colors to elicit certain responses (a certain color or pattern), but we also control the impact of the space through the hierarchies we create. We can create hierarchies within spaces in several ways:

- hierarchy of form (one form precedes another and guides the user toward certain forms and an area of focus)
- hierarchy of color (certain colors draw us toward them)
- hierarchy of contrast (certain contrasts elicit certain responses)
- hierarchy of perspective (forms, colors, and light draw us into the perspective of the space)

In particular, light can be a useful tool to enhance or retreat forms and colors within a spatial design. As Gary Gordon (2003) discusses in *Interior Lighting for Designers*:

> Subjective impressions of space are a function of brightness contrast; the relationship of surfaces that are lighted (the focus or foreground) to those that are left in comparative darkness (the surround or background). It is possible, of course, to introduce general illumination into a room to permit vision. But establishing the emotional impact of an interior through the manipulation of brightness contrast is the real challenge for the creative designer.
>
> . . . Proper attention to the manipulation of brightness contrast as a principal technique for the design of lighting systems results in environments that are inviting, inspiring and supportive of tasks to be performed. (p. 11)

Contrast is probably the single most important aspect of integrating creative lighting into the overall spatial design because the resulting variety adds to the spatial dimension of the project. Even contrast can result in spaces that are too neutral or sterile; low contrast can be dangerous for certain activities, whereas high contrast can cause glare and seeing difficulties.

At this point, form, light, and color are useful tools to mold the space and modulate it as you work through your design ideas. There are a multitude of concepts and techniques that you can use to understand how to manipulate spaces using light, form, and color—concepts much too involved to include here.

DESIGNING THE SPACE, PART I

The best way to fully explore the potential of your concept is to try and "see" it from as many angles as possible. At this stage, full two- and three-dimensional (and even multidimensional) studies are fundamental to being able to capture the design concept fully. Here you might create 15 to 20 perspective views.

Documenting Design Concepts as They Evolve: Keeping the Memory of Ideas as They Develop

Do not throw out your ideas! You might discard them for a particular project, but keep a paper trail of all ideas. You may return to them later as you develop the design, or find them useful in a different project.

In this virtual world, we tend to use the computer to model or sketch ideas. When we find a good idea, we erase the rest. This is a *bad idea*!

Keeping track of your ideas as they unfold is crucial to the good development of design and enhances your capacity to make appropriate judgments and evaluate an idea and its worth.

Ways to save your work include:

- paper versions of ideas (hand-drawn or printed from the computer)
- electronic versions of ideas (saved in JPG or other retrievable format)
- sketchbooks (virtual or real)
- all drawings generated for a project

The problem with erasing ideas as they develop is that we erase potential good ideas lurking among the poor ones. When we draw, we are not the best judges of our own work because we are too subjectively involved in developing the ideas.

So far we have explored the early and developmental stages of the design process. Now let's take a look at space and the user, in preparation for Chapters 6 and 7 where we will develop creative techniques and bring the design toward completion with detail and in-depth development of the design concept.

DESIGNING THE SPACE, PART II: AESTHETIC EXPERIENCES AND INTERIOR SPACES

Until now we have explored general ways to approach designing interior space, as it relates to people and their relationship with the interior environment. We have examined how to integrate research and analysis with the designing of the interior in its early stages, and how to move from plan to modeled space and back again in an iterative process.

The Aesthetic and Human Spirit in Designing

One of the most valuable ways to ensure good design is to integrate the human component into the design of the interior space. As we have seen in the book thus far, different types of interiors demand different human contexts. Our public spaces are not necessarily the same as our private spaces. We live our private lives surrounded by the people and things that

are meaningful to us. When we venture out into the public realm, we use and appropriate spaces and places differently and for different purposes.

Theories and Concepts for Different Environmental Design Types

In the next segments we will look at different perspectives, from various domains, of human perception, reaction, and ways of relating to the interior space. Interior space can be understood from several theoretical contexts, such as in a:

- humanistic or personal context
- cultural context
- social or ethical context
- technical or practical context

Space is a three-dimensional (physical) or multi-dimensional (virtual-physical or virtual) place where people accomplish certain activities and wherein all of the senses are called upon to react. A human can occupy a space statically to:

- sit
- sleep
- wait

Or dynamically when:

- working
- walking
- moving
- talking

As soon as we move, we absorb perceptions of forms, objects, spatial limits, colors, lighting, and shadows. We also experience sounds, touch things and feel textures, sense warmth or coolness, feel a draft, humidity, or smell odors. These are part of sensual and aesthetic characteristics.

Space: Perspectives and Definitions

The word *space* comes from the Latin word *spatium*. Space is a concept that designates a virtual element that contains and surrounds people and objects. Space is synonymous with defined or undefined limits. Space can be contained (interior) or infinite (exterior), informal or formal.

> **BUILDING BLOCK** • *Keep a log, virtual memory stick, sketchbook, or journal of your ideas. Anything you draw has value, even the roughest or smallest sketch or loosest line. You never know when an idea or sketch might become useful. This becomes your "memory" and allows you to go back and retrieve the idea, whether for the project you are doing or perhaps for another project. Many of the sketches and rough ideas you see in this book come from designer's memories and pieces they have conceived. Keep logs in your computer and print out versions of your designs to put into a file that you keep handy. Refer to your ideas and then go back and look at them. You need to see how your design develops as you go along. Not every idea is an original one! But every idea has value . . . you may not use your idea in the project you are doing, but you may adapt it for another project or concept.*

Space can signify many different things in our perception of the world. It can signify:

- a certain distance between two objects, two or more people, two or more walls, or between surfaces; for example, a building occupies a large space.
- volume—this table takes up a small volume of space relative to that one.
- an environment where activities take place
- the representation of place
- visual, auditory, or sensory places (psychological sensations of space)

An interior designer needs to establish the relationship between a user and the optimal ways that his activities can take place within the spatial parameters set by the surrounding environment.

The Architectural Spatial Envelope

Architectural space is defined by the physical and material limits of a particular place or building. These are the major components from which space is constructed and that provide its particular spatial volume. These limits define the space as closed, open, intimate, or expansive. The space can be isolating for those it encloses or feel comfortable and inviting—the same space can evoke very different responses in different people.

Several factors affect the architectural parameters of an enclosed interior space:

- Walls and partitions—divisions that can be composed of various opaque or translucent materials, be thin or thick, planar, curved, textured, and so on
- Floor—horizontal "limit" occupied by the space that helps to determine its limits within the surfaces that surround it; can be finite or transitory, pierced or limited
- Ceiling—horizontal division or "upper limit" that can be as simple as the limit of the vertical surface, or an infinite series of volumes that define the upper limits of the enclosed space; can consist of inclinations, planar elements, different

levels and opacities; and can delineate a space or limit its expansiveness
- Structures and material composition—concrete, steel, or other material structures and their assembly affect the interior "limits" of the space and the available space that we have for planning and designing an interior. Can consist of various columns and floor and ceiling assemblages.

Within the limitations of these three dimensions (floors, walls, ceilings) and the composite spatial assemblies noted, we can find other spatial dimensions:

- openings and access points to other spaces
- visual links to other spaces and the outdoors
- multiple elements that add to the spatial dimension

These openings can be of various sizes, large or small, intrusive or inviting.

The multiple elements that support and occupy the space, including structural columns, objects, and accessories, all add to these dimensions. These elements not only fill the space, they help to define it, create visual relationships, and add to its personality. These elements work with the space and its occupants who appropriate the space as they occupy it over time. As soon as they displace any of the elements, they change the visual relationships and, by extension, the activities and relationships that are within.

Spaces are also transformed by the transitions that occur between them and other buildings and places. There are interrelationships between inside and outside, and between transitional spaces that can be at once interior and exterior to a particular space. These include halls, lobbies, porches, verandas, and so on. In this sense, the threshold of a home, a place, or a building has a large symbolic importance as a place of transition (Abercrombie, 1990; Gallagher, 2007). These transitional spaces are both places of welcome and places of departure. The threshold becomes the "frontier" between the private and public realms, the strange and the familiar. Private and public zones might be defined by thresholds.

Scale and Proportion

Thus far we have talked about human scale and proportion relative to the body and its relationships with objects in space. Space itself has scale and proportion, through its length, width, and height. The interrelationship among these three elements is what gives the interior space its proportional scale. For example, higher ceilings have a sense of expansiveness and give the impression of grandeur, luxury, and importance. Lower ceilings (relative to the width or length of the space) confer a sense of intimacy, warmth, and protection. All these properties of the space inform people and define how they relate to the space.

Other elements that inform how we understand and perceive spaces and that modulate the basic proportions of space include the following:

- The color and material characteristics of the surfaces and elements change our impressions of the space psychologically.
- The acoustic properties of the elements and materials within a space affect our relative sense of proportions and ability to function appropriately.
- The quality and quantity of light affects our visual acuity and perception and intersects with both physical and psychological responses.
- The horizontal and vertical circulation, including changes in level and relative axiality of the space, create a sense of movement.
- The form and shape of the space can affect our perception of it and its relative static or dynamic character. Theoretically, a square form is static, whereas a round, curvilinear, or elliptical form is dynamic. The addition or subtraction of volume within a space adds to its dynamism and produces a complex form adapted to the activities that unfold within.
- Spatial perceptions include all the five senses.

User Needs as "Lived Experiences"

If you recall at the very beginning of the book, there was a little girl in the marina who arrived in the space where I was working. Although I appreciated the space for its functional purpose, a quiet place where I could write, her perception of the space was very different. She exclaimed how beautiful it was. Her perception of the space and mine were quite different. Each person appropriates space for his own purpose and with his own vision, and very often one person's idea of a space is very different from another's. We can force people to use a space in a certain way, but we cannot impose views and perceptions, be they subjective or objective.

No matter what the "user need" might be, the person who is the user has an experience within the space that is real, active, dynamic, and subjective. Actual lived experiences are experiences that happen in the moment, in the actual perception of being in a space at a particular point in time. The space around us is dynamic, meaning that we perceive it as it unfolds around us. People move around the space, or perhaps sit at a desk doing a task, or look at the view and have a perception of it in a moment in time that is different from yours or mine.

Spaces become dynamic when we understand them from this perspective because the space itself is in movement. This means that the person and the space are integrated as one. The space changes as we move through it, and different people relate to the space in different ways. Some people want their objects and belongings statically positioned in a "permanent" sense, whereas others prefer a space that changes from one activity to the next. Each preference is guided by the lived experience of the person using the space.

It is the aesthetic response that we create for people to experience that makes interior design unique.

BUILDING BLOCK • *When first getting any project, get to know the building, the space, and these characteristics. If you are given a project in school for a warehouse, but do not have access to it, go and visit warehouses that are similar to get the feel of the space, its proportions, and relative heights and sizes. You need to feel the space as you would be in it; then transplant yourself into what the user of the potential space might want to experience.*

We are most interested in the intimate relationships that people have with their environment, and we strive to facilitate their experiences through the aesthetic and functional choices that we make.

Space as Place and a Representation of Self

We all have our own ideas about the sense of space. It is important for you to go out and explore different types of spaces, analyze them, and then reflect upon how they make you feel. Space can be experienced as a place where we feel a certain way. We can have a preconceived notion of space and then change our minds after we experience a particular place.

In this next case study (5.4), a student in her first year explores the sense of space as she experiences it. The project was to explore a built interior environment, and the student chose a funeral home. In this narrative, she writes about her first impressions; then how she moves in the space, and how she feels through her experiences.

What emerges from this narrative are the key elements of interior design as they affect the user experience of the space, such as:

- notions of aesthetics, art, poetry, symbolism, sensuality
- notions of comfort on several levels (metabolism, humidity, temperature, air circulation, lighting, acoustics)
- how the space influences psychological and social reactions of people
- how the space operates as a mediator of behavior
- how the human dimension is treated through physical, organizational, psychological, social, and cultural factors
- notions of territoriality impregnated through the ideas of invisible distances, as well as personal, social, and public distances to be respected through the spatial design
- notions of social exchanges are respected and changed from more traditional concepts

What Are the User Needs as Lived Experience?

When we read this case study about the funeral home, we enter into the student's experience and how the space mediated her experiences. In an environment she expected to be hostile, she became enthralled and enjoyed the space despite its difficult vocation. On another level, we must not forget that the space and the users are engaged in a lived, dynamic, and changing place. The interiors that you see in magazines are perfect staged spaces that are not "lived in." People change their environment to suit their lives, whether it is from one moment to the next, from one week to another, or after several years.

We must try, as interior designers, to understand how people live and have lived experiences, in the sense that we must understand how people need and want to live, work, and play, and not only think of them only as "users." Each interior is used by people, and they have subjective reactions and perceptions.

Interior Space Types: A Sampling

We will do a quick overview of different interior space types, and look at some characteristics of each in broad terms. We cannot cover all of the environmental design types here, and there are many other perspectives that you can explore. These descriptions are merely a starting point for further investigation.

We will look at retail environments, health care and institutional design, exhibition design, and tourism, travel and leisure, as a few examples of the many different areas of design that you might consider.

Workspaces and Work Environments

In the course of just 200 years, the workplace has become an essential interior space. The work environment has evolved from its earliest roots in the Industrial Revolution toward a virtual and knowledge-based environment. People work at home, on the run, and in the office. Workplaces have become "workspaces," and these concepts are evolving and changing daily as our ways of working are transformed through transnational and global communities (Amen & Cohendet, 2004; Spain, 1992; Malnar & Vodvarka, 1992; Poldma, 1999). Ways of working have been transformed as we have passed from an industrial age into the information age. The organizational structures of companies and corporations are less rigid and increasingly less static. Globalization and changing business conditions have forced corporations to become transnational players that cross countries and oceans to do business worldwide. This complicates the nature of the work world both at the macro and micro levels. Competition and performance-driven realities have forced companies to think about space as a place of production.

Designing office space and work environments includes considering people's performance at work, the relative flexibility and rapidity with which people need to accomplish tasks, the mobility and efficiency required. New work tools and ways of doing business make the workplace a mobile, flexible, and performance-oriented place. Static objects such as desks, pens, telephones, and paper have been replaced by virtual multitask organizational systems that fit in the palm of your hand. Videoconferencing permits people from different parts of the country or world to organize themselves around a project without having to leave their office. And yet the office is mobile as never before: One can work at home, in the office, on the go, in hotels, cafés, and wherever and whenever it is necessary.

Work environments have come a long way from the limited office designs of the pre- and post-World War II years. The modern era in the twenty-first century has seen some vast changes in work environments, both in the ways that people work and in the ways that workspaces are designed. The rhythm of the work world has accelerated, and spaces must incorporate efficiency and comfort if they are to support people in increasingly stressful work lives. Many researchers study the behavioral aspects of work in the office environment, and designers are constantly designing new ways to live within workspaces (Zelinski, 2002; Stewart, 2003).

In recent years, design issues within a workplace have come to include the ways that architects design the building and how the building is (or is not) structured to support the diverse, constantly changing activities that take place there. The space is then leased to companies who hire others to adapt the spaces provided. New Leadership in Energy and Environmental Design (LEED) certified buildings and sustainable approaches use materials and integrated systems that take into account human requirements now more than ever before. However, fundamental to any building-system approach is the need to understand people and their needs within the workplace. These new systems must be designed considering the people who will be using the spaces and the consequences of systems approaches on varied corporate needs.

New Ways of Working

In the past few years, the workplace has become infused with a new bureaucracy related to Computer Human Interaction (CHI). Although certain work has disappeared, particularly many intermediate and secretarial positions, other ways of working have sprung up. These include contract workers and technical support to run the new systems that can change daily in the workplace. The systems personnel have different requirements and needs from the development or retail aspects of corporate environments, and each division, department, or aspect of the corporation requires a different spatial approach.

People are also working wherever and whenever they can, as work time becomes blurred with leisure time. Some companies remain traditional in style and design, but others welcome new and different ways of designing spaces that incorporate the comforts of home. Meeting rooms are kitchens, offices include sports and activity spaces, restaurants are within office floors. Office spaces can be "narrative, nodal, neighborly or nomadic" as "property and space are beginning to be treated in a new and different way" (Myerson & Ross, 2003, p. 9).

Workspaces are diminishing in size as companies find ways to cut costs and justify the flexible schedules they encourage their workers to take on. Technology is changing how people work, and workspaces are mutating into different forms as never before. Although these spaces are increasingly more ergonomic and suit the needs of the workers, they are also mutating in ways never seen before. In the past, we had essentially two types of office space designs: open offices (secretarial pools) and closed offices (executive and manager offices). However, now we can work in different ways both in closed or open spaces, doing business in numerous ways. Some of these different office plan types include:

- hot line
- telecommuting
- shared office
- satellite office
- free address
- heart
- oasis
- hot-desking
- just-in-time offices
- cockpit office or mobile office
- hoteling or moteling
- touchdown space
- virtual offices
- virtual workspaces

These new ways of working will continue to multiply and change as different ways of working emerge and develop. However, in many cases, these new spaces imply tighter and more flexible workspaces, and that the nature of work is varied and fits within a certain design of a desk, space, place, or person. Workers no longer occupy one space their entire work life as they have done in the past. Closed offices do exist, but are not necessarily relegated to the managers and executive personnel alone. No longer do people occupy the perimeter windows as symbols of power, but are more often grouped in the center with window walls to allow sunlight to filter into the entire space.

In the design of large-scale projects, and in particular office and institutional design, planning is the first step. Planning must be done first to ensure that code requirements and safety issues are met, and that the design program requirements are followed. Only then do we move on to the three-dimensional space. During the planning, you as the interior designer must be able to:

- anticipate the requirements and detail required for the plan
- understand, visualize, and inform the user/client of what they are getting in terms of space alloca-

tion, user requirements, services, equipment, and amenities

If the client is developing a new office, for example, you need to assess and develop plans for:

- adequate workspace layout, storage of equipment and personal articles
- adequate interrelationships among workstations, among the workspace and peripheral yet necessary service needs (photocopiers, printers and computer interfaces, or other equipment)
- adequate proximity from the workstation to required services (coffee, personal care, office tasks, the people working with a particular person in the space, or from a particular space to another location entirely)
- quality environmental characteristics (comfortable ventilation, noise levels that are tolerable, personal comfort levels are met, the office is an anchor for the flexibility required)
- adequate flexibility for the multiple and changing needs of the worker, the workplace, and the work, wherever it goes

No matter what type of design you are asked to do, the result must be an actualization of the virtual idea the client has of the space and its potential for a given purpose. The corporate identity is ingrained within the design, while user comfort and personnel needs are met.

Tourism, Travel, and Leisure: Hotels, Bars, and Eating Establishments

When it comes to hotels, bars, and eating establishments such as cafés and restaurants, we consider space as a place for meeting, exchange, and enjoyment of a variety of activities. As leisure increases in the lives of some, it is integrated with the work environment for others. Travel is no longer limited to holiday seekers and foreign visitors. The shrinking globe means a nomadic existence for some while work is done 24/7 around the world. Tourism, travel, and leisure have become big business in this global economy as commercial establishments compete for both business and tourism dollars.

WRITING ABOUT FIRST IMPRESSIONS OF A FUNERAL HOME

In *The Poetics of Space* (1964), Gaston Bachelard writes:

> How concrete everything becomes in the world of the spirit when an object, a mere door, can give images of temptation, desire, security, welcome, and respect! If one were to give an account of all the doors one has closed and opened, of all the doors one would like to open, one would have to tell the story of one's entire life. (p. 224)

As soon as I arrive at the exterior of the building, I hesitate. Nothing gives away the vocation of this place, this business, its identity. The facade is somber and discreet. However, I am at the right address. Then I suddenly see the calligraphy of the signage on either side of the entrance, poetic quotes inscribed next to small letters that are spelling the name of the funeral home—I realize that I have arrived. I verify the address once more to be sure and I enter; my exploration of this space has begun.

What a nice surprise! Upon my entrance, even before I can objectively write about what I see, a series of sensations overwhelm me. I had always avoided this kind of place, a place where negative, serious, cold, somber, and heavy atmosphere surrounds the activity of death, sadness, farewells, and funeral rituals. And yet here, on the contrary, there are palpable sensations of calm, peace, and warmth that one would not expect. A serene, comforting, and warm atmosphere greets you, and the space is neither sad nor cold. A space that is ideal for meditation or to reminisce about death and the loss of a loved one. No disagreeable odors greet me as I have experienced in other such places (candles, lamps, flowers, stale cigarette smells, the perfumes of people long gone), smells I did not realize I knew until I did not sense them here. One could say that in those places you could "smell death" . . . here you do not even feel this negative sensation.

While consciously becoming aware of these sensual experiences, I know that I should orient myself toward either the left or the right, the directions presented to me in the foyer. The space that I am in is actually a very confined space and yet one does not feel closed in. There is a warm carpet on the floor and a semi-open wall in front of me that creates implicit limits from which I can see what happens beyond, and I can sense larger spaces beyond this entrance space. I have just enough information to know that there are other spaces beyond these walls but not enough information to know what is there.

And what a pleasure to discover that the walk-through I am being guided along has several pleasant surprises for me, as others who enter this space! I sense different things in this space as I walk through it, a certain spirituality and positive energy that entices me, allowing me to have a new and different appreciation for the mystery and spiritualism that can surround death and the spirit of hope leading into other realms.

As I move through the space, these sensations and experiences become stronger and more palpable. The ceiling is very high, the space is vast and open, and the abundance of natural light and the interrelationship of interior and exterior are informed by the light as it plays with the shadows formed by the architectural features. Without naming a specific religious experience, one can sense that this space is reserved for spirituality, meditation, and compassion.

This dynamic circulation guides us as we move through the spaces gradually.

I note the coat check and the reception/office to the left, but the openings and lighting entice us toward the right. Each movement leads us to new experiences within the space. After I have made the tour of the space, I then arrive through a walkway to the spiritual space of the main hall. In this hall I revisit the sensations I have already had, again impressed by the height and how the luminosity of the space gives me a sense of spirituality, infinity, fluidity, respect, and solitude. The textures, colors, and details create this atmosphere that is comforting, soothing, and engaging. (Sylvie Bélanger class notes, 2000)

Designing interiors in this sector remains innovative, as different actors and players (architects, designers, clients) think up new ways to entice people to these different establishments. New and dynamic interfaces such as LED lighting and virtual reality experiences are driving innovative design concepts that lift people out of their daily milieu into new and exciting experiences in the public realm. We will briefly consider hotels, restaurants, and bars/nightclubs with these contexts in mind.

Considering Hotels

We live in an era of increased travel and mobility as the world traveler becomes part of an increasingly nomadic society. Despite economic challenges, people are moving around the world for work and pleasure more than ever before as air travel to distant countries becomes ever more accessible. On the one hand, the world economy and telecommunications make it much easier to travel for work. Leisure time has also decreased, necessitating comfort and convenience when arriving at a destination. Hotels have become more versatile places, accommodating multiple traveler types and needs, from adults to children. The hotel is no longer just a place to sleep. People want to have a unique hotel experience, including shopping, spa treatments, relaxation, and entertainment, among other evolving needs.

Designing hotels is a complex process because of these changing consumer requirements. The hotel exists as a mini-community where the public side of the hotel is only one aspect of the total design. On the one hand, the back-of-store and support services are essential for the well-being of guests and the smooth operations of the services provided. In-depth knowledge and research of both management and operations are necessary for the interior designer to provide a balance between aesthetic and functional requirements. On the other hand, the front-of-store, or retail side, of the hotel has become multidimensional, becoming as varied as the traveler it caters to. Gone are the massive multi-chain and institutional settings of past hotels, as each new hotel type provides sumptuous and consumer-driven amenities to sell their service to potential clients. Added value in

hotels comes from catering to every need and desire, from family services to business home-away-from-home atmospheres, to sophisticated and elegant settings customized for every need.

Considering Eating Establishments

The pleasure of eating is guided by ambiance and appetite. Both are vital to the success of a restaurant because the ambiance guides the pleasure of eating and the senses are enhanced by a complete and aesthetic environment.

Recently there has been a new term called *fooding* to describe the complete experience of dining: "There are those who use the name 'fooding' to describe what has come to be looked on as an art of living and enjoying the cook's creations in a carefully arranged context" (*Restaurant Decors*, p. 6).

In bars, clubs, and discothèques, the vocabulary used to describe these environments often includes words such as *lounge, chill-out, nightclub*, and *cool*. In this design genre, the ambiance is directed toward a theatrical setting in which the bar scene unfolds. The experience is one of immediacy and intimacy within a few moments of entering the space, and all effort is directed toward creating an appropriate ambiance for connection and social activity.

Bars, clubs, and discotheques are planned with intimate knowledge of both front- and back-store restaurant services, understanding the concept of atmosphere creation and with an eye to quick, efficient customer service with a minimum of security problems. The design can be very unique and nothing is sacred. New concepts such as bed-ins and spaces on water add to the allure of these types of designs.

The functional basis of restaurants and eating spaces is supported by an integrated ambiance created by the spatial backdrop that forms the basis for a unique, sensory dining experience (Vaikla-Poldma, 2003). Baraban and Durocher (1989) suggest an understanding of how the various functional components of a restaurant work as a system, and they support a "service systems approach where food is delivered to a customer. . . . Types of eating spaces, subsystems such as accounting, sanitation, and food preparation and storage, and space planning of circulation are all fundamental to understanding the basic elements required of a complete design program" (pp. 15 and 18–24).

Retail Environments

The design of retail environments has undergone enormous transformation since the early 1990s as branding of all types permeates the retail milieu. Because the ultimate retail goal is consumer sales and high profits, all the attention is seemingly directed to the branding of the object and the spatial ambiance. However, this is not sustainable without a thoughtful and functional design that uses lighting, color, and direct manipulation through the layout design to draw in customers and direct them to make purchases despite themselves. In large box stores, the "design" is the absence of design to sell the concept of economy, whereas in high-end retail stores, the sumptuous finishes and soft lighting sell the idea of luxury and uniqueness. And yet sometimes in both cases, the merchandise is very similar!

With globalization, consumer desires are becoming ever more immediate, and physical retail spaces compete with virtual stores that sell more products and services than ever before. This acceleration of goods acquisition allows for consumers to tap into their needs for sensual and exotic products and services through brands that have become easily accessible. Ambiance in both virtual and physical retail environments is what sells, as lifestyles are created and fostered through the acquisition of goods.

In such a rapidly changing retail climate, the life cycle of store designs is extremely short. The quick turnover of merchandise and fierce competition requires retailers to renew their image constantly. The life of a typical retail space is on average three to five years, and although the priority is the presentation and sale of a certain product, brand attraction is playing an increasing role in store design.

Although the primary purpose of retail spaces is as a place of exchange between customers and retailers, stores are also becoming seductive places that aim to attract customers over time. This means enticing people into the store and providing an experience that they will appreciate and return for,

thereby buying more goods in the process. Retailers are increasingly making the store design an adventure, a seductive place where people would want to shop. This act of seduction begins in advertising, on the street, and in the exterior places where the retail space presents itself. The store creates a backdrop with its design, where form, color, lighting, and texture all integrate to transform the brand into a fascinating sensory experience, promoting the product to the fullest. The space transcends the retail aspect and becomes a meeting place, where emotions are manipulated into a positive experience, enticing the customer to buy even more.

Conversely, box stores and discount outlets have their own logic, using a non-designed or warehouse-style space to attract customers who are intent on saving money. But these spaces are also meticulously planned out and designed. From the sharp non-shadow lighting, to the lack of design elements, these spaces entice and manipulate in their own unique way.

Some retail spaces are introducing concepts that promote the store as a place to relax, meet friends, and be convivial. As a way of attracting customers, several larger retail environments offer multiple activities to suit every need. By offering several types of activities (Internet access, entertainment, shopping, eating), the intent is to attract customers with the most variety and cachet. In recent years, the term "retailtainment" has been coined to describe the use of multiple activities in the retail environment to create hybrid retail concepts. Some examples include:

- Internet cafés (free or with a fee) offer wireless Internet connections.
- Multiple "shopping boutique" department stores, where individual retailers group together within a single space, yet separate from a mall-type space. For example, in Montreal, Les Ailes de la Mode is a large department store offering a bistro-style restaurant, a community space in the center of the store with comfortable lounge seating and a pianist playing tunes, a bar, a beauty salon, and family services (changing rooms, support services).

- Bookstores offer cafés and comfortable reading living rooms; television and radio shows broadcast live from cafés, bars, and restaurants; spas and retail spaces are converted to mini concert venues or poetry reading centers; artwork is displayed for sale.
- Beauty salons and spas offer casual eating and retail boutiques that sell the goods you are using.
- Art galleries become retail environments where you can purchase the art, furnishings, and the decorative objects being displayed.
- Hotel-boutiques offer specialty items, from linens to furnishings, for sale so the customer can re-create the same luxury feelings at home; retailers produce "hotel-style" products for sale.
- Shopping malls are diversifying their concepts to suit local and branding needs, and are including cinemas, petting zoos, interior skating rinks, and other attractions to draw people.

Retail environments still provide an array of services, and must have the appropriate front-of-store and back-of-store ratio for product turnover and stock needs. They must provide adequate seating (if appropriate), counter service, changing rooms (clothing), and support spaces for diverse needs.

The designs of retail spaces vary widely, although there is an accepted sense of the design being tailored to the relative economic level of the merchandise. However, this is being constantly challenged by new designs and retail concepts. It is in this realm that the designer and client must work together to develop the program along with the various stakeholders involved with the enterprise.

Sustainability is being incorporated into some retail branding environments, but this depends on the goals of the firm and the real sustainable practices that are provided, whether in diminished packaging, recycling and reusing, or constructing LEED-approved buildings.

Health Care and Institutional Design

The interior design of institutional spaces is a complex integration of design with administrative services that are concerned with various levels of medical care. In this book it is impossible to cover the complexities of health care and institutional design. This is a specialized area of design where the interior designer always works with stakeholders and other specialized consultants in the creation of design interventions that focus on appropriate and healthy settings for different types of medical issues and issues related to an increased aging population. More often than not, architects are the lead in large health care projects, due partly to the complex aspects of environmental, health, safety, and security issues related to the buildings themselves. However, interior designers are finding their place in institutional and health care design. School designs are also undergoing dramatic changes, and these are another form of institutional design where interior designers might form part of the overall design team.

No institutional project can be designed without multiple stakeholders who input the needs of the administrators, the service providers, and the institutions, all of which have a stake in the facility. One of today's main issues is the rapidly aging and deteriorating condition of hospitals, nursing homes, and institutions built in the past 40 years that are still operating and in full use. Even institutions built 15 years ago require renovation with a serious eye to the changing populations. Whether a hospital or an elder care facility, the aging population and changing demographics around the world suggest a different type of user is occupying the institutional spaces of our urban centers.

On a very basic level, newly designed institutions are recognizing the importance of the necessity to "humanize" the interior space, while still providing the care, safety, and security required for the diverse population and health care needs. Interior designers can play a major role within the design of health care environments through the development of expertise that helps integrate the real, intimate human aspects of care through design choices such as color, lighting, and environmental systems within the designed spaces. An important design criteria for institutional design becomes the adaptability of the environment for the users' specific demographic, whether this is related to age, gender, medical situation, or cultural preferences (Poldma, 2006).

SETTING THE RIGHT ATMOSPHERE— MENTAL, PRACTICAL, AND CREATIVE

With all the particular contexts of the project and some preliminary concepts floating around, you can now develop the design to its fullest. We have seen some first ways of getting into the design through modeling and different approaches to scale and sense of the space.

Now you want to infuse your design with creative thinking and the aesthetic elements that will make your design unique. You can use and apply the skills from this book and countless others, but only you can decide which methods work for you.

The Mental Framework

It is important to get into the right mental framework to carry out a design project from the earliest meetings with the client right through to the final installation within the space. Some suggestions include:

1. Setting up the right kind of atmosphere to draw, work on the design, and also just to think.
2. Setting the mood means filtering out bad influences and filtering in good ones. For example, do not get distracted by the Internet or television; these both distract and do not encourage creative thinking. You can set the mood by putting on some music you like as a backdrop to clear your head. Music or musical visuals are good sources of relaxation, whether a DVD in your room or an MP3 player in your ears.
3. Thinking. This requires clearing the head.
4. Organizing the work into segments. Do not try to tackle it all at once.
5. Moving from one aspect of the design to the other. If, for example, you get stuck on the planning, you can move away from the plan and try looking at materials to give you inspiration. Or you can go out for a coffee and look at how different things work together in the world around you.

6. Using timelines and schedules. When things get busy, write down your daily workload and what you need to do. Place the due date for a project in a visual calendar and then work backward, listing the important due dates. This also helps to clear the head.
7. Stopping designing at a certain point, The design process is iterative, and this means that it continues, no matter where you are. At a certain point, you stop designing and move the design to its final version, the solution. This solution is a finite decision made at a particular point in time, for a particular purpose. You will always want to make it better, more finished, and more polished. You will get that chance in the next part of the process.

Setting up the mood means moving into the world of creative idea-making and ideation, and developing the concepts. Let's look at different ways to do this in Chapter 6.

BIBLIOGRAPHY

Abercrombie, S. (1990). *A philosophy of interior design.* New York: Harper & Row.

Albretch, D. (2002). *New hotels for global nomads.* London: Merrell Publisher Ltd.

Allen, J. (1987). *Designer's guide to Japanese patterns.* San Francisco: Chronicle Books.

The Architectural Press. (1970). *Principles of hotel design.* London: The Architects' Journal.

Bachelard, G. (1964). *The Poetics of Space.* Boston: Beacon Hill Press.

Ballast, D. K. (1993). *Interior design reference manual: A Guide to the NCIDQ Exam* (4th ed.). Professional Publications.

Bangert, A., & Riewoldt, O. (1993). *Designers hotels.* New York: The Vendome Press.

Barabon, R.S., & Durocher, J. F. (1989). *Successful restaurant design.* New York: Van Nostrand Reinhold.

Barreneche, R. A. (2005). *Nouvelle architecture commerciale.* Phaidon.

Becker, F. (2004). *Offices at work.* San Francisco: John Wiley & Sons, 2004.

Bérubé, C. (2001 November) FIIDA, PDG de O.V.E. *Les bureaux à l'ère de la nouvelle économie, in* Design Solutions, *Intérieurs*, pp. 33–50.

Boissière, O. (1998). *Boutiques, séduire autrement.* Paris: Telleri.

Brawley, E. (1997). *Designing for Alzheimer's disease.* New York: John Wiley & Sons.

Cassidy, S.-M. (1999). *A place to stay, 30 extraordinary hotels.* Vicking Studio.

Ching, F. (1995). *Interior design illustrated.* New York: John Wiley & Sons.

Ching, F. (1996). *Architecture, Form, Space and Order,* New York: John Wiley & Sons.

Ching, F. (1998). *Design drawing.* New York: John Wiley & Sons.

Curtis, É. (2001). *Hotel interior structures.* Wiley-Academy.

Cuttle, C. (2003). *Lighting by design.* Oxford, UK: Architectural Press.

Davidson, J. (1991). Lighting for the aging eye. *Interior Design.* New York.

Dean, C. (2003). *The inspired retail space, attract customers, build branding, increase volume.* Gloucester, MA: Rockport Publishers.

De Vleeschouwer, O. (1998). *Hôtels étonnants.* Telleri.

Diekman, N., & Pile, J. (1990). *Drawing interior architecture: A guide to rendering and presentation.* New York: Whitney Library of Design.

Felstead, A., Jweson, N., & Walters, S. (2005). *Changing places of work.* New York: Palgrave Macmillan.

Fortmeyer, R. (2007 September). The new age of high-tech hospitals. *Continuing Education*, McGraw-Hill Construction, September 2007.

Fotoussi, B. (1992). *Hôtels.* Éditions du Moniteur.

Gensler, A. (1998). *Developing the architecture of the workplace.* Edizione Press.

Gervais, C. (1999 February). Bureaux : les lieux de réunion, *Intérieurs*, pp.41–47.

Gordon, G. (2003). *Interior lighting for designers* (4th ed.). New York: John Wiley and Sons.

Hall, E. T. (1969). *The Interior Dimension.* Garden City, NY: Anchor Books.

Hendersen, J. (1998). *Workplaces and workspaces: Office designs that work.* Gloucester, MA: Rockport Publishers.

Hiss, T. (1990). *The Experience of Place.* New York: Alfred A. Knopf.

Hospitality Focus (2001 March) Starwood Hotels and Resorts. *Special Issue, Interior Design.*

Kaplan, M. (1996). *The new hotel: International hotel and resort design 3.* New York: PBC International.

Karlen, M. (1993). *Space planning basics.* New York: Van Nostrand Reinhold.

Kaufmann, P. (1999). *L'expérience émotionnelle de l'espace.* Paris : Librairie philosophique J. Vrin.

Kliment, S. A. (2001). *Building type basics for hospitality facilities.* New York: John Wiley & Sons.

Laseau, P. (2001). *Graphic thinking for architects and designers.* New York: John Wiley & Sons.

Lawson F. (1976). *Hotels, motels and condominiums: design, planning and maintenance.* London: The Architectural Press Ltd.

Mace, R. (1997). *Universal design: Housing for the lifespan of all people.* New York State University, New York: The Center for Universal Design. www.design.nesu.edu:8120/cud/pubs/center/books/lifespanhous.htm

Micheli, S. (2004). *Petites & grandes boutiques.* Milan: Actes Sud/Motta.

Myerson, J., & Ross, P. (2003). *The 21st century office: architecture and design for the new millennium.* New York: Rizzoli.

Newton, H. (2002). *Restaurant decors.* Mexico: The Atrium Group.

Pappas, T. (1991). *More joy of mathematics: Exploring mathematics all around you.* San Carlos, CA: Wide World Publishing/Tetra.

Poldma, T. (1999). *Gender, design and education: The politics of voice.* Unpublished Master's Thesis. Montreal: McGill University, Author.

Poldma, T. (2006 July/August). Adapting the interior environment: A case study using light, color and research as catalysts for interior design problem-solving. *Interiors & Sources*, pp. 58–59.

Raymond, S., & Cunliffe, R. (1997). *Tomorrow's office: Creating effective and humane interiors.* London and New York: E & FN Spon.

Rengel, R. (2003). *Shaping interior space.* New York: Fairchild Publications.

Riewoldt, O. (1997). *Intelligent spaces: Architecture for the information age.* London: Laurence King Publishing.

Riewoldt, O. (2000). *Retail design.* New York: te Neues Publishing Company.

Riewoldt, O. (2002). *New hotel design.* London: Laurence King Publishing Ltd.

Rocher, E. (2002) *Bar decors.* Mexico: The Atrium Group.

Rutes, W. A., Penner, R. H. & Adams, L. (2001). *Hotel design, planning and development.* New York: W. W. Norton & Company.

Rus, M. (2001 January). *Get a room! Interior design* Hospitality Awards.

Ryder, B. (2005). *New bar and club design.* New York: Abbeville Press Publishers.

Serfaty-Garzon, P. (2003). *Chez soi, les territoires de l'intimité.* Paris: Armand Colin.

Shobata, Y. (1993). *New hotel architecture: Modern hotel design: A Pictural Survey.* Meisei Publications.

Smith, D. H. (1978). *Hotel and Restaurant Design.* Design Council Publications.

Sommer, R. (1967). *Personal space: The behavioral basis of design.* London: Prentice Hall International.

Special Interior Design, Hotel Design. (2001 October). *A joint hospitality supplement from the editors of Interior Design and Hotel Magazine,* pp. 266–345.

Stewart, M. (2003). *The other office: Creative workplace design.* Amsterdam: Frame Publishers and Basel, Birkhauser-Publishers for Architecture.

Stungo, N. (2001 September). Hotels: Everyone's at it, *World Architecture, 99.*

Tetlow, K. (1996). *The new office: Designs for corporations, people & technology.* PBC International.

Tremblay, D-G. (1995). *Organisation du travail et technologies dans les bureaux d'hier à aujourd'hui.* Presses de l'Université du Québec.

Verderber, S., & Refuerzo, B. J. (2006). *Innovations in Hospice Architecture.* New York: Taylor & Francis.

Vischer, J. C. (2005). *Space meets status: Designing workplace performance.* London and New York: Routledge.

Vodvarka, F., & Malnar, J. M. (1992). *The interior dimension: A theoretical approach to enclosed space.* New York: Van Nostrand Reinhold.

Weishar, J. (1992). *Design for effective selling space.* New York: McGraw-Hill.

Welsh, S., & Beautyman, M. (2007 November). X-ray vision: The diagnosis for hospitals and clinics. *Interior Design, 78*(14).

Wong, W. (1972). *Principles of two-dimensional design.* New York: Van Nostrand Reinhold.

Wong, W. (1993). *Principles of form and design.* New York: Van Nostrand Reinhold.

Young. P. (2000). The age factor. *Azure.* Toronto: Azure.

Ypma, H. (2000). *Hôtels extraordinaires.* Hachette.

Zelinski, M. (1998). *New workplaces for new workstyles.* New York: McGraw-Hill.

Zelinski, M. (2002). *The inspired workspace: Designs for creativity and productivity.* Glouster, MA: Rockport Publishers.

Chapter Six

CREATIVE GENIUS IN DESIGN PROBLEM SOLVING

Objective

Throughout the book, we have seen different ways to jump-start design thinking, whether through brainstorming in the early stages of the design process, or moving from known to unknown aspects of the design. In this chapter we will reexamine various thinking tools that use creativity to help foster different design ideas during the various project phases. We will look at the following concepts:

- Using the creative process to jump-start interior design thinking.
- Using design elements and fundamentals to generate design ideas through creative thinking processes.
- Fostering creative thinking during the different stages of the design process as a means to guide creative ideas and to judge developing designs.

MAPPING THE UNKNOWN ASPECTS OF THE DESIGN PROCESS

One of the points we have discussed throughout the book is the natural movement during designing from the known to the unknown and back again. In this chapter we will look at different tools that will help us to develop these more unknown aspects of a design. We might ask ourselves what a space might look like or how would it feel. As we develop designs, we explore possibilities by trying out our ideas within the space, trying always to envision the space, its occupants, what they do, and how we can fit them together.

In some ways, we are doing what Edward De Bono (1995) calls *po*:

Po is . . .

*Po*ssibilities

*Po*tential

Sup*po*se

Hy*po*thesis

*Po*etry

. . . Po . . . suggest(s) multiple possibilities. . . .

. . . Many years ago I invented the new word *po* as a formal indication that a provocation was to follow. A provocation is a statement that we know to be wrong but which we use in order to jerk us out of our usual thinking so that we can form new ideas. . . .

. . . Possibility is always creative. Possibility always moves forward from "what is."

(pp. 131–133)

De Bono suggests four ways to explore possibilities:

1. The search for standard or routine solutions. These solutions are available to us and we search our minds to find the appropriate solution or way forward.
2. Here we move from a very general statement of what we need to a specific solution. We can also use general statements to move backward from where we want to be to where we are.
3. This is the creative approach. We deliberately create new ideas and then seek to modify them to suit our purposes.
4. This is the design or assembly approach. We put together different elements to achieve the desired purpose. These elements may be obtained from standard sources or through creativity. (pp. 135–136)

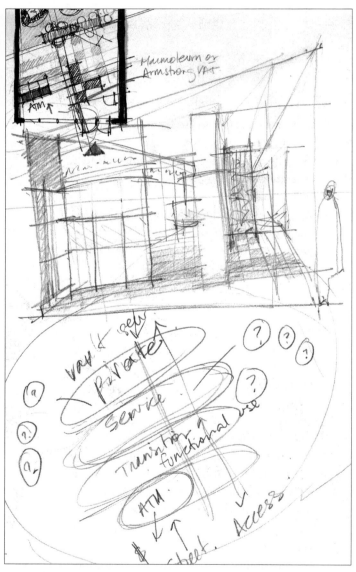

Figure 6.1a • Plan and sketches of a preliminary design idea

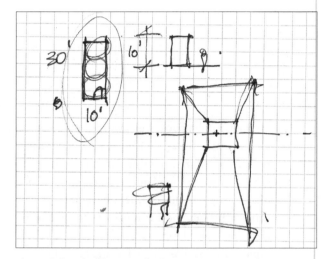

Figure 6.1b • Blocking out a basic space to sense scale

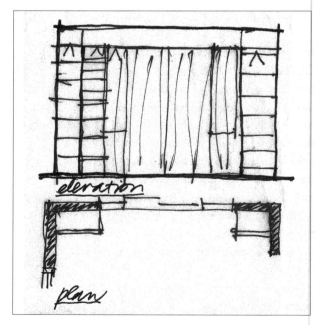

Figure 6.1c • Plan and elevation of a window wall

We use these approaches as we design interior spaces. We can refer to this as "thinking as doing." Using De Bono's four concepts, let's examine what we might do to put them into play through a sketch plan and its iterations:

1. Lay out the space based on functional concepts we examined in the research and analysis phase. We can start with the plan and fit the various components we have determined are required. Figure 6.1a shows an example of how to plan out a space looking at needs and requirements.
2. Develop the design criteria and then create the design concept. Create a concept statement from the design criteria as a general overview of what you want to achieve; then model this within the space itself.
3. Try a new idea on the space to see what it might be like.
4. Try the design idea with an organizational principle that brings together the functional layout with the new idea.

As we apply these four approaches, we move from thinking-as-doing toward doing-as-thinking. Each time we try a different way of seeing the design, we develop more ideas (Figure 6.1a through d).

GENERAL CONCEPTS: THE CREATIVE PROCESS IN INTERIOR DESIGN THINKING

We will look at creative processes and how to generate ideas by applying this type of creative thinking and problem solving to interior design projects. Interior designers use several methods to convert creative ideas into built realities. The designer's personal experience shapes each creative idea as well as the subsequent aesthetic environment that is created. Whether this creativity is innate in an artistic sense, or whether it is a way of organizing ideas into a new way of understanding interior space, each is a form of creativity in problem solving.

There is recognition that the creative process is a necessary part of design problem solving. Creative thinking includes generating ideas during the design

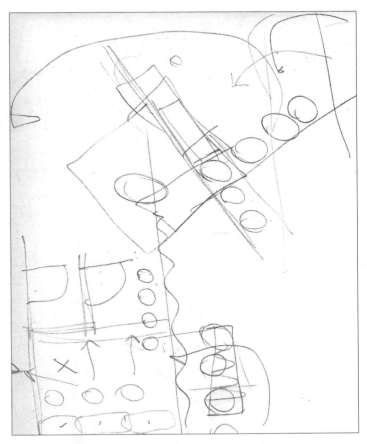

Figure 6.1d • Different ways to resolve an entrance point

process and using the design fundamentals of form, shape, and pattern to guide you. The creative part of design exploration includes both the physical form of the space, and your own intuitive, creative thinking that helps you to think of different ways to solve the problem at hand.

Over time, a wide range of personal and professional experiences help the designer to foster creative ideas. Some of these ideas come from plans, others from a visualization of the space; still others come from the different ways that you use art, form, space, and material to create the concepts that you envision.

Many design ideas, indeed the "creative spark" that we often have for a design concept, happen away from the design task itself. For example, Malnar and Vodvarka (1992) talk about how creative practices use techniques to stimulate the mind, and speak about John Dewey and his book *Art as Experience:*

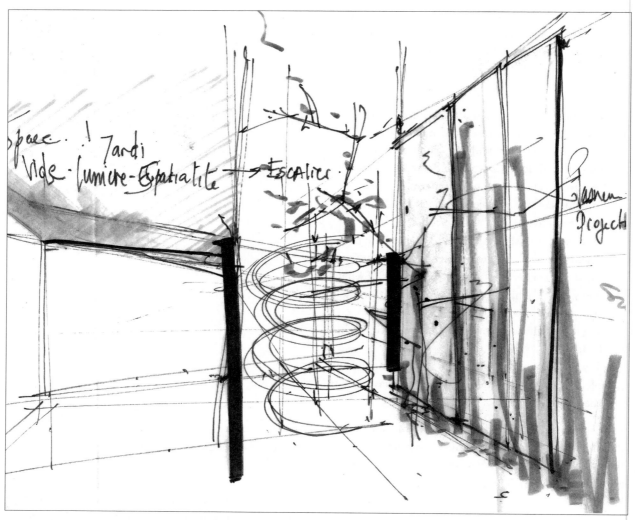

Figure 6.1e • Another way to conceptualize space altogether

To develop such sensitivity to underlying relationships, and their visual manifestations has long been a goal of design education, leading to inventions designed to stimulate the creative mind. . . .

. . . One's ability to sense the larger reality is critical to the design process. Indeed Dewey suggests "it is the context of every experience and it is the essence of sanity . . . once that reality is sensed, the designer must convert it into a perceivable reality." (p. 28)

If this is true, then what you experience helps to frame the creative ideas that you generate. Your experiences need to be as varied as possible to foster your creative mind.

Moving into that unknown territory of creating is something most designers all experience in one form or another at some point in their design process thinking. It is where you explore and discover new things, or document ideas that you want to try out, experimenting with the forms and features of the project. The creative process is a process that is recognized as a vital component that produces design ideas that ultimately transform perceptual and intangible ideas into tangible realities (Arnheim in Margolin & Buchanan, 2000; Bilda & Demirkan, 2003).

Developing Ideas about Interior Space Using Creative Thinking and Design Principles

Before we go any further, we should put the creative process into the perspective of the interior design project. Using creative thinking means thinking about the interior space and the user simultaneously. At this point you might ask questions such as:

- How do I make the space interesting?
- How can I create an experience for people that they will enjoy?
- How can they move in and through the space, and do what they need to do?

Creative ways of thinking about the design include:

- thinking about the movement within the space
- using organizing design principles to guide people through the space
- understanding the design as a metaphor for objects found in nature or in other aspects of life
- understanding how people perceive the space, the objects within, and the nature of their activities
- using what we learn when speaking to clients, users, and others to inspire us into thinking about potential design solutions

We can organize space creatively, build creative inspiration into our designs, or use known creative problem-solving techniques to adapt required functions into spaces that may not really be suited for them.

We will begin by looking at the nature of the creative process and then examine specific techniques and examples of creative problem solving as it relates to interior space.

THE CREATIVE COMPONENT OF THE DESIGN PROCESS

Creativity in design is not just about the creation of a novel concept for an interior space. Nor is it about the creative flair of an artistic genius. Creativity in interior design means using inspiration, as well as design thinking, principles, and fundamentals to solve the design problem in unique ways. Your goal is to create the design and to understand the design problems in

ways that your user and client may not imagine, but that solves their problem in a new way while integrating their priorities and preoccupations.

Creativity in interior design includes being inspired and thinking about new or novel ways to make the space better, about reaching out to people, and using interior design as a catalyst for change.

Sources of inspiration are all around us, and we draw on them every time we embark upon a new design. For some, it is art; for others, math or music. Still others use childhood memories, nature, or social activities as sources of inspiration. Just as each individual is unique, so are the experiences that shape and inspire us.

Steve Morris (2006) discusses how creativity in graphic design means exploring realms outside one's own personal comfort zone:

> . . . If you exist only in a fishbowl in the design industry, and all you read is the standard design publications, your ideas will be relatively small. You have to think outside of what you're used to. . . . I think that the definition of creativity is that every human being is very creative, and exercises that creativity. That doesn't mean that they do it for a living. And anyone has the ability to problem-solve at any level. It's just to what degree. And if you're openly willing to express it. (p. 150)

The same is true for interior designers when they are creative problem solvers. Problem identification and problem solving require creative thinking because the work of integrating an interior spatial environment with the objects and people within and around the various activities for which we design is complex, and the solutions are not always evident.

About the Nature of Creativity

We often think of creativity as something a lonely artist does, shut away in his studio until he emerges with his latest work of art. But in interior design, creativity happens when designers bring people together to work on complex problems effectively. Some years ago, in a PBS television series called *The Creative*

Spirit, Paul Kaufmann (1992) suggested, on the show and its accompanying book of the same title, that:

> . . . Creativity is not . . . something that is entirely individual. It involves reaching other people. It's a social fact, not just a psychological one. Creativity is not something a person keeps in the closet: It comes into existence during the process of interacting with others. (Kaufmann, 1992, p. 26)

Being creative means thinking and doing the design in different ways, by searching for ideas and possibilities. Renowned psychologist Howard Gardner (1992) has said that we usually consider people to be creative in something. He suggests that:

> A person isn't creative in general—you can't just say a person is "creative." You have to say that he or she is creative in X, whether it's writing, being a teacher, or running an organization. People are creative in something. (p. 26)

Like Morris, he qualifies the notion of being creative "in something" or to what degree. Goleman, Kaufmann, and Roy (1992) cite Gardner and evolve this idea about creativity in the context of Gardner's ideas:

> The textbook view of creativity . . . doesn't make any sense at all. I think that you have to watch a person working for a while in a particular domain, whether it is chess, piano playing, architecture, or trying to run a business or run a meeting. And you have to see what they do when problems come up and how their solution is achieved. Then you can make your judgments on whether that person is creative or not. . . . People who are creative are always thinking about the domains in which they work. They're always tinkering. They're always saying, "what makes sense here, what doesn't make sense? And if it doesn't make sense, can I do something about it?" (Goleman, Kaufmann, & Roy, 1992, p. 27)

Interior designers are creative when they problem solve, look for function and pattern in spatial contexts, or look for new or different possibilities. This is tinkering in Gardner's sense of the word.

BUILDING BLOCK • *Carry a sketchbook with you in your daily life. Sketch anything and everything that you see. Look around you at the world, be it nature, the urban city, or the sky. It can be small or large, black or colorful, but it should be real paper and markers or pencils that you use. You can use it alongside a computer-generated sketch, but do not ignore the paper sketch. It is a prime example of tinkering. And don't forget to use color: We live in our interior spaces with color and this is part of our design palette!*

> *You can also do this type of tinkering with a laptop or portable recording device of any kind. Keep track of your ideas as they emerge into your head— do not wait for rational thinking to take over, as this dulls the creative process. Get your ideas into some type of visual or written form as soon as you can!*

Sketch out your ideas in a sketchbook, especially if you want to do things immediately in virtual form. This is an essential form of tinkering, as we think by transmitting our ideas from head to drawing paper.

Sketching and drawing are parts of our tinkering language, our means of communication with ourselves and others. The initial idea brews in our heads and when we transform from head to model or sketch, whether real or virtual.

Designing with Creative Thinking Tools and Methods

We use our creative design thinking in different ways. Sometimes we just want to brainstorm ideas, but at other times we need to apply our research and analysis using creative thinking to integrate the design elements into a proposed design.

In previous chapters, we have seen how we can generate ideas with others or alone, using brainstorming and artistic visual tools. Sometimes when discussing a design problem with a client, ideas may pop into your head, and hopefully you can sketch them out immediately. Who hasn't heard of the dinner meeting with the paper napkin becoming a sketch pad? At other times you may be working with other designers on a project and several people come up with different ideas. This type of group brainstorming is a great way to step out of your own design process and try out new things.

Ideation: The Process of Generating Ideas

You will also find that ideas often come up when you least expect it. For example, you are working on the layout plan of a space, and you just cannot get seven workstations into a space where only five will fit. Then you walk away and take a break, and suddenly you can see the solution in your mind's eye. You should immediately rush back to your sketch pad or computer and get the idea down. This is the creative process at work and this form of ideation helps to produce the first ideas that we have. Creative ideas require stepping away from what you know and exploring the unknown, uncharted territory where only you can figure out what will make your particular project tick! The more ideas you generate, the better your chances are of developing good ones.

When I was in school, we were instructed, "Ideate! Ideate! Ideate!" We were told to unroll a sketch paper roll and with a thick black marker draw anything and everything that came into our heads. I suggest that you do this at least once during the designing process, putting yourself under a time limit. The pressure to sketch, say, 20 ideas in 45 minutes will generate ideas quickly. The first step to ideating is to generate ideas. Robert Ornstein (1991) explains how we must generate many ideas to find the occasional good one:

> Creativity is part of evolution, and it works in a way similar to natural selection, in which there are random variations, some of which prove useful and are "selected" by the environment. People generate many ideas, almost at random, a few of which are appropriate and become selected. Chance plays a great role in both the generation and evolution of ideas. Generation *of ideas is the primary stage*. People who have many ideas are more likely to have creative ones. A useful creative idea is rare.

Campbell emphasizes:

> The tremendous amount of nonproductive thought must not be underestimated. Think of what a small proportion of thought becomes conscious, and of conscious thought what a small proportion gets uttered, what a still smaller fragment gets published, and what a small portion of what is published is used by the next intellectual generation. There is a tremendous wastefulness, slowness and rarity of achievement.
>
> Thousands of small and wrongful ideas prepare the way for an occasional useful one. Thomas Edison supposedly evaluated his progress on an invention by saying that he knew a hundred ways that wouldn't work. *Creativity involves hard work and the relentless generation of ideas and thoughts to produce a few that pass evaluation. Evaluation is the assessment of an idea's worth.* It is perhaps more important to recognize a good idea than it is to possess one. (Emphasis in the original.)

Avoiding Blocks to Creativity

One of the biggest stumbling blocks to generating creative ideas is the rational response "I cannot do it," or "I am not creative." How do you know if you do not try?

So my advice is *try to do it anyway!* Often students tell me, "My sketches are not nice," and they

---

BUILDING BLOCK • *Here is a simple exercise that you can do, whenever and wherever you are. One of the best ways to begin generating ideas is to temporarily leave the research behind and draw little sketches, smaller than a playing card. These sketches should be random and loose, in a sketchbook with a black marker. Even they are rough and not great, you need to loosely sketch ideas as they come into your head. Label the page with the date and project; add images and ideas that come to mind from the research or analysis you have done. NEVER throw out your sketches and keep the journal—you never know what little sketch may be useful later on!*

try to hide them and not show them to me. So what? You must remember that even the roughest of sketches brings out inspiration. The messiest ideas and sketches can be the best sources of a creative spark. We need to draw or map out many ideas to be able to sift through them and see which idea has the most promise.

No matter what the scope of the project or the nature of the design, an exciting way to develop creative ideas is to look at the project as a whole. When developing designs, it is always a good idea to think about all the possible components at once.

I just presented one exercise to you to try, but there are many others. And which exercises interest you depend a little on who you are and how you think. All designers have certain thinking modes that differ from others, and there are many who believe in what is called the creative spirit. Let's explore this thinking and the idea that we have certain attributes that we use to develop creative thinking and problem solving using what some call a *creative stew*.

The Creative Stew

A few years ago in the PBS series *The Creative Spirit*, Daniel Goleman, Paul Kaufmann, and Michael Roy (1992) suggested that there are many different aspects to creativity and that these make up a "stew" of creative moments that we collect and use. Teresa Amabile (in Goleman, Kaufmann, & Roy, 1992) talks about this stew:

> . . . Being creative is kind of like making a stew.
> . . . There are three basic ingredients to creativity.
> . . . The essential ingredient is expertise in a specific area: domain skills. These skills represent your basic mastery of a field. . . . The ingredients of creativity start with skill in the domain—and the expertise.
> . . . Many people have a flair for something . . . with the proper skill development, even an average talent can become the basis for creativity.
> The second ingredient in the stew is . . . creative thinking skills: ways of approaching the world that allow you to find a novel possibility and see it through to full execution. . . . [T]hese

creative thinking skills include being able to imagine a diverse range of possibilities, being persistent in tackling a problem, and having high standards for work.
> . . . Finally, the element that really cooks the creative stew is passion. The psychological term is *intrinsic motivation*, the urge to do something for the sheer pleasure of doing it rather than for prize or compensation. (pp. 28–30)

Goleman, Kaufmann, and Roy (1992) develop ideas on how the creative process works, and talk about renowned psychologists Howard Gardner and Mihaly Csiktszentmihalyi. They suggest that some of the many creative traits include:

- Creativity is ageless.
- Creativity means listening. Having a conversation is a form of talking and also listening, learning about your client and user needs through conversation. But this also means listening and learning through listening.
- Creativity requires information gathering. Gathering accurate information is essential to early, preparatory stages of the creative process. The more good information you have about a problem, the better the chances of devising a solution. (p. 38)
- Creativity requires taking risks.
- Creativity requires learning from the risks taken.
- Creativity means being open to new experiences; learn to embrace anxiety and use it to help you to problem solve.
- Learn to develop "flow" (Csikszentmihalyi, 1997; Kaufmann, p. 46). This can include "states of mind;" for example, keep a childlike spirit, or create a flow in the mind, like water . . . (Goleman, Kaufmann, & Roy, 1992, retrieved and in summary form, pp. 30–50)

Mihaly Csikszentmihalyi (1997), another renowned psychologist, explores creativity and develops the idea of creative flow, the place "where people are at their peak. Flow can happen in any domain of activity"(p. 46). He has published several books on creativity and develops the concept of "flow" extensively in his seminal book, *Finding Flow* (1997). The concept of flow is tied to three things: how flow comes about, what constitutes the creative nature of a person's experience, and the locations where flow occurs. Here we have an excerpt of Csikszentmihalyi's concept of flow:

> Imagine, for instance, that you are skiing down a slope and your full attention is focused on the movements of the body, the position of the skis, the air whistling past your face, and the snow-shrouded trees running by. There is not room in your awareness for conflicts and contradictions; you know that a distracting thought or emotion might get you buried facedown in the snow. And who wants to get distracted? The run is so perfect that all you want is for it to last forever, to immerse yourself completely in the experience. . . .
>
> . . . [T]his complete immersion in an activity may occur in a social interaction, as when good friends talk with each other, or when a mother plays with her baby . . . in these moments what we feel, what we wish, and what we think are in harmony.
>
> These exceptional moments are what I have called flow experiences. The metaphor of "flow" is one that many people have used to describe the sense of effortless action they feel stand out in moments that stand out as the best in their lives. Athletes refer to it as "being in the zone," religious mystics as being in "ecstasy," artists and musicians as aesthetic rapture. Athletes, mystics and artists do different things when they reach flow, yet their descriptions of the experiences are remarkably similar. (pp. 28–29)

This concept of flow is important because it is a means by which designers realize ideas to their full potential, whether interiors or other design projects. Flow may occur during the various stages of the design process, when you begin to see things coming together, or when a "Eureka" hits as you discover an idea, a possibility, or the design concept. I refer to flow moments as Eureka moments (Vaikla-Poldma, 2003) and this Eureka moment is captured in a certain way of thinking and doing that helps us to create interior concepts. We can create concepts when we are

not in these moments, but often when things come together it is because of how we relax, let our minds go, and allow creative acts the chance to occur. It is also important to realize that these moments are not always present, and that they are not always necessary, either. But they are possible and probable.

The Influence of the Surrounding Environment

Another interesting aspect of this idea of flow is how the environment affects your creative and problem-solving abilities. According to Csikszentmihalyi, not only are we capable of finding flow, but that flow and creative thinking can be helped along by the surrounding environment. There are two ideas *within* this one concept: We need flow to create and be creative as designers, and we can also create environments that allow flow to occur for others.

Here in another excerpt from *Finding Flow*, Csikszentmihalyi (1997) talks about the influence of the surrounding environment on one's capacity to find flow and the influence of our location in this experience:

> Everyday life unfolds in various locations—the home the car, the office, streets, restaurants. In addition to the activities and companionships, locations also have an effect on the quality of experience. . . .
>
> For many people, driving a car gives the most consistent sense of freedom and control; they call it their "thinking machine" because while driving they can concentrate on their problems without interruptions, and resolve personal conflicts in the protective cocoon of their personal vehicle. . . . Different rooms in the house also have their particular emotional profile, in large part because each is the setting for a particular kind of activity. (pp. 43–44)

The environment can play a crucial role in helping people do their activities, and this may include helping people to find flow. Setting the mood to design can be as easy as taking a walk, shutting down all distractions, or putting on headphones to shut out the world.

Different Creative Intelligences

Finally, Howard Gardner suggests that there are many different types of creativity, as he terms "multiple intelligences" (in Goleman, Kaufmann, & Roy, 1992, pp. 72–80). Gardner provides seven "intelligences" to consider, and suggests that creativity is a cultivated skill as much as an innate trait. He names these seven intelligences as follows:

- Language
- Math and logic
- Music
- Spatial reasoning
- Movement
- Interpersonal intelligence
- Intrapersonal intelligence

Notice that interior designers may have traits or more than one of these intelligences, but essential to an interior designer's creative thinking is the concept of spatial reasoning.

Notice also in the past few ideas about creativity that we develop creative skills using both skills and talent, and these are essentially grouped together with the idea of passion.

Levels of Creative Thinking

Generating creative ideas begins any time you are working on a project. Typically we generate ideas after the preliminary design program is done or the project parameters are set. Too often we jump right into the space itself, putting aside the research instead of using it to help gain insight into the creative potential of a project. One of the basic ways to create concepts is to let your mind wander and create an environment where you can begin to conjure up possible ideas for your interior space.

There are three levels of brainstorming and concept creation that can help you to really get into the project:

- First-Level Brainstorming: Fostering creative thinking during the earliest stages of the design process (free, spontaneous ideas that flow from initial project thinking)

- Second-Level Creative Work: Generating creative ideas about the project during the designing phase (both within and outside of the space)
- Third-Level Creative Thinking: Moving into the space and developing aesthetic concepts for the space in greater detail and with material design elements in mind.

Why three levels? In interior design, we need to plan and use our logical skills to fit functions within a space, particularly in large-scale projects. However, it is important to step away from this, daydream, and let the mind wander. So we need different places in the design process where we can feel that we can do this. We can ideate and brainstorm in the early stages of the design process (first level), or we can do this when developing ideas within the space (second level). We can also do this when we move into designing the three-dimensional space and develop design details and figure out how things should work together (third level).

Each time we suspend our designing even temporarily and try ideating or brainstorming ideas, this allows us to:

- verify that our ideas make sense
- explore freely in the unknown territory of the design process
- filter out ideas floating around in our heads
- come back to the design with a clearer head and hopefully one or two new ways to solve the planning problem

Let's look at some examples of exercises we can use to foster creative thinking and creative processes.

Different Techniques and Exercises for Generating Ideas

We looked at examples of first- and second-level brainstorming in earlier chapters. Here we will examine various techniques that can be used at all three levels. The different techniques and approaches here come from many different sources. Some you might already know, such as using design elements and principles; others may be new.

Examples of Exercises

There are an infinite number of techniques and approaches that one can use to generate design ideas. When a teacher suggests that you should come up with 10 to 15 different sketches or concepts for a particular problem, it might seem daunting at first.

The following techniques will help unleash your creative genius. These different examples are presented in a loose order—meaning that when you are stuck and need some inspiration, you can try any one of them to help generate some ideas. Some are related to the space and some are not. Each method uses the words and concepts of the previous research and analysis as a catalyst for ideas.

Ask Questions

Hanks and Parry (1991) suggest that the "ability to ask questions is the most important creative skill" (p. 79). They quote Suzanne Langer, who says that the "treatment of the problem begins with its first expression as a question. The way a question is asked limits the ways in which any answer to it may be given. A question is merely an ambiguous proposition; the answer is the determination" (p. 79). They also suggest that there are some good key words that you can include when asking questions.

Who? What? Why? When? Which? Where? How? So What?

Earlier on I suggested that there are many basic questions that we must ask as designers—these can serve here as catalyst for idea generation.

??? → ?? → &*$?%$!*&%$/ → Eureka!

Questions are vital because by asking them, we stimulate our creative thinking skills. As Hanks and Parry suggest, "When you do not ask questions, nothing happens." (p. 79)

Conceptual Doodle

A conceptual doodle is any sketch that transforms an idea in your head onto paper. It can be generated in many ways and may be inspired by a:

> **BUILDING BLOCK** • *A great way to stimulate design thinking: Ask a simple question and then group the answers as a series of key words on paper or a visual board. Get your friends together and answer the question spontaneously.*
>
> *For example: What does _____ mean to you?*
>
> *The _____ can be whatever your project is: house, home, dining, shopping, working.*
>
> *Generate key words that pop into your head and then have someone put them on a board, paper, or panel. See what different ideas the various participants come up with. Debate the issues as they arise.*

- word
- action
- space
- silly thought

A conceptual doodle is meant to express ideas and thoughts in the drawn form as you envision the interior space that you are creating. In Figure 6.3, the doodle expresses the designer's ideas for the plan in three-dimensional spaces.

Peter Koenig (2000) refers to the conceptual doodle/diagram as "the heart of the schematic phase of the design. It is the designer's first marks on paper after research and programming have taken place. They allow the designer to examine many different ideas at this preliminary stage of the design process." (p. 65)

We create conceptual doodles for many reasons and often develop our ideas from them. We may or may not show them to clients, but they can be very useful in explaining ideas, especially when the client cannot visualize the design idea.

Concept Sketches

Concept sketches are more refined doodles, usually of the space in very small format. They are usually small, hand-drawn sketches in a sketchbook or on tracing paper. Sometimes they can be computer generated.

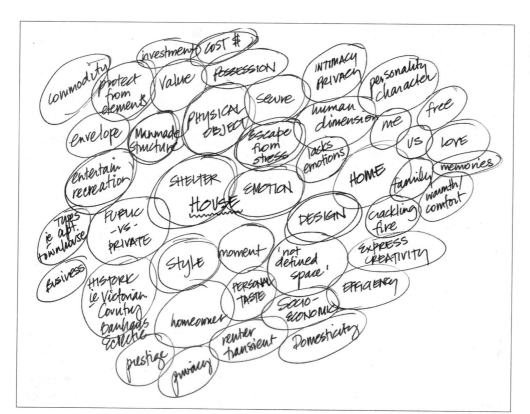

Figure 6.2 • Example of asking questions in the form of a bubble diagram

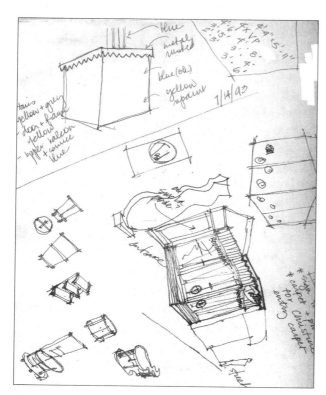

Figure 6.3 • Example of a conceptual doodle

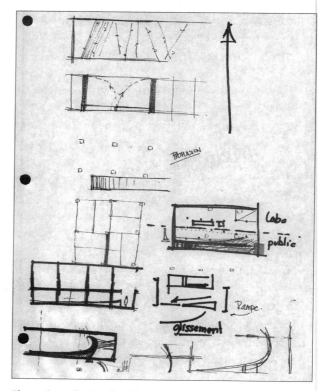

Figure 6.4 • Sketch of an idea

The purpose of the concept sketch is to try out your ideas on a different scale and completely out of context. In Figure 6.4, the space is big and wide, and the designer wants to explore the space immediately in a very small scale.

Macrocosm ➔ Microcosm

Another way to stimulate creative thinking is to change the scale of your project. This can often provide a new perspective on an idea. For example, if the plan is at 1:100 scale:

- Blow it up to a larger scale to try a new idea, *or*
- Look at the problem from another vantage point, *or*
- Try out your idea in one medium and scale and then in another form. For example, if you tried it in a plan drawing at 1:50 scale, perhaps try it out in real model form at 1:20.

Paul Koenig (2000) writes about the importance of trying things out in different ways and from more than one perspective:

When working on preliminary designs, I recommend moving from the macrocosm, or overview,

> **BUILDING BLOCK** • *Inspirations and building blocks: Watch movies; think about the other end of the scale.*
>
> *To understand the idea of microcosm ➔ macrocosm,*
>
> *1. Watch the movie* Powers of Ten *by Charles and Ray Eames (1977). This movie is a must for understanding how scale affects us.*
>
> *2. Understand the other end of the scale. In the book* The Elegant Universe, *other dimensions are considered as vital to understanding the galaxy. Brian Greene talks about the telephone pole, and how we see it as an object in the distance. However, the bugs crawling on the pole see it in full dimension as their habitat. Think about differences in scale when you design: To design for an elderly person is different than for a young adult.*

to the microcosm, or smallest detail. When first working with conceptual/doodle diagrams, beginning design students are tempted to jump to preconceived notions for design solutions rather than letting them develop through the natural course of design evolution. They often have the tendency to work backwards by coming up with a design decision and then doing conceptual/doodle diagrams to support the end result. This, of course, entirely defeats the purpose of the diagram. The use of the conceptual/doodle diagram is not only critical in the design development phase but will serve as proof of a logically conceived and functional preliminary design solution.

Geometric or Organizing Principles

Generate a design idea from an organizing principle. If we take the same sketch from the microcosm ➔ macrocosm example, we can see how the sketch develops into a plan using geometric principles.

Many designers and architects use organizing principles to shape their designs. The design of Volkswagens and coffeepots, art and graphics, all come from geometric principles (Elam, 2001). There are many sources of inspiration for geometric principles. Although it is impossible to review them all in this book, here are a few examples. You can explore this further in the texts suggested here, and also in your classes when you study design elements and fundamentals.

The Golden Section

One of the fundamental organizing principles is the proportional principle known as the Golden Section. The Golden Section is a mathematical organizational principle that we use in design and architecture when we want to organize spaces, forms, and the movement of one element within another in a logical sequence. The Golden Section (Ghyka, 1977; Pappas, 1998) is a geometric proportion used in logic and aesthetics, and is an elementary idea from the ancient times of the Greeks and Vitruvius. As Ghyka (1977) develops the definition, this proportion is one of several that "is the quantitative comparison between two things. . . . The simplest asymmetrical section and the cor-

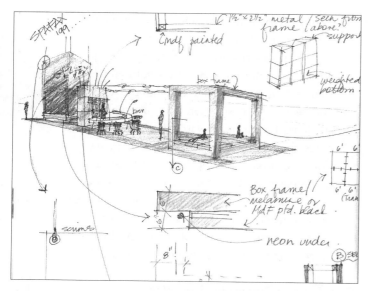

Figure 6.5 • Example of this type of microcosm → macrocosm sketching (exhibition booth concept: refer to Case Study 1.3 in Chapter 1)

responding continuous proportion: the Golden Section" (pp. 1–3). Figure 6.7 shows the Golden Section as it unfolds geometrically.

To be able to understand and use these geometric principles requires research and an understanding of their use beyond the scope of this book. I include these here as a possible means of generating ideas, or as a means to organize first geometric ideas when you develop them. Geometric and organizing principles should be studied and used whenever the ideas call for an intentional proportional study, or whenever ideas can be formed using the shaping of these ideas through a geometric principle. The Golden Section, Gothic Master diagram, and other geometric forms are useful when you know how they are used, and what proportions they generate.

Using the Principles of Form and Design

Developing creative techniques using the principles of form and design means shaping spaces using visual and fundamental basic design elements such as the point, line, and shape (circle, triangle, square, and so

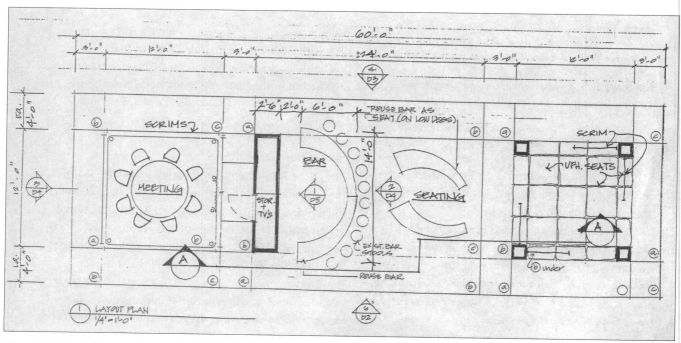

Figure 6.6 • Plan of the exhibition in Chapter 1, showing a geometric organization (refer to Case Study 1.3 in Chapter 1)

on) to organize the forms within a space. This can be done either in two-dimensional planning or three-dimensional spatial concept creation.

This design thinking is taken from fine arts, where the basic concept of form as linked to the line, shape, and dimension of fundamental elements is found in all art and design (Itten, 1983; Gatto, Porter, & Selleck, 1978). Gatto et al. suggest that the elements and principles used to make fine art are basic design elements and principles. These are the fundamental tools of the designer, and the basis for all good design (pp. 9–11).

Design Elements

According to Gatto, Porter, and Selleck (1978), the basic design elements are line, color, value, shape and form, space, and texture. These elements can be both the source of creative thinking in art and a basis for designing spaces.

Forms such as circles and lines act as spatial organizers when they are put into plans. We can use the inspiration of forms such as circles to organize concentric spatial designs. If we begin by looking at the circular form and its pattern repetitions, for example (Wong, 1978; Wong, 1993), we can then explore the similar pattern in the plan of the space.

We can use any or all of these design elements to generate an idea. For example, we might have a plan drawn and have a hard time imagining an interior space from that plan. A simple line sketch creates a form that then takes shape, generating negative and positive space relationships. Design elements help both create the initial form and also help to refine the form as it takes shape.

Concepts of Harmony, Repetition, Rectilinear, or Radial Patterns

Wucious Wong develops concepts of two- and three-dimensional design using design elements and principles in his seminal books, *Principles of Two-Dimensional Design* (1972), *Principles of Three-Dimensional Design* (1972), and *Principles of Form and Design* (1993). Wong names several different ways that we can organize shapes and forms using design principles:

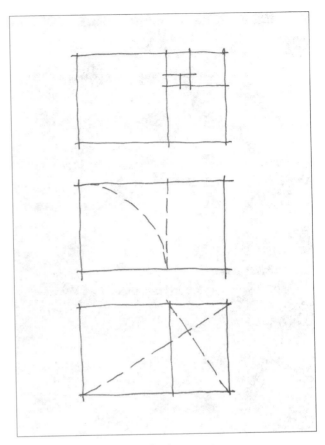

Figure 6.7 • The Golden Section in geometry

- Two-dimensional designs: repetition, structure, gradation, radiation, contrast, space
- Three-dimensional design: serial planes, prisms, linear frameworks, wall structures

These variations of a structure can be used individually or multiplied in many ways. The placement of a form or shape changes its very position; how we put together open and closed spaces, shapes, and forms modifies the visual and tactile experience of the potential user. These are forms primarily used in sculpture and graphic design, but interior designers can draw inspiration and use some of these principles when first organizing the space design and layout.

Spatial Organization

The potential of relational elements of form and shape are important possibilities to consider when designing. Depending on how you move and change forms, you can organize them in different ways (Ching, 1979). This is known as spatial organization. Form can be directional positioned strategically or guided by other aspects such as a point, a focal shape, or a direction. It can be transformed, transplanted, repeated or copied, or changed through its very shape and dimension (Ching, 1979, p. 66).

Let's examine how form and art principles guide the development of ideas and the spatial organization in Case Study 6.1.

Patterns for Generating Ideas

If we carry on with this idea of form and organizing principles, we can use patterns to help us generate ways of seeing our designs creatively. First, we will speak about patterns as useful to help organize the design planning and spatial organization. Second, we will look at patterns within the two-dimensional aspects of design such as wall coverings and other materials that we use to shape interior space.

Patterns as Organizing Principles

Patterns can be found in nature, in geometry, and in repetitive designs that we generate on our own. Artist M. C. Escher often used form, pattern, and multiple repetitions of symbols and designs to create his art. We can take two- and three-dimensional representations of various forms and create patterns, delineations, and movement from them (Wong, 1972; Wong, 1993; Allen, 1988; Rengel, 2003). In this idea of pattern, space is sculpted using a pattern or organizing principle that is repeated and represented within a space, or used to actually shape the interior space itself.

Patterns as Motifs

People have used patterns to adorn their interior environments and objects for centuries. Cultural uses of patterns vary widely. Patterns as motifs are patterns as we would find them in materials and on finishes such as wall coverings, carpets, or textiles. Pattern designs are used to adorn walls, floors, and ceilings when applied to surfaces and as a means to create and support a certain style or taste (Rodemann, 1999).

We can also be inspired by patterns used in culture and throughout history. For example, Japanese patterns are organic, simple, and beautiful, and can inspire and be used to generate an idea within a spatial design (Allen, 1988). Patterns can be sources of inspiration, or a means to represent visually ideas and movement for people who might otherwise not be able to visualize concepts and ideas that are more abstract. Patterns are also useful as a means of adornment, if not overused.

Montage and Collage

We can use the design elements and organizing principles we have explored thus far, and sculpt out forms using color, texture, light, and space as facilitators for our ideas. We can express our ideas through either the montage of found materials or the creation of a collage made of found images, objects, or materials. We already have explored multiple types of collages in earlier chapters.

An early pioneer of this type of thinking was Johannes Itten (1995), who incorporated these ideas within courses that he taught at the Bauhaus. He taught various concepts about design elements such as "clair-obscure" (dark-light) and color, and how materials and texture form the basis for stimulating ideas at the Bauhaus (Itten, 1995, p. 45).

Collage and the montage of textures that overlap, of either chosen or found materials, is a great first means to explore possible form relationships. Collage can be used to inspire ideas for the first development of conceptual ideas, whereas montage can help with initial interrelations of material relationships in space. Montage is a useful technique to consider when designing or just trying to put things together.

Collage

We saw examples of collage and spoke about this technique in detail earlier in this book. Collage is a media with infinite possibilities, and it allows you to express and represent emotional expressions visually. The other exciting thing about collage is how, by using found images, you can easily represent images you may be trying to express in the space but that you may find hard to do. We are not all good perspective

STUDENT DEVELOPMENT OF A COMMUNITY LIBRARY FOR CHILDREN

In this case study, the student develops a concept based entirely on form, line, and color as inspiration for this children's library in a community setting. The project consisted of creating a dynamic and economic solution in an existing library space within a community center. The library needed a face-lift and animating elements for children, as well as better functional organization between the children's reading activities and the library services aimed at adults.

The following three sketches show the form and line development, the emergent concept in sketch form, and the final library interior space during construction. The student benefited from a real project scenario, and afterwards the student participated in the project as consultant through to the completion of the construction, as a graduate. (Note: ethical issues were very carefully organized with and outside the project parameters through the local library committee and the university.)

Figure A • Concept for the children's library; the concept taking shape through line, form, and color development, using artistic forms

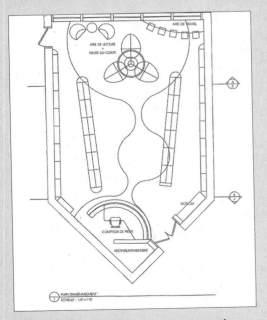

Figure B • The sketch of the interior perspective

Figure C • The final interior photo

renderers nor are we able to draw perfectly immediately. Making a collage to represent an idea or a concept can help you to use found images to express your concept in its initial stages.

We saw examples of collage earlier on in the book. I often suggest to my students that showing the material choices in interior environments means representing them as they would be in proportion to how you would actually see them in interior spaces, as overlapping cuts sized approximately in the real proportions that they would be used within the space.

Doodling Outside the Box

Try sketching ideas in another way. In *Design Yourself!*, Hanks, Belliston, and Parry (1977) suggest many ways to see things differently using sketches, including doodles, copying, changing the size, drawing something in detail, overlapping objects when sketching them, or changing and modifying the shapes that you use. Here is an example of brainstorming/daydreaming in sketch form:

It is important to be able to generate ideas, walk away, and daydream. There are many different techniques for visual thinking that can also be a catalyst to idea-making. These include night dreaming, daydreaming, and imagination games that you can play.

Inspiration from Nature, Daydreaming, and Childhood Thinking

Having fun is an important component of creating. Reaching back into childhood memories offers a place for us to play, to have fun. Daydreaming is a means of keeping our childhood thinking alive. In *The Sense of Wonder*, Rachel Carson (1956) explores how we can do this through the exploration of nature and the world around us. Exploring nature does not necessarily mean going out into the country. It means taking a minute to look around and see nature as it manifests itself in your world. Try and think back to your childhood and what you loved, enjoyed, and found wonder in—bring this back into your mind. Let your mind go and allow a sense of wonder to return. As Rachel Carson notes:

Exploring nature . . . is largely a matter of becoming receptive to what lies around you. It is learning again to use your eyes, ears, nostrils, and fingertips, opening up the disused channels of sensory impression.

For most of us, knowledge of our world comes largely through sight, yet we look about with such unseeing eyes that we are partially blind. One way to open your eyes to unnoticed beauty is to ask yourself, "What if I had never seen this before? What if I knew that I would never see it again?" (p. 52)

Visual Brainstorming and Doodling Techniques

Different authors talk about visual brainstorming and mapping as a means of generating ideas. We looked at some of these in earlier chapters (Hanks & Parry, 1991; Margulies, 2002) when we explored visual brainstorming and visual mapping techniques. This is similar to doodling, but the difference is that visual brainstorming actually tries to replicate what you see in your head into a concrete form. In a doodle, the concrete form is not really important. Here we will review some basic visual brainstorming and mapping techniques: visual mapping, concept maps, bubble diagrams, and dialogue sketching.

Visual Maps

Visual mapping is a specific drawing tool that maps out what you "see" in your head. There are many ways to create visual maps and we have already

> **BUILDING BLOCK** • *As a designer, I like to work late at night on ideas and concepts, or planning spaces that are hard to fit. Sometimes I give up frustrated and head off to bed. And wouldn't you know it, the answer comes to me just before I fall asleep. I get up out of bed, grab my sketchbook or a graph notepad, and jot it down, or else I will forget and my idea will be gone. Often I cannot see for the darkness, but I sketch or write it down anyway. It is really important to get up at that moment—the idea may be the solution to the problem!*

explored some methods in earlier chapters. Visual maps integrate words, thoughts, pictures, and ideas that generate new patterns and ideas. We can create maps alone, while others are talking, or when brainstorming in a group. As Nancy Margulies (2002) suggests:

> The ability to put thoughts into images as well as words enhances thinking skills and actually improves intelligence. . . . Mapping while others speak requires us to listen not only to the flow of words, but also for key ideas and their relationships. (p. 14)

The types of maps we create depend on what uses we need them for. The visual map can be a completed series of sketches, or a structure that you fill in when you work on a project.

Concept Maps

Concept maps are a means to quickly document what you are thinking and yet what may not be very clear yet. Concept maps differ from bubble diagrams in that they are free flowing and do not necessarily try to organize the activities and spaces. They usually include words, and are not necessarily used to develop spatial ideas, although they can provide a catalyst for multidimensional thinking at times. They are a form of visual map in that they represent visual ideas from the head, but are not related to specific spaces or areas as bubble diagrams usually are.

Concept mapping puts ideas down on paper as they evolve in your head, as a means to reflect what we do as designers—we see things in our head and use spatial plans to map out our ideas. I have frequently used them in my own designing and also in design research. When I need to put words and ideas into order, I visually reorganize them as concept maps. For example, in the early stages of a more complex design problem, you might use a concept map to organize the different users within an office space, or understand the hierarchies and political relationships of the different employees. You may use concept maps to help organize the research that exists only in words, as a link to bubble diagrams or space ideas that you develop later on.

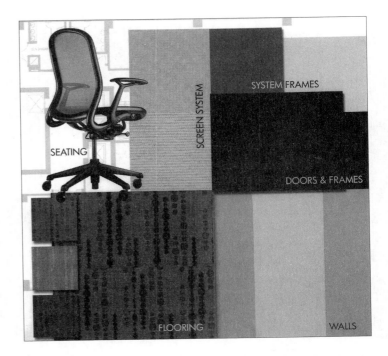

Figure 6.8 • Sample board using the overlapping and proportional techniques of collage

Dialogue Sketching

We can also brainstorm and try out our ideas by speaking to a friend, colleague, or teacher, and the ensuing dialogue can become a catalyst for your design. If you are stuck, seek someone else's advice. A former student came to see me when she was having trouble breaking out of her ideas. While we talked, we generated a visual sketch together. She later told me she was inspired by our talk; it had provided a much needed breakthrough and enabled her to draw her plans. The sketch we created together allowed her to see the three-dimensional total of a space that does not exist, and that she was having trouble visualizing.

Kinesthetic Mapping

We have also introduced kinesthetic mapping earlier on. In a kinesthetic map, you plot out the movements of people and look for circulation patterns. Kinesthetic maps are two-dimensional representations of dynamic movements in the space, a means to "see" the reality of the active spatial components. These are very useful when we are not familiar with how the people move through a space in a particular

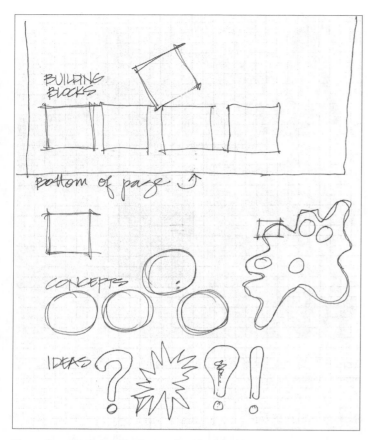

Figure 6.9 • Example of brainstorming/daydreaming

Figure 6.15 shows an example of a complex bubble diagram.

Creative Intuition

Another technique, although not often recognized or understood, is intuition. After you have generated different ideas on paper, you intuitively know that certain ideas have more potential than others. Hanks and Parry (1991) speak about intuition as a means of solving problems. A great example is when things go wrong and you see a different way to use something that has failed. People see that something has potential and they know "in their bones" that this will be successful (Hanks & Parry, 1991, p. 84).

Intuition is a hard one to explain because we must learn to hone and develop it on our own. Let hunches and ideas that are not logical or rational play a part in your design thinking. Too often we rely solely on methods rather than allowing our intuition and hunches to play a role in our designing.

Perhaps your idea just needs a quick spark—you can try something purely by intuition or chance. This can also help you creatively solve your problems. You never know if you do not try.

Changing Media

Sometimes changing the media you usually use helps foster new ideas. If you always sketch on paper with a black pen, move to large markers on newsprint. If you always create your ideas in the computer first, try sketching on paper, or creating a collage either on paper or virtually using video or photo media.

Videos

To be able to visualize the space, videos are a useful means to see the space three-dimensionally in real time. At first this can be helpful, especially if we do not understand how to draw in three dimensions or are having trouble visualizing an interior we are working with.

Model-Making and Maquette Studies

Model studies or form studies can often be an inspiration for the three-dimensional form development of

design, or when we need a catalyst for our ideas, as the actual circulation patterns can be sources of inspiration. This circulation map in Figure 6.13 is an example of a kinesthetic map.

Bubble Diagrams

We explored bubble diagrams as organizational drawings; now let's look at them as creative catalysts for designing. We often use bubble diagrams to jumpstart planning, and before we block plan too far in a project. Bubble diagrams are also a quick and easy way to transfer words, spatial configurations, and schematic groupings into a series of organized groups that can help bridge the gap from research to possible spatial configurations. They are not meant to be too developed, and are meant to help place space within the context of the research in its earliest stages. Figure 6.14 shows an example of a spatial bubble diagram.

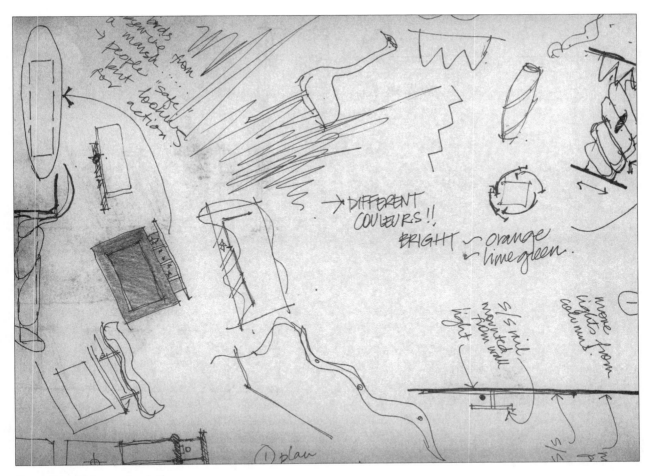

Figure 6.10 • Nature as inspiration

interior space. They are also the easiest way to develop and make explicit material/object relationships. When we need to see the interior and try out our material ideas, models and maquettes are the best way to visually represent our ideas. We have seen examples of this throughout the book, as in Chapter 5, Figures 5.21a, 5.21b, and 5.21c when we saw how the student sketched an idea, made a paper and cardboard model, and then sketched what she saw in perspective.

Material/Object Relationships

Studying materials that inspire certain feelings can bring about ideas for a space. For instance, you could be redesigning a hotel lobby that is defined by historic columns and plaster ceilings. The material evokes opulence and inspires choices such as wenge wood and a dark palette of rich materials. This in turn becomes the catalyst for the hotel name, logo, and overall concept.

Photography: Exploring Multiple Contexts

You can use inspirations found in objects through photography and juxtapose these inspirations with your design to get a different context for your concept. You can take photographs of things that you see, completely out of context, and use these for inspiration in designs. This transfers the objects into a new context, as the object is situated into a different realm entirely.

For example, Michael Joannidis used a keyhole as inspiration to design the pattern and detail for a focal point in a restaurant/club design. The original keyhole inspiration is shown here in Figure 6.16 and the use of

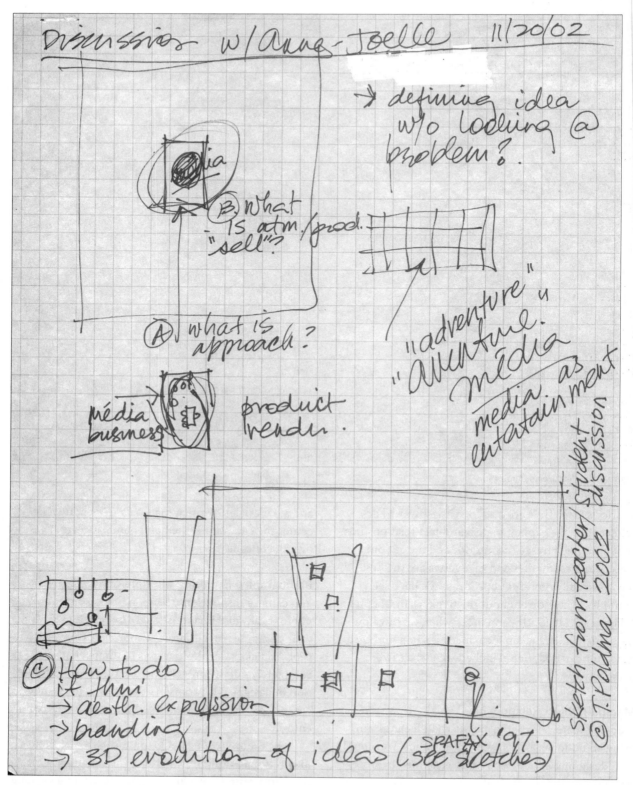

Figure 6.11 • Example of a visual map

the inspiration in the final design is shown in Figure 6.17.

Other Techniques for Creative Problem Solving

Here are some other techniques to help formulate problem-solving skills when away from the design task. You can then return to the task and see the design problem or issue in a different light.

Develop a Metaphor for the Concept

A metaphor is a means of expressing a concept that parallels the design intent. Several creative thinking texts explore this concept (Koberg & Bagnall, 1981; Hanks & Belliston, 1990; Hanks & Parry, 1991). Hanks and Belliston (1990) define a metaphor as follows:

> A metaphor is a comparison of the meaning and attributes of one thing to the meaning and attributes of something else. . . . To learn from a metaphor, the learner must take charge; he must act

and make some decision, take some risk. He does not manipulate, but invests something of himself, so that growth may result. . . .

. . . Use a metaphor to generate new meaning from old or unfamiliar concepts. Put the

Figure 6.12 • **Concept mapping example**

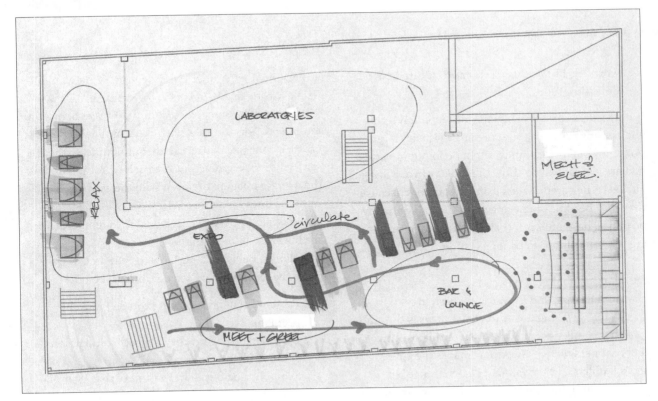

Figure 6.13 • **Kinesthetic map example**

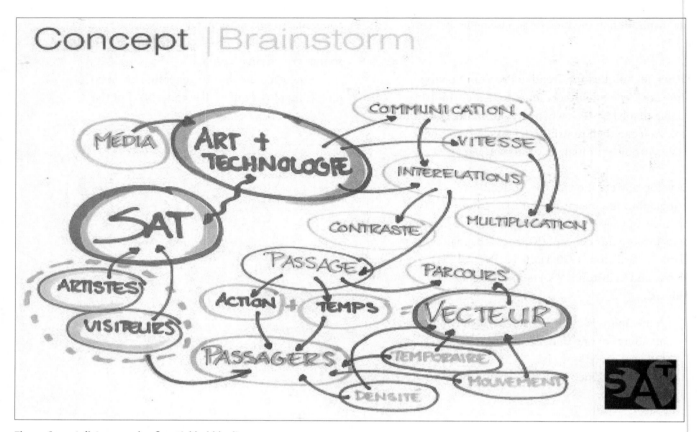

Figure 6.14 • Julie's example of spatial bubble diagram

words "is like" between things to create new relationships. (pp. 123–124)

It is a visual expression of your idea in literal terms and is useful in giving the concept a visual reference point. Metaphors can most often be found in nature and are a great way to show the intent of your design. However, be careful when using metaphors because they may become cliché, meaning they may already be in use, have outworn their usefulness, or maybe are too "in fashion" to be long lasting.

Develop an Analogy: Synectics

Hanks, Belliston, and Edwards suggest, in *DesignYourself!*, that a way to create ideas is through *synectics*. Synectics is a way to see problems from a different perspective. *Synectics* "makes the strange seem familiar and the familiar seem strange" (p. 121). If you are designing the interior of an appliance, you

are making the familiar seem strange. What would it be like to live in an appliance, for example?

So we create analogies of things to see them a different way. For example, when I encourage students to create a concept, I often ask them to immerse themselves in the design, to put themselves in the mind of the user, to imagine themselves in the space as if they were the ones living there. This is a type of analogy, of the synectics. We displace ourselves temporarily to see how the space might be.

Hanks, Belliston, and Edwards cite four ways to make the familiar seem strange. These include:

1. Personal analogy—putting yourself into the problem
2. Direct analogy—identify a direct comparison to your problem
3. Symbolic analogy—find a symbol that is similar to your design concept

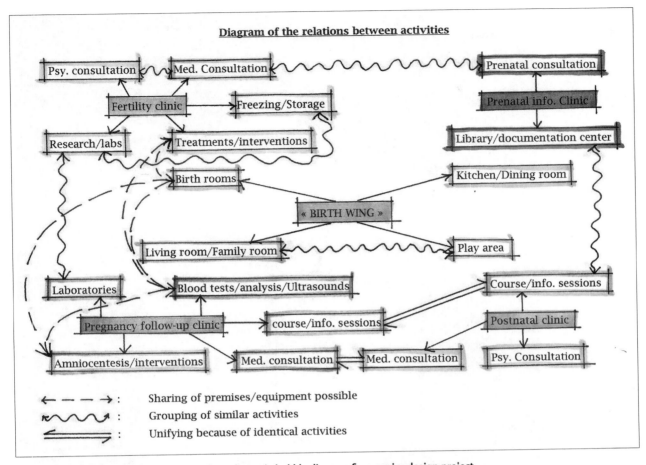

Diagram of the relations between activities

Figure 6.15 • Justine's example of a complex schematic bubble diagram for a senior design project

4. Fantasy analogy—wish fulfillment (pp. 122–124)

An analogy helps you to see the design in a different way. For example, you can come to understand what it is like to have special needs by using a wheelchair for 48 hours. You will learn and understand the issues of barrier-free design, particularly if this is part of your concept.

Bionics

Bionics is the process of applying nature to man-made things (Hanks, Belliston, & Edwards, 1978). This technique is used extensively in industrial design to inspire the design of products. It is rarely used in interior design, but I mention it here because sometimes it is useful to study animals as a source of inspiration to help us in our spatial designs. For example, lighting

concepts have been linked to the light-emitting capacities of fireflies (Hanks et al., 1978, p. 128). We can look to nature and its animal processes to inspire us in our designing. There are many more creative brainstorming techniques out there . . . find them!

"Doing as Thinking" and "Thinking as Doing"

All of these techniques are not useful if you do not explore design in your own way. You are the one who will develop your own creative and problem-solving styles and skills. You can inquire, understand and learn, research, analyze, and design. You can also daydream, imagine, and create. These are all tools in the design process. The key trigger is to understand that these tools come with a combination of trying, effort, and learning how to ask questions, but also knowing when to "let go."

Figure 6.16 • Project inspired by a traditional goldfish bowl, design by Michael Joannidis

Figure 6.17 • Detail inspired by the goldfish bowl idea, design by Michael Joannidis

Considering "thinking as doing" and "doing as thinking" means exploring and moving in between what you think and what you draw or model. Move back from your initial ideas within the unknown, but be prepared to implement the best ideas in your designs. Do not be afraid to try things out. Do not fear the unknown, as it is often through exploring the unknown that new ideas develop. The next step is to judge and evaluate your ideas, decide on the final concept, and implement it in the space. We will look at these aspects of the design process next.

BIBLIOGRAPHY

Arnheim, R. (2000). Sketching and the psychology of design. In V. Margolin & R. Buchanan (Eds.). *The idea of design: A design issues reader.* Cambridge, MA: MIT Press.

Bilda, Z., & Demirkan, H. (2003, January) An insight on designers' sketching activities in traditional versus digital media. *Design Studies, 24*(1), 28–50.

Carson, Rachel. (1956). *The sense of wonder.* New York and Evanston: Harper & Row.

Ching, F. D. K. (1979). *Architecture: Form, space & order.* New York: Van Nostrand Reinhold Company.

De Bono, E. (1995). *Teach yourself to think.* London: Penguin Books, 1995.

Elam, K. (2001). *The geometry of design: Studies in proportion and composition.* New York: Princeton Architectural Press.

Gardner, H. (1982). *Art, mind, and brain: A cognitive approach to creativity.* New York: Basic Books.

Gatto, J.A., Porter, A.W., & Selleck, J. (1978). *Exploring visual design.* Worchester, MA: Davis Publications.

Ghiselin, B. (1952). *The creative process: A symposium.* London, UK: New Amsterdam Library.

Ghyka, M. (1977). *The geometry of art and life.* New York: Dover Publications.

Goleman, D., Kaufmann, P., & Roy, M. (1993). *The creative spirit.* New York: Plume, Penguin Books.

Greene, B. (2000, 2003). *The elegant universe.* New York: Vintage Books.

Hanks, K., Belliston, L., & Edwards, D. (1978). *Design yourself!* Los Altos, CA: William Kauffmann.

Hanks, K., & Belliston, L. (1990). *Rapid viz: A new method for the rapid visualization of ideas.* Menlo Park, CA: Crisp Publications.

Hanks, K., & Parry, J. (1991). *Wake up your creative genius.* Menlo Park, CA: Crisp Publications.

Itten, J. (1995). *Le Dessin et la forme.* France: Dessain et tolra.

Koberg, D., & Bagnall, J. (1981). *The all new universal traveller. A soft-systems guide to: Creativity, problem-solving and the process of reaching goals.* Los Altos, CA: William Kaufmann.

Koenig, P. A. (2000). *Design graphics: Drawing techniques for design professionals.* Upper Saddle River, NJ: Prentice Hall.

Laseau, P. (2001). *Graphic thinking for architects and designers.* New York: John Wiley & Sons.

Margulies, N. (2002). *Mapping inner space: Learning and teaching visual mapping* (2nd ed.). Tucson, AZ: Zephyr Press.

Miller, S. F. (1995). *Design process: A primer for architectural and interior designers.* New York: Van Nostrand Reinhold.

Mitton, M. (1999). *Interior design visual presentation: A guide to graphics, models and presentation techniques.* New York: John Wiley & Sons.

Ornstein, R. (1991). *The evolution of consciousness; the origins of the way we think.* New York: Simon & Schuster.

Rengel, R. (2003). *Shaping interior space.* New York: Fairchild Books.

Rodemann, P.A. (1999). *Patterns in interior environments: perception, psychology and practice.* New York: John Wiley & Sons.

Vaikla-Poldma, T. (2003). *An investigation of learning and teaching processes in an interior design class: An interpretive and contextual inquiry.* Unpublished doctoral thesis. Montreal: McGill University, Author.

Wong, W. (1972). *Principles of two-dimensional design.* New York: Van Nostrand Reinhold.

Wong, W. (1972). *Principles of three-dimensional design.* New York: Van Nostrand Reinhold.

Wong, W. (1993). *Principles of form and design.* New York: Van Nostrand Reinhold.

Chapter Seven

EXPRESSING AND REFINING IDEAS FROM 2-D TO 3-D TO SOLUTIONS

Objective

This chapter will focus on how the different steps of the design process culminate into the final design solution. The final design comes together as we finalize our ideas, and this chapter explores how you shift from reading about theory and practice to seeing in-depth design solutions. We will look at examples of the last stages of the design process, when the design is reproduced for presentation to a client or for critique to a jury of teachers or professional peers. Examples of design projects show how we make the transfer from virtual to built reality. Case studies of student projects show how created client briefs and actual building scenarios are used.

DEVELOPING THE IN-DEPTH COMPONENTS OF THE DESIGN

Developing the in-depth components of the final design is the last step in the development of the original design concept. You have decided on a concept, and by now you have probably made some preliminary choices regarding materials, finishes, lighting, and equipment. In this final stage, you review the choices that you have made, create in-depth details of your ideas, and refine the spatial concepts.

Projects in this chapter were done using AutoCAD, Photoshop, and various hand-drawn sketches. Students currently use Cinema 4 and SketchUp for most 3-D development. The virtual tools used are constantly evolving. This is just a snapshot of the full range of design communication tools that might be used and would change over time with future technological developments. Different schools will use different techniques and processes.

As we begin to formalize the concept into its final stages, we need to expand on certain design elements that have been developed to date. Perhaps you have a lighting concept, but it is not well thought out; or maybe you have chosen some materials, but have not considered all of the material choices that might be possible for the space. Or perhaps you have been so wrapped up with the space that you have forgotten that the people need to sit at a table, but no furnishings have been finalized.

At this stage, you take stock of what decisions have been made, and what final decisions remain in relation to your design concept. In-depth components of the design include (but are not limited to):

- specific finish selections
- final furnishing selections and accessories

- complete desired or required color and lighting effects
- detail development for custom furnishings, design elements, and custom architectural features
- follow-through of the design concept through all possible communication means

The case studies will help us to see these concepts actualized. For example, in Chapter 5 we saw a design concept for an artists' exhibition lounge workspace, as the student created a series of iterations of her first idea. Then in Chapter 6 we saw the exploration of these concepts as the designer developed the ideas. Here we will look at how the design develops in greater depth to the final solution that she presents.

For one last time, we take stock of the design itself and begin making decisions. Each idea is judged and evaluated as useful or not for the final concept. At this stage, you decide which ideas stay, and which ideas are discarded or left in the background. You become the judge and jury on which ideas, details, and project elements are vital to present to the client.

Refined Concepts to Realizable Solutions

The design is done and you are on the last stretch of the project! You have worked through the research and analysis phases, developed the design toward a final design solution and concept, and are working on the elements of the design that will give it depth and breadth. You are ready to complete the last phase of the design process.

This is the final stage before you finish the design and present it either in class to a teacher or jury, or to a client. In either situation, the design leaves your personal domain (where you have worked on it alone or with other designers) and enters into the public realm (the design recipient). You are putting the design out into the world to see what others think of it, how they will judge it, and what they will do with it.

This detailed final concept is needed to communicate your design intent, and to allow the project to go to the next stage, the implementation of the concept into a built reality. By "detailed," I suggest here that you have conceptualized and identified the

ideas, how the materials fit together, what custom fittings and fitments you would like, and how they will look and be built.

There are several things that can be done to add depth to your concept, and make sure that it is thorough. To further refine your concept, you can:

- develop final specifications and choices for the lighting plan
- choose the final materials and finishes that you need to show your intentions
- develop the final layout of the furniture
- develop the details of the built-in elements and how they will fit into the space
- create in-depth views of the space, including the components you have designed
- virtually model the space with in-depth detailing of the ideas
- create the final versions of the views and visual elements of the presentation
- create specific details of how things will be selected, fit together, or built, depending on the complexity of your concept ideas

At this point, and before the final presentation is completed, it is a good idea to go back again to the program and analysis, and consider what aspects have been integrated into the concept. We tend to get caught up in the design ideas and can lose sight of the supporting ideas that initially inspired our thinking.

BUILDING BLOCK • *One way to understand the depth required at this stage is to project yourself into the space. If you were to use the design, how would you arrive, move through it, what would you feel? Think about the design as if you were going to be in it tomorrow! How? Possible ways include filming your work as you develop it, print out the plans and drawings if they are in a computer, or try to sell your ideas by trying to show the concept to someone who knows nothing about the project. Showing the project to someone else forces you to appropriate the spaces as your own.*

Developing a Design Three-Dimensionally to Its Fullest

At this final stage of the design process, we expand our design thinking to develop the design in depth, using our knowledge of detailing and material intersections, form development, and light modulations. We need to be sure that we represent the design accurately in its final form while also conveying the concept accurately. With new technologies, we can also virtually walk our clients through the space in multiple dimensions.

Using Color, Light, and Materials

Color and light are major design elements that complement the development of the form and spatial characteristics. In Figure 7.1 and Case Study 7.2, we see how the designer overlays the lighting concept on the plan to show us her lighting ideas and then, with perspective, illustrates how the concept feels. In Case Study 7.3 we see how the designer develops a color concept that integrates form and lighting.

At this stage it is important that we get across the feeling of the space by expressing it in visual drawn form, or superimposed within the actual space itself, if possible. Color and light are the major means by which we can express the forms and ideas that we have, and our choices should work together to support the design intent, function, and the forms that we are proposing for the space. Color and light (with materials) can also define the overall concept quite dramatically, as we see in Case Study 7.3, Figure D.

In Case Study 7.3, Figure D, the designer is trying to express in a flat static form a lighting idea that is active and dynamic, meaning that the lighting is moving to the activity within the space, rather than merely lighting an object or part of the space.

Detailing the Interior Space

When finalizing our designs, we should detail the concepts to reflect the actual design development. This does not mean making technical details as in working drawings, but rather to work through what the various components will look like and how they will be constructed in a conceptual sense. This is the pre-technical detail, if you like.

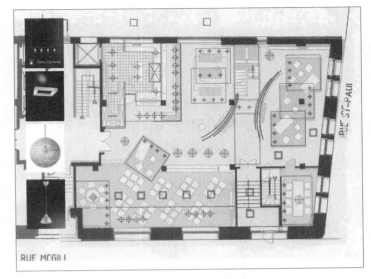

Figure 7.1 • Reflected ceiling plan overlaid on design plan

Another aspect of detailing the interior space is how we fine-tune and add softness, comfort, humanity, and sensual aspects to the space through the material choices that we make. Using Case Studies 7.1 and 7.3, let's look at the project in terms of the detail development. For the exhibition art space, the designer developed full details of the flexible seating that can be moved around to transform the space from an artists' work area to a rave dance floor and then back to an exhibition space.

In Case Study 7.3 we see how the designer develops the detail for the movable seating.

For her school concept in Case Study 7.3, the student develops full furniture details. For example, she designs cubes for the students to store their belongings. In Figure F, we see how she presents a thought-out cubicle design. In Figure G, she develops seating for the public areas. Finally, in Figures H and I we see detailed development of the library.

Detailing ideas at this stage not only confirms that you have thought of all the potential aspects of the project; this type of detailing also offers you as the designer a means to clarify and modify things relative to the original design program.

Mapping the Final Parts of the Design Process

At this late stage, you develop and finalize the project and make it ready to present to a client. You need to

An Exhibition Space

In this last conceptual stage of a combination work-space/exhibit/bar, the student has developed several components of the project in detail, including:

- the lighting plan and concept
- the technical aspects of the mobile furniture
- the detail material and finish choices

In Figures A and B we see the final concept expressed in plan and elevation.

In Figures C and D, we see the evolved concept in detail form. The designer has developed the movable system design right through to the connections and possible configurations. The designer develops the bar area, the movable seating that delineates the space in different ways, and also the movable wall, which we see conceptually and also in developed detail.

Finally, here in Figures E through I, we see how the plan modifies into several configurations.

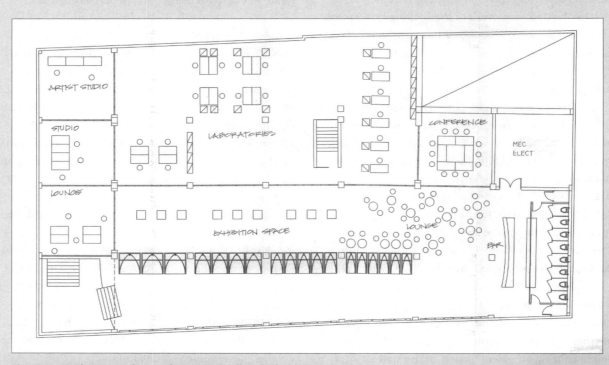

Figure A • Final concept plan, student artist's collective design

Figure B • Final concept elevations, student artist's collective design

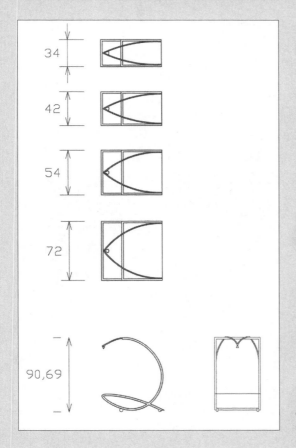

Figure C • Detail of wall division/seating unit; student's design

continued on the next page

continued from the previous page

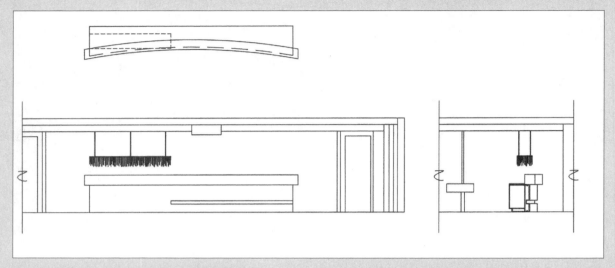

Figure D • Final concept detail bar, student's design

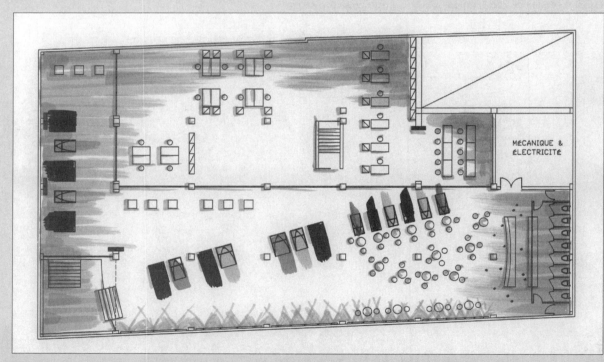

Figure E • Laboratory and artists' collective workspace plan A

Figure F • Laboratory and artists' collective workspace perspective

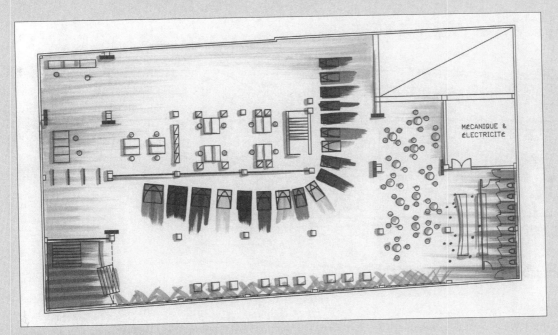

Figure G • Exhibition plan option B

continued on the next page

continued from the previous page

Figure H • Exhibition perspective B

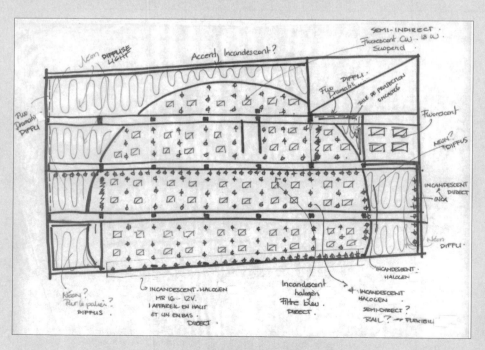

Figure I • Reflected ceiling plan for all plan options

The Art Book—An Internet Café, Library Complex

In this project, the student develops a design concept for a multi-use Internet-library-café in a recycled building, using sculptural forms and light as inspiration. Here we see a series of presentation boards, from first ideas to plans, then elevations and perspectives. Note in Figures A through D how the presentation captures the essence of what the designer is trying to convey. The presentation is clear, with plans laid out functionally, and includes perspectives that illustrate her use of natural light in both day and night views of the space. She develops a movement through the space that is exciting, and we sense this through the design development, from the lighting through to the finishes and material choices.

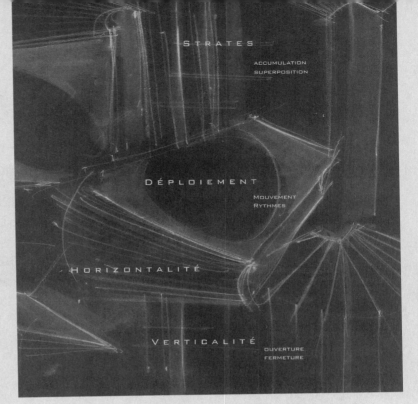

Figure A • The form and shape of an interior environment can be created using artistic elements and properties.

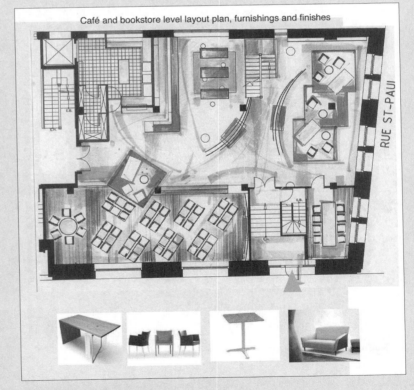

Figure B • Plan of interior space

continued on the next page

continued from the previous page

Figure C • Elevation of the interior

Figure D • Perspective of the interior day and night

An Alternative School Design

This project began with extensive research on school types, the school environment, and best practices that form the foundation for this concept development. This is a primary school for five- to twelve-year-olds, located in a suburb of a large city. The site is an old mansion with an existing extension that, when renovated, can service the new school concept and its needs. The design concept is created using knowledge gleaned from school reforms implemented in the nearby urban area, with particular attention to creating an environment that is community oriented and where parents are valued and involved. The concept takes into account student well-being and self-actualization in learning, while providing a safe, secure, and stimulating learning environment. The interior design is considered to be support for learning through experience, and self-awareness through exploration.

Figures A and B show the detailed plans, which demonstrate a flexible space concept. There are three floors, with two dedicated to classrooms for kindergarten and elementary grades, and with the third providing flexible spaces for activities such as exhibitions, fine arts, music, and offices.

In Figures C, D, and E, we see the development of the concept in its overall plans and perspectives.

In Figures F and G, we orient ourselves and see the details, the materials, the furnishings, and the overall detailed intentions.

Finally, Figures H and I show us how we can make this space multifunctional and how the design details make the spaces flexible.

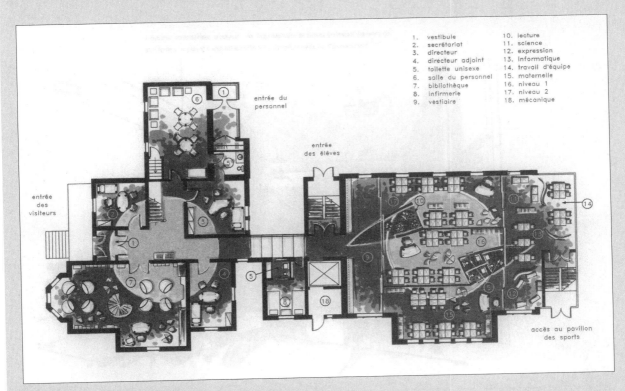

1. vestibule
2. secrétariat
3. directeur
4. directeur adjoint
5. toilette unisexe
6. salle du personnel
7. bibliothèque
8. infirmerie
9. vestiaire
10. lecture
11. science
12. expression
13. informatique
14. travail d'équipe
15. maternelle
16. niveau 1
17. niveau 2
18. mécanique

Figure A • Plans of the proposed concept

continued on the next page

continued from the previous page

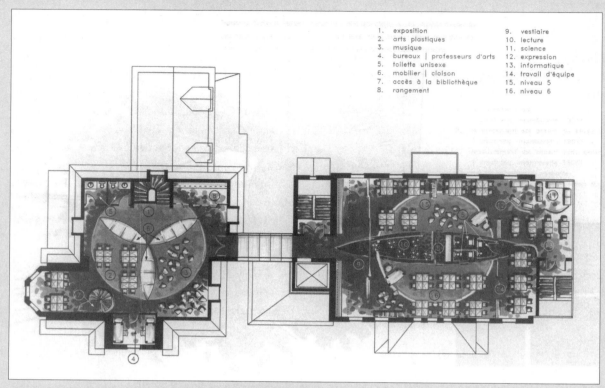

1. exposition
2. arts plastiques
3. musique
4. bureaux | professeurs d'arts
5. toilette unisexe
6. mobilier | cloison
7. accès à la bibliothèque
8. rangement
9. vestiaire
10. lecture
11. science
12. expression
13. informatique
14. travail d'équipe
15. niveau 5
16. niveau 6

Figure B • Plans of the proposed concept

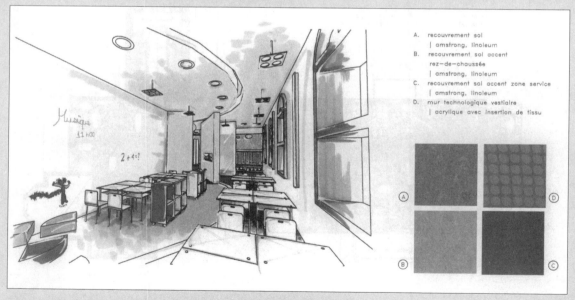

A. recouvrement sol
   | amstrong, linoleum
B. recouvrement sol accent
   rez-de-chaussée
   | amstrong, linoleum
C. recouvrement sol accent zone service
   | amstrong, linoleum
D. mur technologique vestiaire
   | acrylique avec insertion de tissu

Figure C • Perspective views of the interior

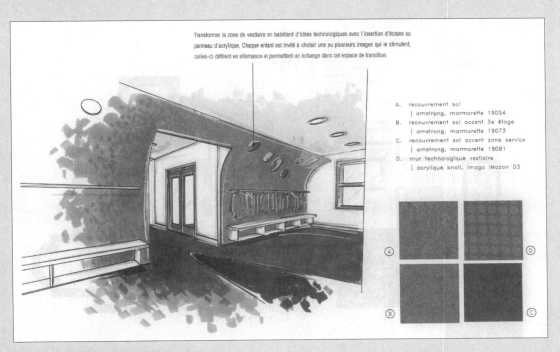

Transformer la zone de vestiaire en babillard d'idées technologiques avec l'insertion d'écrans au panneau d'acrylique. Chaque enfant est invité à choisir une ou plusieurs images qui le stimulent, celles-ci défilent en alternance et permettent un échange dans cet espace de transition.

A. recouvrement sol
   | amstrong, marmorette 19054
B. recouvrement sol accent 3e étage
   | amstrong, marmorette 19073
C. recouvrement sol accent zone service
   | amstrong, marmorette 19081
D. mur technologique vestiaire
   | acrylique knoll, imago iMozon 03

Figure D • Perspective views of the interior

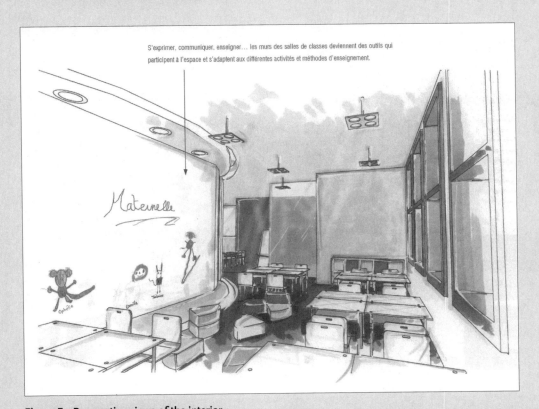

S'exprimer, communiquer, enseigner… les murs des salles de classes deviennent des outils qui participent à l'espace et s'adaptent aux différentes activités et méthodes d'enseignement.

Figure E • Perspective views of the interior

continued on the next page

continued from the previous page

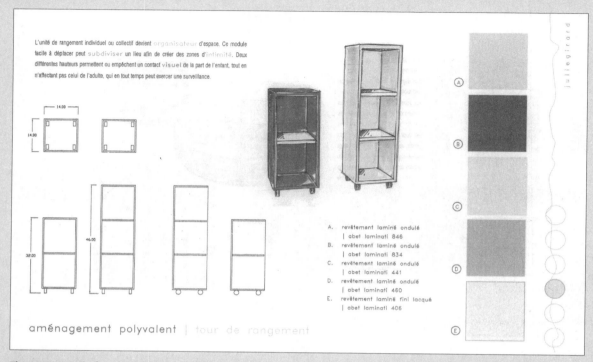

Figure F • Detail of custom design elements

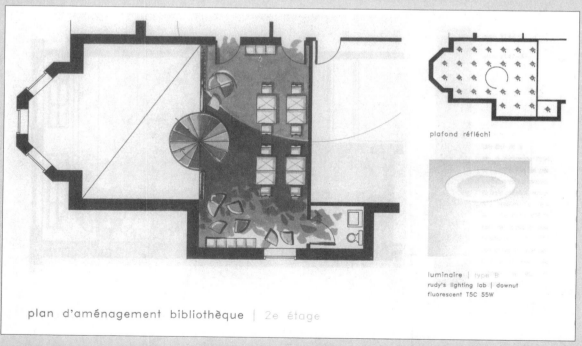

Figure G • Plan of detail area in library with reflected ceiling plan and choice of luminaire

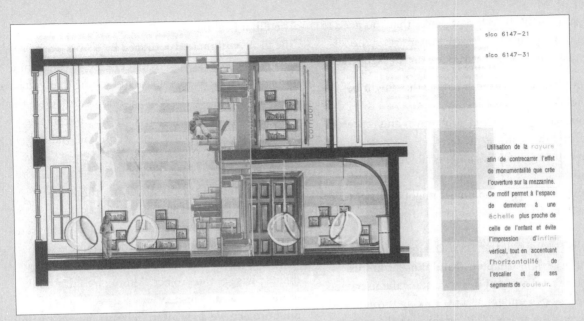

sico 6147–21

sico 6147–31

Utilisation de la rayure afin de contrecarrer l'effet de monumentalité que crée l'ouverture sur la mezzanine. Ce motif permet à l'espace de demeurer à une échelle plus proche de celle de l'enfant et évite l'impression d'infini vertical, tout en accentuant l'horizontalité de l'escalier et de ses segments de couleur.

Figure H • Detail section/elevation of library space

Figure I • Section detail of the interior

put together all of the relevant pieces that you need to communicate your final design. You must do the following tasks to ensure that you are on the right track:

- Complete all relevant drawings that might be needed.
- Make sure things are clearly drawn and represented, and that color is included.
- Have material choices and detail ideas that are realizable.
- Show the interior and how it might look, whether as a drawing or in virtual form.

The Walk-Through of the Final Design Concept

As we have seen in Chapters 5 and thus far in this chapter, the final concept must work for the users and be a place we can understand by walking through and experiencing the space. Walking through the space three-dimensionally makes it come alive, and we use tools such as perspectives, modeled interior designs, and renderings to create a facsimile of the actual interior space as a means to represent visually what we might experience within the space itself.

In Chapter 5 we talked about walking through the space as a means of generating ideas, and developing several views to explore the potential of the design as well as develop our ideas. At this stage, the walk-through is another means of verifying that all the aspects of the project have been dealt with. At this stage of the design concept, the walk-through is you taking yourself through the concept and the communication tools that you have used to get your idea across to a potential client.

Refining Final Design Concepts

Finally, the design comes together for presentation. We saw in some of the case studies how the students presented their concepts, with all of the pieces in place, from plans to two-dimensional representations (elevations, materials, graphics) and three-dimensional representations (videos, perspectives), all with the goal of communicating the design to the viewer. At this stage, you are making snap decisions and final judgments as the ideas are refined and integrated into the overall presentation.

The Final Evaluation by Others

The project ultimately is judged by others, whether it is your peers, teachers, invited critics, or clients and potential users. At this stage, everything that you have worked for is put to the test, as people will judge the ideas, their worth and value, and their pertinence from a program point of view, economic viability, social value, or aesthetic beauty.

The Post-Design Process: Moving the Project Toward the Built Reality

The next stage is the post-design process—the transfer of the design concept toward the built reality through the technical drawings and contract documents phase of the project. Although in this book we do not venture in-depth into this stage of the built project, we do want to examine how detail and contract drawing development are an integral part of the design process, in the work that follows the concept development.

The post-design process is a continuation of the design process. We should never conceptualize without thinking about how things will actually be built, specified, or organized when it is time to transfer the design in the reality of the built environment. For example, in Case Studies 7.1 and 7.3, we show how in-depth detailing helps us to work through our first design ideas, and is also shown as part of the final design concept. By selling our detailed ideas to clients alongside an overall concept, we can prepare the groundwork for budget and construction details we need to execute later on. In Case Studies 7.1 and 7.3, the projects, although designed as a concept, were also detailed in-depth, with movable walls or flexible furniture concepts. If we remember that part of our job is to respond to client briefs and user needs, naturally we design concepts to their fullest. Designing this way means specifying both products and furnishings, and also designing custom-detailed architectural elements and furnishings.

Considerations within the design process, before we finish the design, include:

- choosing materials and thoroughly identifying their specifications for future use

- developing details with a mind to actually building them further down the road
- making sure that the client sees all of the choices that you have made
- providing samples of all of the finishes and samples/photos of proposed furnishings
- integrating sustainable practices within the final concept development through the final material and detail development choices in a holistic way (Winchip, 2007)

In these last stages of the design process, everything comes together and it is a good time to take stock. Integrating the design with appropriate choices means getting back to the reason for the design in the first place, and helping the design move from virtual idea to tangible reality. What was the design approach? A sustainable one? An economic one? An aesthetic one? Each design process approach implies choices along the way.

We will now move into the post-design process stage in Chapter 8, and also review the actual, live experiences of the users after the space is actually built. We will also build on the ideas of contexts in design approaches further in Chapter 9.

BIBLIOGRAPHY

Ballast, D. K. (2007). *Interior design reference manual: A guide to the NCIDQ Exam*. Belmont, CA: Professional Publications.

Ching, F. D. K. (1975). *Building construction illustrated*. New York: Van Nostrand Reinhold.

Collier, B. J., & Tortora, P. G. (2001). *Understanding textiles*. Upper Saddle River, NJ: Prentice Hall.

Cuttle, C. (2003). *Lighting by design*. Oxford, UK: Architectural Press.

DeChiara, J., Paneiro, J., & Zelnik, M. (1991). *Timesaver standards for interior design and space planning*. New York: McGraw-Hill.

Hall, W. R. (1993). *Contract interior finishes*. New York: Whitney Library of Design.

Mahke, F. H., & Manhke, R. H. (1993). *Color and light in man-made environments*. New York: John Wiley & Sons.

Wilhide, E. (2001). *Materials: A directory for home design*. Gloucester, MA: Rockport Publishers.

Winchip, S. (2005). *Designing a quality lighting environment*. New York: Fairchild Books.

Winchip, S. (2007). *Sustainable design for interior environments*. New York: Fairchild Books.

Chapter Eight

FROM PROCESS TO REALITY

Objective

In this chapter we will explore two aspects of the design process we have not explored in-depth to date: How we move the project toward the built reality, and how we intend our designs to be lived in as real, experienced spaces.

Throughout Chapters 1 to 7, you have explored the design process, from earliest ideas to the final project concept. Now we will examine how the design project is built and contextualized within the complex issues of our lived environment. We will move into the final stage of the design process and then the post-design process. We will also examine theoretical foundations that underlie how we do what we do, and introduce you to some basic ideas.

EXPLORING THE BUILT DESIGN PROJECT

First, we will look at the final components of the design process, and how the project moves from process to built environment. We will also consider how people react to the designed space, and how we learn from the built project, whether as part of post-occupancy assessment, or as designers dealing with deficient work who reflect upon the result of the design itself. And although we may have built the design, the design process keeps on evolving as we judge the design and its success, and build the next one learning from the first.

Second, we will reconsider the idea of design intentions, and how the design becomes experienced in the real world. In the latter part of the chapter, we will introduce some theoretical concepts related to the idea of lived experiences in space. What are these experiences? What are they and why is this important

to understand as a designer? Although we are concerned with comfort and satisfaction as psychological aspects of well-being, we are also concerned with how people's well-being can be enhanced through our design intentions. This is a more philosophical approach, grounded in the lived realities of people who occupy space as subjective human beings. We will introduce ideas such as ethics here, and speak about sustainable practices again.

When we discuss lived experiences, we reenter the theoretical realm. We design spaces, yes, but we also affect how people "live" as real people, with feelings and emotions, and very real needs that are constantly changing and dynamic. As we design these spaces to be used and lived in, we integrate the dynamic aspects of human behavior, meaning that the movement and activity that people do is hard to design around. We will introduce some philosophical concepts such as phenomenology, which is the understanding of lived experiences as real, dynamic aspects of living. What is a lived experience in design in more philosophical terms? Why is this concept an important one to understand at this stage of the design process? These are added, in-depth perspectives that we include here because the design process is more than selecting physical elements to satisfy requirements.

We will begin the chapter by looking at how projects are detailed and built, revisiting case studies we have explored previously. We will consider post-occupancy processes and what we need to know to complete the built project. We will then discuss how to critically reflect on the designs we create. These more philosophical ideas balance the more pragmatic, everyday things we need to address as designers when we move our designs from concepts to realities. Designing is not a perfect process, and with each project we gain experience that allows us to know what to do better next time. This self-assessment requires critical reflection, both during and after the design process has been completed for a given project.

BUILDING THE DESIGN: THE POST-DESIGN PROCESS

In today's world, designing has become very complicated. Building a design project is an entirely different process than it was even 20 years ago. Although some projects are designed and built quite simply, such as the kitchen remodeling in Chapter 3, more often than not, projects have a complexity inherent in their designing and particularly in their production. This means that the design is transferred into the built reality through a multitude of processes that are not always easy. For example, in Case Study 3.3, the client's allergies and concerns about natural materials complicated what might otherwise have been a simple renovation, and rightly so.

Another aspect of design implementation is the relative time component associated with different parts of the design process. Throughout this book, you have seen how we design an interior space, and

it seems as if this would be the bulk of the work. When you are in school, you spend most of your time learning techniques, how to do research, and how to design. This might also give you the impression that the bulk of your time in practice is spent on these things. However, the reality in actual project development is that the designing is usually but a small part of the much larger process of getting the project built and occupied by the users. The time spent on the designing often depends on the interior type. For example, the design of work environments varies from full design of the space to planning that has already been designed, whereas in restaurant and bar designs, the design concept forms the major component of the process.

The Design Project in the Built Stages

After the design project has been approved by the client, you move into the post-design process of getting the project built. At this stage, you communicate the design to other players and stakeholders, including contractors, architects, engineers, and specialists. For example, in restaurant design you may be part of a larger team headed by an architect who is in charge of building the space, a project manager who manages the entire project, a team of mechanical and electrical engineers who coordinate the interior environmental systems including HVAC, electrical, and lighting systems, and lighting and kitchen specialists brought in for the detail of the kitchen design and lighting effects.

Another example is the case study of the exhibition kiosk that we discussed in Chapter 1. In this particular project, the interior designer was the lead, and the team of consultants included the contractor, the events coordinator, the graphic designer, and lighting and media specialists.

A Review of the Phases of the Design Process

In Chapter 3, we presented the various stages of the design process. Let's bring these concepts back and see what they consist of.

I. Pre-Process
- Fact-finding mission; get to know the client

- Understanding the client needs and project parameters prior to the research phase (as explored in Chapters 1–7)

II. Design Process

The last stage of the design process (stages 1 through 5 have been explored in previous chapters) is the implementation of the design and the post-design assessment. This process consists of implementing the final design into technical or construction plans and executing it through pricing and construction. This stage includes:

- Implementing the final design concept
- Creating the means by which contractors can build on the site (plans, details, modeling)
- Understanding changes as part of the implementation process
- The post-design assessment (post-design process)

III. Post-Design Process

The post-design process consists of the following components:

- Evaluating the design after it is finished/built
- Post-occupancy evaluation (after people have moved in; looking and assessing the viability of the design)
- Planning for the next project, integrating feedback on the actualized design

In interior design practice, these phases of the implementation process are usually reorganized into production phases after the design has been approved by the concerned stakeholders, such as the client/user and/or the project management team. We might find the following aspects of the project in one of several phases of the design process:

- contracts, documents, and production phase
- project execution phase
- post-project phase (also known as post-occupancy evaluation phase)

Let's have a look at each part.

How Design Projects Are Built

The implementation of the final design means changing gears in the design process. You have completed one stage of the design process and are moving into another, the post-design process. You transfer the design into technical details, technical or construction plans, and then finally execute it through pricing and construction of the project itself.

At this stage, you need to prepare information by creating the means by which contractors can build on the site, suppliers can order materials and furnishings, and clients can coordinate purchases and moves for the new spaces. This includes the development of technical plans, elevations, sections, specifications, and details as required. You will need to detail all aspects of the design both in visual and verbal terms.

Sometimes things move very quickly in industry; even so, drawings and other communication tools that clearly explain the design are imperative if the concept is to be implemented well and accurately. In visual terms, this means developing documents that can be issued to other consultants for coordination purposes, and to contractors for the pricing and eventual construction of the project. This includes developing full sets of working/construction drawings that may include:

- detailed plans of the overall space and its construction, interior systems, lighting and electrical/IT needs, communication, and security issues
- detailed elevations and ceiling plans showing all of these components in three dimensions on a two-dimensional drawing
- details of all architectural features of the space and of all built-in features, fitments, and custom furnishings
- specifications and documents that explain the various designed elements such as lighting choices, materials, custom features, and components that require specifications (specialty components, built-in elements, equipment, and its integration into the overall planning and detailing)
- specifications and details concerning purchased and ordered items, and the coordination of same

At this stage, the depth of your design will become evident. If you have created a vague concept, you will have difficulty developing the details that you need.

> **BUILDING BLOCK** • *While designing, try to envision the built space right from the beginning. A well-proposed concept is already in the detail and construction development phase. A good exercise to do while designing is to document the actual specifications and choices right off the bat. You need to make decisions while in the conceptual development phase so that you will know how they impact on your choices. Ask yourself: Can I detail this the way I am designing it? Can a contractor build it, and if not, can I teach the contractor how to build it through my own knowledge of building? If you do not have this knowledge, your ideas may not stand up to the scrutiny of builders or other consultants. Research your choices in terms of their viability as much as their maintenance, safety features, or other characteristics that you may investigate.*

Integrating Thinking into the Process

At this stage of the design process, you will have met with the client and the design will have been approved, with or without changes due to cost, technical issues or timing, and construction constraints. Changes are normal at this point in the process. However, the more thought out your concept is, the easier it is to implement changes that do not disrupt the design. Too often interior designers design concepts that are neither practical nor cost efficient. By the time the design has been created, if it is not viable, it creates problems for the client and project down the road. It is important to understand the cost implications of design decisions made earlier on.

Some designers feel that cost considerations hamper the creative aspect of designing. This may be true, but if you think about the practical aspects as an integral part of the creative process and integrate them early on, your design will be based on thinking about all the parts of the process in an integrated way. Then after the design is done and the project is moving toward a built entity, you do not have to back-pedal and figure out how to make the design fit the more constraining issues of the project, such as cost and time.

This is difficult to understand in school, especially because many design studios do not use real projects or real project scenarios. However, do not worry about it at this point because real work experience is what is required to be able to consider cost and time issues. These come with the experience of doing actual projects in practice. This is why in this book we present these concepts from the point of view of practice through a limited number of examples. Changes are a standard part of the design process, from the moment we begin the design until the user occupies the space. People are constantly adapting their environment and this is part of the process (Vaikla-Poldma, 2003; Poldma 2007).

We will now take a look at how these final stages are implemented by revisiting case studies of actual projects built, and how time, schedules, and costs impact the decision making that occurs.

People, Schedules, and Time

As we move the design toward the built project and a final designed environment, you will find that this takes a considerable amount of time. Although the design may have taken a certain amount of time to create, getting the project actually built is a much longer and more complex process because the design transfers into the public domain. When we move the design toward the built product, we enter into a series of relationships with other people who become involved in the project. You have to be able to deal with them, know who the proper players are, and be able to judge what is relevant within the project development and what is not.

The Various Players

There are a host of new players who enter into the picture at this stage. If you have ever been in design practice, you may have already met some of them during the design process. In the design production phase their role becomes much more important and present. You may deal with architects who are designing the building or are in charge of the project, engineers who are specialized in the various components of the building systems, and various service providers for systems, communication, and various specialty needs specific to the project. Some of these players and their roles are:

- Project manager
- Architect
- Interior designer
- Structural engineer
- Mechanical engineer
- Electrical engineer
- General contractor and subcontractors
- Service providers (communication systems, IT systems, security systems)
- Lighting consultant
- Other specialists who are specific to a project (kitchen, lighting, institutional, decoration, hotel, exhibition, hospital, facility planners, psychologists, graphic designers, media specialists, etc.)
- Product suppliers and distributors
- Furniture suppliers and distributors
- Accessory suppliers and distributors

Most projects always involve the first seven people listed; others become involved depending on the context specific to that project. To illustrate this point, if we use our previous case studies as examples, we can see how the players vary from project to project. For example, in the kitchen case study in Chapter 3, the players were:

- the interior designer
- the kitchen speciality company specializing in natural materials
- the contractor and his subtrades
- the finishes and cabinet suppliers and manufacturers

In the office case study in Chapter 4, the players consisted of:

- tthe client IT specialty team
- the client coordination team
- the project management team
- the landlord
- the architect
- the engineers (mechanical, structural, electrical, and systems)

- the systems providers (IT, communication, alarm, and security)
- the interior designer
- the contractor and his subtrades (drywall, construction, electrical, plumbing, finishing, installation)
- the finishes manufacturers and suppliers
- the furniture systems providers

All of these different consultants play a specific role in moving the design through to completion, and their respective roles must be clearly identified both on paper and on the construction site.

For example, you may have selected certain finishes for your project. At this stage, the product manufacturers and suppliers must be consulted for their input on maintenance and installation, or perhaps the timing of orders and deliveries or for the way the item will be purchased and coordinated with the general contractor. You must be able to identify the people who will support the choices that you make, give the best price to the client, and accurately represent your intentions in the chosen materials and furnishings. When installed, you need to create a way to instruct your client on the proper maintenance of the finishes, whether through a meeting or by leaving a manual with the instructions with the client.

Ethical implications include making choices that are competitive and transparent to the client. For example, you have designed the interior selecting a certain carpet, and have specified the manufacturer and supplier. The project goes out for pricing and suddenly you have three other suppliers contacting you with more competitive prices. What do you do? Do you ignore the requests? Dump your first supplier? Does your client have a friend who wants to undercut the supplier with an inferior product? These are all ethical issues that impact on the design decision making. Our choices in terms of the various players are influenced by our own convictions and how we adapt the design to the built version of the project that we envision. We will look at these types of ethical issues in more depth in Chapter 9.

Schedules and Time Issues

As we develop the project, time becomes a critical factor. No matter the size and scope, from small to large and complex commercial projects, time plays a large part in determining the capacity to carry through to successful completion. Projects are always scheduled for completion within a certain time frame. This time frame can be driven by the opening date of a boutique or the move-in date of new employees into an office. No matter what the project, time is a major constraint. It is imperative that you develop knowledge and experience for dealing with time issues as they develop over the course of the project. There are real contract issues at stake when time elements are not respected, and this must be taken into consideration at the outset of the project.

Along with time constraints, projects usually have imposed schedules, and this may hamper the more conceptual side of the design process. Projects are often scheduled, especially when they are large and involve many players. In Figure 8.1 we see an example of a typical time schedule.

In school you are also faced with time and scheduling conflicts. For example, one student creates her final project with an acute awareness of the time constraints imposed by the school schedule, her other courses, and her various commitments. She develops a time schedule to organize herself so that she can produce the design within a realistic time frame. In Figure 8.2, we see her time schedule sketch.

Building the Final Design Project

The detail drawings are done, and the schedules are determined. You have also put the project out for a bid, or have gotten prices through one of several different methods available locally. What happens next? At this stage, the project players get together and organize the work for the construction to begin.

Let's take the example of the food court, first explored in Chapter 2, to see how a project moves from the final design stage into construction and the final built environment (Case Study 8.1).

Post-Occupancy Evaluations, Assessments, and Post-Design Processes

After a project has been built, the interior designer should return to the site and assess the relative success of the project as built. Normally, as-built drawings are done to record changes that may have occurred during the course of construction from the original drawings. A post-occupancy assessment should also be made of the design project; this assessment can take several forms. Some designers prefer to do a post-occupancy evaluation (Winchip, 2007) whereas others create deficiency lists and evaluate using more informal assessment tools. Still others create what are called "punch lists," and many designers do informal personal assessments of the relative success of a design after it has been implemented. Each assessment aims to review what has been built, how it suits the users, what was been done well, or what might require improvement. However, when projects become larger and more complex, formal assessments tools such as the post-occupancy evaluation are needed to verify that the design concept has been implemented appropriately and thoroughly. Let's look at the various tools available.

Deficiency Lists

Deficiency lists are created with contractors and clients to verify the original design program and contract documents from a built interior perspective. Some designers use punch lists, which are also a form of deficiency list. Both list the elements and features of the built space that need review or correction. The designer, the client, and the contractor do a walk-through of the space and identify every aspect that does not comply with the built specifications and the contract. There may also be changes that the designer must document, and that need to be clarified, as they relate back to the original contract. All these procedures compare the built result to the design as it was produced in the technical drawings, contract documents, and issued specifications.

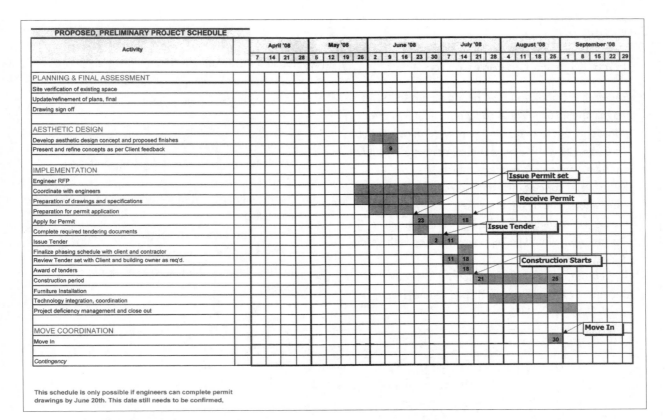

Figure 8.1 • Time schedule for a construction project

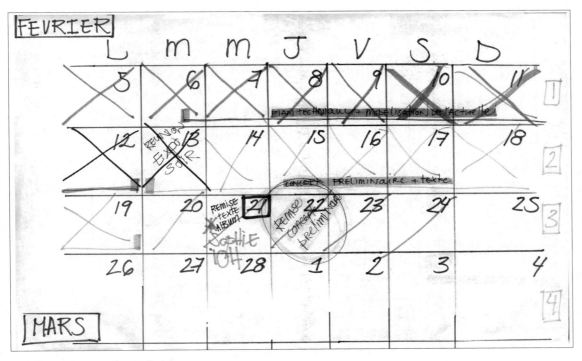

Figure 8.2 • Josiane's time schedule

Food Court Construction

Earlier in the book you saw the food court in its sketch stages and also as a final concept in actual interior photos. To get to that point there were many stages. Three people worked on technical drawings and a full contract documents package, which was coordinated with several consultants, the project manager, and contractors. The designer worked closely with both the project manager and the clients to ensure that the design intent would be kept while dealing with severe budget constraints.

From this approved concept, full contract documents were created and specifications were developed for everything from architectural features to environmental systems to all custom and purchased furnishings. These include:

- all details of flooring, columns, ceiling elements, handrails, and waste bins
- details for the food kiosks, lighting, and mall corridor treatments
- graphic signage and movement (using lighting and color)
- seating type, layout, and details, including maintenance and production issues
- flooring layout, maintenance, and layout of pattern

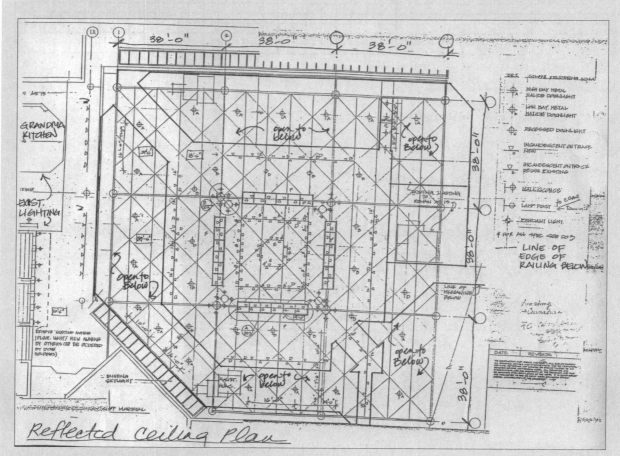

Figure A • Working drawings: Talk of the Town food court, 2000

- overall coordination of the renovation while the mall stays open throughout the construction period

The final technical plans are extensive. Figures A and B show some of the plans and details of the space itself.

Details include identifying and detailing several design elements within the project.

The project goes out for competitive pricing, organized by the project manager. The consultants, clients, and the designer review the bids when they come in, and they are negotiated with the clients until the final price and concept are agreed upon. Based on this agreement, the interior designer prepares the final drawings for construction.

Recently the food court and its surroundings are under design and construction development again. In Figure C we see further development of details, where AutoCAD-drawn plans are superimposed with hand-drawn sketches to work out an idea.

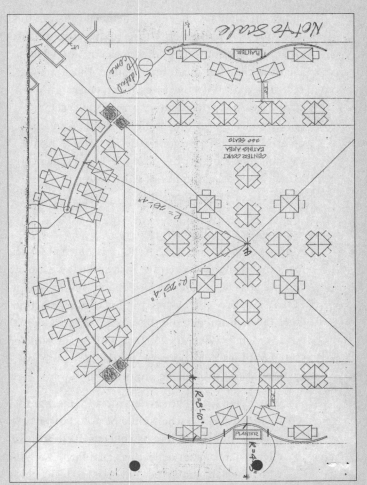

Figure B • Working drawings: Talk of the Town food court, 2000

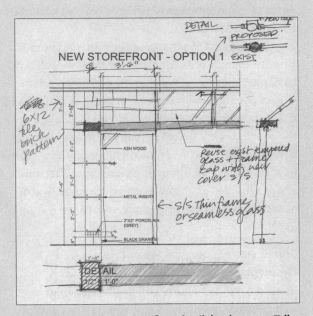

Figure C • New column/storefront detail development; Talk of the Town food court, 2008

The changes are part of the new redevelopment of the space. There are concepts in the works for a new hotel and a full redesign once again of the interior mall and food court areas. This is an excellent example, attests Michael Arnold, of how a quality design allows for developments and change over times, and how an interior is a living and changing place.

Post-Design Assessment

A post-design assessment is done by interior designers in conjunction with the deficiency list. In this assessment, the designer returns to the client and user and looks at what works, what does not, and what might work better in a future project. This is a more reflective and subjective assessment, where the designer returns to the iterative part of the design process once more. The interior designer wants to determine whether or not the design intentions are valuable, and whether the newly designed space actually helps the user live or work better, more efficiently, or more enjoyably.

Post-Occupancy Evaluations

A post-occupancy evaluation (POE) is a formal assessment that brings together the post-design assessment and the post-occupancy walk-through with the client. POEs are "a process for determining user satisfaction with the environment and the success of the built environment" (Winchip, 2007, p. 306). Susan Winchip (2007) outlines a clear process for the POE both in traditional and sustainable projects as follows:

> The design team should develop a POE program that identifies (1) who should be asked to participate, (2) information to be collected, (3) the most effective means for collecting the information, (4) when the data should be collected, (5) procedures for rectifying any problems, and (6) a means of dissemination. Conventional building projects generally involve the client and users of the space in the POE. For sustainable projects, these individuals should be asked to participate in the POE, but other people who should also be included are the contractor, engineers, architects, suppliers, community representatives, and any other stakeholders. (p. 306)

In essence, the post-production process considers all of the stakeholders through the deficiency/punch list, the designers' own reflection on the project, or the POE, regardless of the type of design project. Regardless of whether you do a formal POE or assess the project more informally through punch lists or deficiency lists, you should always do a post-occupancy assessment of the design.

Changing and Shifting Interior Design Foundations

As we move the design into a built reality, we should also take a critical look at how people actually live in the designed environment that we have created, and what this means in terms of design intentions. We discussed our design intentions in Chapter 5, and after the project is built, this idea comes back for consideration. Is the design working for people as they use the space? Are they able to use it as a supportive place where they can do what they need to do?

Earlier in the chapter, we discussed how when we move into the built reality of a project, we assess its relative success or failure using assessment tools and deficiency lists. In essence this deals with the practical issues, such as the replacement of burned-out lamps, and whether or not the space suits the person and is comfortable. However, on a more philosophical level, our goal as interior designers is to create an environment that allows people to have lived experiences that are enticing, exciting, and perhaps beyond what they might have imagined.

As I suggested earlier, we "live" in environments that are changing and dynamic, and yet we still tend to design interior spaces as static places where we expect people to behave in a certain way. This idea of design is changing rapidly worldwide, as we see people appropriating spaces in many different ways, in dynamic ways, and also in ways different than we may have intended. We increasingly design to suit transitory activities, multiple uses and contexts, and an array of new ways of seeing interior spaces.

The Phenomenological Idea of Real, Lived Experience

The concept of phenomenology will be explored as it relates to interior design. Why is this concept an important one to understand within the design process? What is a phenomenological experience of space?

The idea of "real, lived experience" comes from an aesthetic perspective of philosophical ideas situated in phenomenology (Shusterman, 1997; White, 1998; Vaikla-Poldma, 2003). When we speak of real, lived experiences, we make our aesthetic design decisions considering the ways that people live in and appropriate space, integrating their activities as changing and dynamic acts that are experienced in everyday living.

A Phenomenological Design Approach

People live in spaces every day, they are happy or sad, and we design for them with this in mind. We design for human response that is a subjective, lived experience that we all have, meaning that we live life experiencing space as wonderful or reacting to it as negative, usually subconsciously. We also design with design intent, and this can be affected by how we appropriate the very act of designing itself. Both the subjective experience of space and the subjective act of designing affect how designs are created.

We will build toward this idea of phenomenology by examining three ideas:

1. Understanding the social construction of space
2. Determining how changing concepts of time and space affect how we design interior space
3. Developing a phenomenological approach to designing interior space (involving the designer and the design act)

What Is the Social Construction of Space?

As we design, we shape and mold more than the physical and psychological components of interior spaces. We design space to respond to more affective and subjective human needs such as feeling better and living well. We are on the tip of supplying value systems as we design to reflect the values of the society that we live in. The idea of design here is universal in that design should be accessible to the most people possible, and should be an integral component of thinking when constructing buildings and designing interiors.

We also socially construct the spaces that people inhabit. From the moment of birth, spaces shape who we are and how we function as people of a particular culture or society. The social constructions of space and place create, at least in part, the social roles and relations that govern how we live, work, and play (Poldma, 1999). When we design interior space, we enter into a complex human way of being that is influenced by the ways we socially behave with one another. These social relations are influenced by our values. There are social constructs that often govern social and power relations between men and women, and these become manifest in the space that we design. For example, in Chapter 4 we discussed Shirley Ardener's ideas (1981) about the social considerations of space as a place that is accessible to some but not others. Sometimes we unconsciously design spaces that create divides between people, or alternatively, bring together people who might otherwise not intermingle. Sometimes we also create spaces that hinder certain activities while encouraging others. And we may not even be aware that we are doing this if we are not reflecting on what we do when we design.

And it may seem that we are sometimes forced to live in spaces that perhaps we do not enjoy. As Joy Malnar and Frank Vodvarka (1992) suggest:

> Man seeks to make sense out of his surroundings and to define and locate himself with respect to these surroundings. To this end, humans are directed towards organizing their environment, giving it significance, and assessing their position in the altered structure that ensues. . . . A designed space, by definition, is meant to encourage and facilitate certain kinds of behavior within it, and communicates that fact through the use of codes. But clearly spaces undergo a change of significance when used by persons who no longer accept these codes, especially spaces that failed their users. In any case, spaces are subject to individual interpretation, itself a product of expectation. (p. 290)

If we design interior space with this idea in mind, we then acknowledge the more lived, actual experiences of space as driving design intentions. We see here how space is built as much physically as socially on our expectations, and is based on our subjective acceptance or rejection of the space as a place (through our interpretation). Perhaps spaces do and should change, and if so, then perhaps static designs are no longer a valid means to create interior spaces. Let's look at this possibility next.

How Do Changing Concepts of Time and Space Affect the Interior Space?

If we understand that space, when designed, contains subjective responses influenced by social codes and constructions, then we use underlying values grounded in the idea that space is a physical place that interior designers replicate, fill in, and finish, such as a container.

New Considerations—Taking Up Space

But what about wanting to change the space immediately for different and complementary uses? What about the exterior and interior interplay of the street, the exhibition hall that imposes itself on the kiosk, or the view of the store into the mall? What about the ways that we play at work, the way we transform our cars into working environments, or how we work 24/7 around the world from the comfort of our homes? We saw how students tried to create new ways to think about how taking up space means creating flexible and changing spaces that reflect the multiple needs of the people who move through it. Spaces may be used for multiple purposes simultaneously, transformed for different needs, where immediate physical surroundings become a place for worldwide communication, where space might be transformed immediately for upcoming activities, or where space transcends time.

Space and its uses are changing rapidly in our new, emerging global world. In 2005, I explored the intersection of the social aspects of space with the idea of lived experience, and how in this new era we should perhaps reconsider the meaning of "space" as a place that is dynamic and constantly changing. In collaboration with Magda, one of my doctoral students, and as part of my own post-doctoral design research, I developed an argument for the idea that global changes are shifting the very nature of designed interior space, which has become less static. We

examined (Poldma & Wesolkowska, 2005) how sociological, anthropological, and cultural geographical perspectives identified space as increasingly "intrinsically tied to lived experience" (p. 56). We presented the argument that a phenomenological perspective considers what it is to be in a state of actual, lived experiences, and how our perceptions are subjective and bound by our particular point in time. We talked about Dholakia and Zwick (2003), who write:

> In the age of new media and mobile communication, we have thus moved from spatialized time, where the nature of the activities is predominantly governed by the structured logic of the place (one reads in the library, one studies in the classroom, one eats in the restaurant, etc.) to temporalized space, where the nature of the activities of its inhabitants define the place (a restaurant becomes a playground, a coffeehouse becomes an electronic mall, a train becomes a workstation, etc.).

Subsequently:

> In spatialized time, the subject perceives place as the primary mode of identification against "others" such as the environment, people or work processes. In temporal space, the predominant mode of identification is through the experience of time fragments, temporally demoting place to a physical backdrop. . . . Thus people, whose life experiences overlap and intersect, blur the boundaries of place and space/time relations. (Poldma & Wesolkowska, 2005, p. 56)

So, no longer do we design a space to fit people into; rather, people have lived experiences that transcend time and space, and in ways beyond our capacity to design interior spaces. Digital worlds are transforming the very nature of how we experience and interact with other people and within environments (McCullough, 2004). We work digitally and virtually from home and communicate around the world 24/7, and we play while we move locally or globally, doing what we need to do anywhere, anytime. Indeed, we may be working while in our pajamas in our bedroom, and playing while at work.

People's lived experiences increasingly govern what shapes a space takes on, as spaces become more flexible and changing. Figures 8.3 to 8.20 show a reconceptualization of what it means to be a moviegoer. The student who is developing her final project concept begins by using some of these critical ideas in her questioning, by investigating how people experience the cinema. The sketches show both a design development and a reconceptualization of the inter-relationships between people, objects, and inhabited interior spaces. The figures illustrate, moreover, the full development of a cinema concept, from the the initial site selection to the rough ideas to the design development and, finally, to the fully developed concept and details. In the end, we see how the design revolves around the idea of a complete interactive spatial experience.

In the profession, many designers are rethinking how space might be considered. For example, Adrienne Rewi (2004) explores how designers are changing the boundaries of space through their designs, as a means "to accommodate change" (p. 11).

She considers what different designers and architects think about flexible and multifunctional spaces. She explores what Tara Roscoe thinks about how we assume what interior design is about and how this becomes what people think about space:

Challenging previously accepted common practices may be easier said than done, considering how much we have invested in the status quo. "Some people assume all living rooms need a sofa and all offices need desks," Roscoe says. It should always be second-guessed, and designers need to lead their clients through that process. It has become more difficult in the past 10 to 15 years to implement ideas that are outside the box because of the focus on the bottom line, but if interior designers want to move beyond cranked out tried-and-true formulas, they have to allow for that in the project process. . . .

. . . [D]esks or walls can become computers or television screens, a wall can be illuminated or changed in color with the push of a button.

. . . Roscoe is unsure that people are sufficiently aware of or prepared for how these advances will impact on the spatial order of offices and homes. (pp. 12–15)

Indeed, even in this book, we considered home and office activities separately and in different chapters. The work environments we studied only reflected the work that people did while at the office. Whereas the office design we explored in Chapter 4 appears to be a traditional work environment, in reality the office personnel move frequently and the designs include flexible spaces for revolving personnel and temporary functions. The actual design integrated new modes such as overlapping office spaces, mobile workstations, and flexible, complex IT systems. The design reflects the reality of one particular office and, regardless of the designed office space, people work as they need to and transcend the physical space to do the work that they need to do.

In the twenty-first century, spaces are fast becoming "intelligent" as the visual image takes over text as the prime communicator (Riewoldt, 1997). As Otto Riewoldt suggests:

The borderlessness of the technological world is thoroughly at odds with the containing structures of buildings: virtual reality by its very essence has less and less need for architecture. . . . The digital revolution is based on simultaneity, synchronicity, permanence, immateriality, immediacy and globality. . . . The global enterprise of the future will be a composite, changing network of autonomous units. . . .

. . . [D]igitalization is burning up space: space for working and living in. Virtual corporate structures need less office space, fewer parking spaces, and fewer facilities for the public." (1997, pp. 7, 9, and 11)

These ideas about changing work modes and ways of understanding the ways we take up space mean that we as interior designers need to think about what people actually do and how we can best support their activities when designing a space. If we are no longer putting things into a space for static activities, but rather creating a backdrop for a myriad of activities to

Figure 8.3 • Series of sketches and existing interior views of the student's design project development

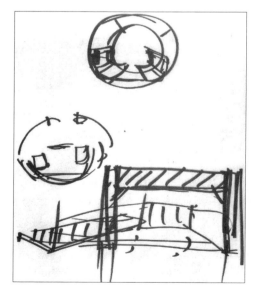

Figure 8.4

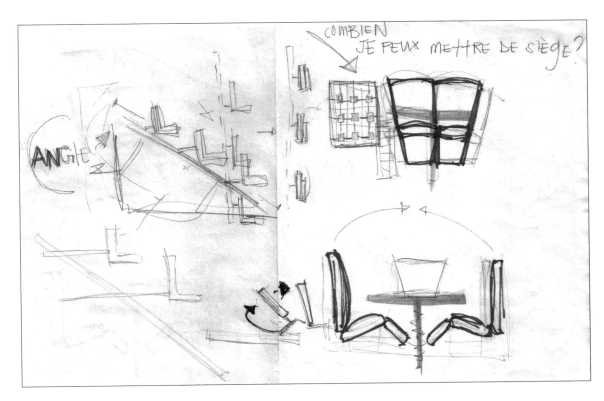

Figure 8.5

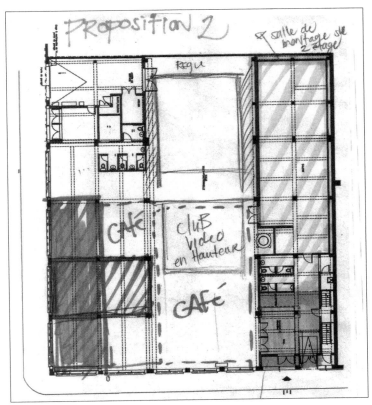

Figure 8.6

Figure 8.7

Figure 8.8

Figure 8.9

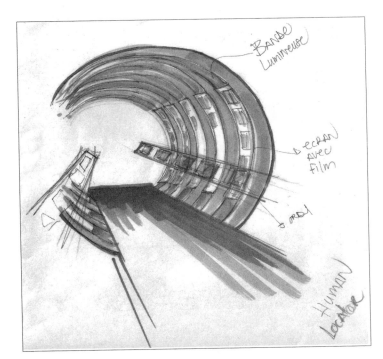

Figure 8.10

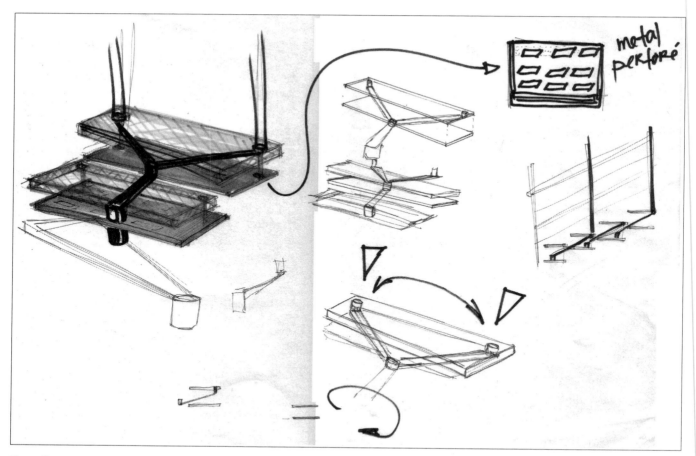

Figure 8.11

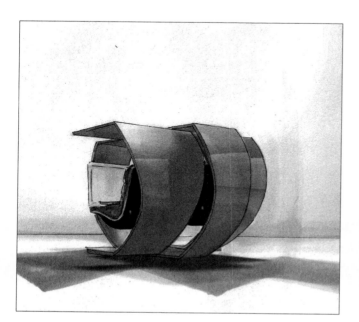

Figure 8.12

Figure 8.13

Figure 8.14

Figure 8.15

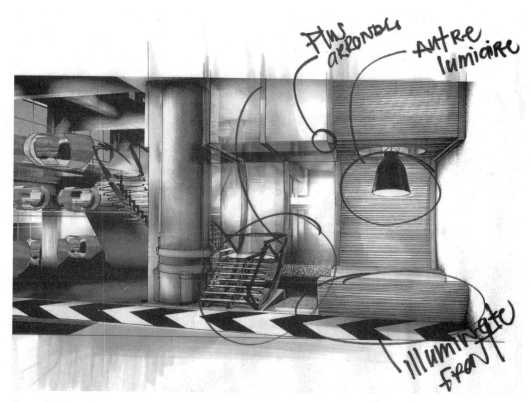

Figure 8.16

Figure 8.17

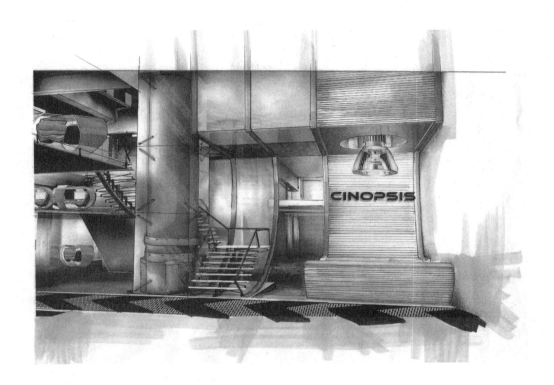

Figure 8.18

Figure 8.19

Figure 8.20

unfold, then we are considering how space is taken up rather than designing within a controlled place. Thus, we arrive at the third idea explored here: the idea of phenomenological lived experiences in spaces.

Developing a Phenomenological Approach to Designing Interior Space (Involving the Interior Designer and the Design Act)

When we speak about a phenomenological approach to space, we have to situate this idea within a definition of what phenomenological is. In its simplest sense, it means considering how people have subjective responses to spaces as they experience them in real time and as actual experiences. Paralleling this idea are the emerging ways in which designed spaces are radically changing from static containers to live, flexible, and changing environments. We consider two concepts as phenomenological:

- The design act as phenomenological

- The designed space as a phenomenological experience

Let's examine these concepts.

When we design interior space as a place of change and as a supportive dynamic environment, our approach to designing is essentially phenomenological in that we aim to create lived-in, dynamic spaces that people can appropriate and use to live better and do their jobs more efficiently (Franz, 2000; Vaikla-Poldma, 2003). (Note that philosophically "to live better" means to live a good life and is derived from Wittgenstein [Shusterman, 1997]. The concept of phenomenology has its roots philosophically in hermeneutics and the writings of renowned philosophers such as Edmund Husserl, and developed further by Martin Heidegger [Heidegger, 1971/2001]. For the purposes of this book, the philosophical presentation of ideas will be limited to the more pragmatic aspects of the experience of space, as suggested by Richard

Shusterman, and examined here by Jill Franz as a pragmatic view of how we might understand these concepts in interior design [Shusterman, 1997; Franz, 2000].)

When we design with a phenomenological stance, we see the interior space differently. We think about the space as a live and lived place, and incorporate the following thinking into our design process:

- Understand dynamic thinking and complex problem solving
- Capture the idea of "actual lived experience" in the ways that we design the interior space
- Understand the tangible, lived acts of experiencing space
- Understand the design act as a phenomenological intention
- Understand the designed space as the product of multiple processes and as an integrated process with other processes

If the things that we experience are not bound in time and space, as thought in the past, then they exist in our awareness in a particular point in time and change each time we move around in space. This is a phenomenological stance, as expressed by Maurice Merleau-Ponty in his seminal book, *Phenomenology of Perception* (1958; 1945). When we design with this perspective, we accept that the space is a place where things will happen independent of what we might intend. This means that we do our best to support the range of activities that we know our client and user wants and needs, and we do so anticipating what design elements will support these activities. Because they are dynamic and changing, our design solutions must also be flexible, capable of changing, and transcending time and space.

Understanding the Philosophy of Phenomenology (the Designer's Stance and Intention and the Experience of the Space)

People make meanings of their lives within the spaces that they use and inhabit. When we live within our homes or work in different types of environments, our means of self-expression are through narrative (language) and visual arts forms (art and artistic objects). To design a space appropriately, a designer needs to understand people, and their experiences frame the potential use and design of a particular space. The designer must mesh a spatial and visual framework with the meaning making and life-world of the potential user. These aspects of the interior designer's research and approach to design thinking are grounded in phenomenology and psychology.

An interesting way of considering this idea of life-world is explored by Maurice Merleau-Ponty (1945; 1958), who suggests that each person has their own way of moving, experiencing, and seeing interior space. Merleau-Ponty presents the relationship between perception and the body in space thus:

> Our own body is in the world as the heart is in the organism. . . . When I walk around my flat, the various aspects in which it presents itself to me could not possibly appear as views of one and the same thing if I did not know that each of them represents the flat seen from one spot or another. . . . I can of course take a mental bird's-eye view of the flat, visualize it or draw a plan of it, but in that case too I could not grasp the unity of the object without the mediation of bodily perspective: it is the flat "seen from above," and the fact that I am able to draw together in it the habitual perspective is dependant on my knowing that one and the same embodied experience can view successively from various positions. (p. 235)

Merleau-Ponty goes on to state that this perception is subjective and bound in part by bodily movements in space, as grounded in experience. He explores the example of the cube, and how rationally we can understand the concept of a cube, but our experience of it is a "collection of lived through correspondence" (p. 236).

Phenomenology understood as direct experience (Merleau-Ponty, 1958) and the concept of meaning making in our life-world (White, 1998) thus become part of what interior designers might want to research and understand. Not only do users perceive certain visual cues and psychologically relate to them as positive or negative experiences (which have perhaps been manipulated by designers to help us think these things), but they also experience meaning making through the appropriation of spaces and objects, and through the attachment of meaning to things (Csikszentmihalyi & Rochberg-Halton, 1981). Psychological needs and psychological reactions to space are fundamental to human interaction in space. There are a host of personal needs that people need to satisfy, be these associated with memories (Bachelard, 1958), personal territorial needs (Sommer, 1969), or more fundamental needs such as surrounding ourselves with objects that help us to find meaning in our lives (Csikszentmihalyi & Rochberg-Halton, 1981).

Perception plays a large role in the achievement of meaning making through the vehicle of experience. And life-world experiences frame all of the above.

The Transformation of the Spatial Experience

Interior spatial experiences include sensual responses, visual attributes that create psychological reactions, and feelings or emotions that can be generated by responses to spaces and the people who occupy them. For example, interior attributes—including the nature and use of materials, the change of exterior to interior, and concepts of order in space—are fundamental to understanding how space can transform the psychological and physiological responses we have.

One role of the design process has always been to learn to understand the user in a personal, almost intimate sense. For example, when I was a student, I remember being told to think about what it would be like to be in the place I am designing. I now suggest to my students that to be able to create, an interior designer must dialectically deal with the visual reactions that people will have and understand how the users' direct experiences will affect their sensual experience of the space. A phenomenological approach offers possibilities to explore space both in terms of the individual understanding of self as part of the interior experience, but also in terms of our own relationship to the social world.

The Concept of Experiences in Space as the Foundation for Activities

If we consider that experiences shape activities, and that we use activities as one of the contexts in designing interior space, then we might also consider the nature of these experiences. Experiences can be the result of a multitude of actions in our daily lives, be they virtual, physical, personal, or social (McCullough, 2004; Mitchell, 1993; Latour, 2005). Experiences can be the result of:

- activities that we need to perform; for example, a certain task
- how we feel about a place, a space, and our perceptions of and reactions to it
- the relationships that people have with objects and the interaction between their memory of it and their experience of it at any given point in time; this is relative to age, gender, and whether or not the experience is one of action relative to the object itself or a reaction from the self to others (Czikszentmihalyi & Rochberg-Halton, 1981, p. 112)
- our desire for constant experiences and order (work, weekend chores, play)
- our desire for changing and moving experiences
- our desire for contact with others
- our desire to experience things, events, people, and situations
- how we understand and accept the visual and sensual environment that surrounds us

When we design physical space, we also support the engagement of people with various types of experiences, from the simplest task to the most complex interrelationship of people, objects, activities, and subsequent responses.

The Designer and the Design Act as Phenomenological

Finally, when we design in the phenomenological sense, we transplant ourselves into the lived situations of the people for whom we are designing. We create designs using our rational mind (to create plans and solve functional problems), our creative mind, and our human senses. Related to our creative mind is the ability to design different possibilities, and this happens during our exploration of ideas within the unknown aspects of the design process as we explored in Chapter 6.

When we design considering the senses, we enter into the life-world experiences of people. Gaston Bachelard (1958) suggests how designing can help create places where memories are created when he suggests that "thanks to the house . . . a great many of our memories are housed" (p. 8). Bachelard implies that our inner self is related to spatial memories that are formed in our homes and living spaces. Bachelard uses the idea of the house as a "repository of memories" to associate interior space with humanity on a very personal level. If you consider that homes store memories, and that through these spatial memories you can form an association with your past, then you can also create new memories by designing spaces that reflect the way that people want to live.

We develop memories and use them to both live within spaces and to design them. White (1998) suggests that this is because, as Husserl noted, "Most of the things in our . . . life-world are immediately experienced by us as mentally significant things" (p. 5). It is vital that these experiences are understood when we design spaces. We need to understand that not only are the people living in interior spaces users but there are also dynamic and active people, and that the human side of designers adds their lived experience to the design situation. And yet, whereas designers need to feel the emotions and sensual experiences that Bachelard and others speak of, they also need to be able to step back and objectively provide the best concept for a project through their interpretation of these emotions and responses.

TRANSFORMING THE DESIGN CONCEPT

You have now seen how we transform the design concept into a built reality, and what design intentions mean as people experience the space in real time. Spaces are lived in, transformed, and used by people who add their own subjective views and experiences to the mix.

Throughout the book, we have alluded to several aspects of design thinking that form how we see space: sustainable aspects, cultural and social contexts, and ethical considerations. We will explore these dimensions in more detail in Chapter 9.

BIBLIOGRAPHY

Abercrombie, S. (1990). *A philosophy of Interior design*. New York: Harper & Row.

Amin, A., & Cohendet, P. (2004). *Architectures of knowledge: Firms, capabilities and communities*. Oxford: Oxford University Press.

Ardener, S. (Ed.). (1981). *Women and space: Ground rules and social maps*. New York: St. Martin's Press.

Bachelard, G. (1958; 1964). *The poetics of space*. Boston, MA: Beacon Press.

Ballast, D. K. (2007). *Interior design reference manual: A guide to the NCIDQ Exam* (4th ed.). Belmont, CA: Professional Publications.

Ching, F. D. K. (1975). *Building construction illustrated*. New York: Van Nostrand Reinhold.

Cohen, D. (1977). *Creativity: What is it?* New York: M. Evans & Company.

Csikszentmihalyi, M., & Rochberg-Halton, E. (1981). *The meaning of things: Domestic symbols and the self*. Cambridge, UK: Cambridge University Press.

Dholakia, N., & Zwick, D. (2003). *Mobile technologies and boundaryless spaces: Slavish lifestyles, seductive meanderings, or creative empowerment*. Paper presented at the HOIT.

Feld, S., & Basso, K. H. (1996). *Senses of place*. Santa Fe, NM: School of American Research Press.

Foucault, M. (1967, Spring). Of other spaces. *Diacritics*, 22–27.

Franz, J. (2000, July 8–12). *An interpretive–contextual framework for research in and through design: The development of a philosophically methodological and substantially consistent framework*. Paper presented at the Foundations for the Future: Doctoral Education in Design, La Clusaz, France.

Guerin, D., & Martin, C. (2001). *The interior design profession's body of knowledge: Its definition and documentation*. Original Report prepared for the Association of Registered Interior Designers of Ontario (ARIDO). Toronto: ARIDO.

Hall, W. R. (1993). *Contract interior finishes.* New York: Whitney Library of Design.

Heidegger, M. (1971; 2001). *Poetry, language, thought.* New York: HarperCollins.

Latour, B. 2005. *Reassembling the social: An introduction to actor-network-theory.* New York: Oxford University Press.

Malnar, J. M., & Vodvarka, F. (1992). *The interior dimension: A theoretical approach to enclosed space.* New York: Van Nostrand Reinhold.

Margolin, V., & Buchanan, R. (Eds.). (2000). *The idea of design: A design issues reader.* Cambridge, MA: MIT Press.

McCullough, M. (2004). *Digital ground: Architecture, pervasive computing and environmental knowing.* Cambridge, MA: MIT Press.

Merleau-Ponty, M. (1945; 1958). *Phenomenology of perception.* London: Routledge.

Mitchell, C. T. (1993). *Redefining designing: From form to experience.* New York: Van Nostrand Reinhold.

Ornstein, R. (1991). *The evolution of consciousness: The origins of the way we think.* New York: Simon & Schuster.

Poldma, T. (1999). *Gender, design and education: The politics of voice.* Unpublished Master of Arts thesis. Montreal: McGill University, Author.

Poldma, T. (2007). *Living in complexity: First-year design studio experiences.* Paper presented at the IDEC 2007 International Conference: Design and Social Justice, Austin, TX.

Poldma, T., & Wesolkowska, M. (2005). Globalization and changing concepts of time-space: A paradigm shift for interior design? *In-Form 5: The Journal of Architecture, Design and Material Culture.* The University of Nebraska–Lincoln.

Rewi, A. (2004). Beyond Walls. *Perspective, the Journal of the IIDA.*

Riewoldt, O. (1997). *Intelligent spaces: Architecture for the information age.* London: Laurence King Publishing.

Segal, P. (2006). *Professional practice: A guide to turning designs into buildings.* New York: W. W. Norton & Company.

Shusterman, R. (1997). *Practicing philosophy: Pragmatism and the philosophical life.* New York: Routledge.

Steeves, H. P. (2006). *The things themselves: Phenomenology and the return to the everyday.* Albany, NY: State University of New York Press.

Vaikla-Poldma, T. (1999). *Gender, design and education: The politics of voice.* Montreal: McGill University, Author.

Vaikla-Poldma, T. (2003). *An investigation of learning and teaching processes in an interior design class: An interpretive and contextual inquiry.* Unpublished Doctoral thesis. Montreal: McGill University, Author.

White, B. (1998). Aesthetigrams: Mapping aesthetic experiences. *Studies in Art Education, 39*(4), 321–335.

Winchip, S. M. (2007). *Sustainable design for interior environments.* New York: Fairchild Books.

Chapter Nine

DESIGN SENSIBILITY, AESTHETICS, SUSTAINABILITY, AND ETHICS

Objective

In this chapter we explore and develop in depth essential contexts that inform the design process. Chapter 8 introduced the idea that our world is changing, and how the design process must also allow for change and difference. In this chapter we will look at how different contexts are necessary to grasp this changing world and what this means in terms of the design process.

AN EMERGING PARADIGM SHIFT IN THE DESIGN PROCESS

We live in an era of transformation, a paradigm shift in the world in terms of global technological communication and mass consumption. Ways of doing things that we have literally taken for granted for the past hundred years are shifting. This changing society demands different ways of seeing and using interior space, ways that include new dimensions such as virtual experiences and global connectedness. This affects our ideas about design sensibility, about aesthetics, and about sustainability, all concepts bound by an ethical design approach.

We will explore five aspects of this paradigm shift:

1. What is this paradigm shift, and how does this impact on interior design both as a profession and as a discipline in evolution?

2. What are these new and emerging ideas and concepts in terms of design sensibility, design processes, and design intentions?

3. What are the ethical implications of these changing times?

4. What is our social responsibility with regards to the design choices that we make?

5. How do we design integrating sustainable thinking and ethical concerns?

We will look at what this paradigm shift is and how interior design is contextualized through the four concepts of design sensibility, social responsibility, ethics, and sustainability. We will examine these ideas through case studies and examples of projects that put these ideas into practice. When we speak about design intentions here, we need to think about a sustainable and universal approach that supports design for all types of people and all types of situations (Mace, 1997).

Ethics becomes a fundamental component of the design process as we consider our choices in terms of who we are designing for, what ethical issues can and do arise, and how we can design for the broadest possible population. We cannot ignore the political and economic aspects of the environment that drive design process thinking as much as psychological or physiological needs do. The social aspect of an increasingly crowded world with cultural and fundamental subjective differences must also be taken into consideration.

We cannot escape the fact of our dwindling world resources and what this means in terms of the everyday design decisions that we make. For example, we cannot begin a design without considering how much of what is already there should be saved, recycled, or reused. Integrating sustainable design practices into design processes is essential to designing appropriate and sustainable interior environments (Winchip, 2007). We need to ask ethical questions alongside design questions, broadening the way we think about how we use materials in a sustainable manner (McDonough & Braungart, 2002).

As we have seen throughout this book, when we design, we factor in multiple contexts and ideas, from design elements and principles to psychological, social, and practical needs. We do so with certain value assumptions about our society. Our fundamental beliefs govern our lives, our values determine who we are, and ultimately underpin the realities that we create for our lives and ourselves.

It is in this spirit of values that we introduce the concepts of ethics, sustainability, and design for all people in the universal sense. Before exploring these ideas further, let's understand how this era in which we live is changing, by understanding the changing society as going through a paradigm shift.

Defining the Concept of a Paradigm Shift

We live in an era of shifting paradigms. In *From Power to Partnership*, Montouri and Conti state that "the twentieth century has seen some of the most dramatic changes in history. . . . [T]his massive outburst of human creativity . . . is so overwhelming . . . there is a massive paradigm shift" (1993, pp. 5–7).

Montouri and Conti define *paradigm* as

A set of assumptions about reality. These assumptions are so pervasive we don't even know that they're just hypotheses. They form an invisible set of beliefs about the world; beliefs that we take to be reality, and they function as a compass that guides our lives at an unconscious level. (pp. 8–9)

The impact of global marketplaces on the production and acquisition of goods; notions of users in mass markets and advertising; changing lifestyles and the impact of technology on living; changing social roles and patterns of family: These are all current world changes that affect our lives daily.

How Is This Paradigm Shift Manifested?

These paradigm shifts into a post-industrial society have had a profound impact on the way that design is produced. Cityscapes are changing at the macro level, while people's lives and the social nature of their existence are also changing dramatically at the micro level. Lives have become more insular, technology oriented, and less community based. And yet, global changes and virtual realms make possible a whole new range of relationships among people, objects, and the environment. Experiences are increasingly mediated by information and communication technologies, and this has an impact on both interior design concepts and spatial configurations. Social norms are changing as new and perceived psychological relationships affect both the self and our relationships with other people.

Returning to Design Sensibility and Aesthetics

Although we are engaged in these shifts, we must remember that we design for a client or user, creating an interior space, object, or building. The root of our profession is situated in the design intentions that guide our decision making, and these intentions are based in concepts and processes that integrate aesthetic thinking and values that govern the choices that we make.

How can we explore and develop a design sensibility that informs our design process thinking in the context of this complex and changing world? How can our design sensibility capture the aesthetic intent and meaning that we need to bring to the project, while understanding the ethical contexts that it requires? Developing a design sensibility enables us to see the broader picture, even though this may not be evident at first. However, it is through understanding design sensibility that we come to appreciate ethics and complexity in design projects. Let's examine this idea further.

Developing a Design Sensibility through Design Process and Inquiry

Tracee Vetting-Wolf, a product designer, is concerned about how design is understood in the workplace and in society. She explores the way that design sensibility informs our thinking and how we use the design process to inform our decision making as a complex process. Tracee considers the design process as a rich and inquiry-based process. She believes that we must develop a design sensibility and make others aware of its usefulness and value through our own reflection and how we inquire during the design process.

Case Study 9.1 explores how Tracee sees the design process theoretically, and how her own classroom experiences with Gunther Dittmar of the School of Architecture at the University of Minnesota helped her to develop design sensibility.

As we see from the different examples in Case Study 9.1, students find their own unique ways to explore the same design problem. They develop a design sensibility using simple paper and geometric forms they manipulate.

In the following case study (9.2), we see how the student in interior design develops a design sensibility through the development of a concept of healthy eating for an exhibition booth design.

Design sensibility evolves from this type of exploration. Ideas about "goodness" are developed using aesthetic forms and passages that guide the user through the interior spaces and forms that are created. Aesthetics integrate with form and feeling that transform the concept into an experienced reality that adds meaning to the food being sold.

Design in a Global World

In this era of paradigm shifts, design sensibility shifts from the purely aesthetic experiences we see with the two case studies to including issues dealing with the social, sustainable, and ethical contexts of the design process. These contexts are increasingly integrated into the design process as we consider sustainable approaches or universal needs as integral parts of intentions, alongside client needs, building contexts, and functional relationships. Whether it is the way that we choose materials, deal with social issues within the project, or design for special or delicate situations, we are adding new complexities to the design process that we need to understand and reflect upon.

Values in the Design Process

When we look at social, sustainable, and ethical contexts in the design process, we return to the issue of values and how they impact on our design process thinking and subsequent design interventions. Our values shape our behavior and attitudes, and socialize us into behaviors that, in turn, determine the designs that we create. These are underlying values, in that we are not always aware that they influence our design decision making.

A good example of the effects of underlying values in design thinking is how gender is thought of in terms of design. We like to think of design processes as value-free. And yet, as Daphne Spain (1992) explains, in many cultures, social roles determine status, status determines power of one gender at the expense of another, and these power relations are entrenched in the design of interior spaces. When spaces represent the social constructs of school, home, or the political environment, people are manipulated by the belief systems that are perpetuated through the design solution in the first place (Spain, 1992). Let's examine how gender and spaces are social and political next.

Space as Social and Political

In her book *Gendered Spaces*, Daphne Spain (1992) suggests that the socially and mutually dependent

Tracee's Ideas about Developing the Design Process through Design Sensibility

Design sensibility is a multifaceted skill and talent that leverages creativity and logic, and has defied concise definition due to the variability with which it is acquired and practiced. Design sensibility can be understood as a layered effect of knowledge and practice. Design process is a practice that affords design sensibility. Design process and design sensibility afford design knowledge. Design knowledge feeds design process and outputs products of knowing.

I. Process: Making Process Palpable (Progression Exercise)

When I was in graduate school getting my master's in architecture, we did an exercise developed by a professor there (Associate Professor Gunter Dittmar, College of Design, Department of Architecture, University of Minnesota; http://arch.cdes.umn.edu/faculty/Roster/GunterDittmar.html). The exercise effectively demonstrates design process and inquiry in an understandable way; it represents an abstract example of design process that others can understand, particularly if they actually do the exercise. As simple as this may sound, it is incredibly powerful. Not only do you start to realize what you know but you start to realize that there is a lot more to know and that you can consciously uncover it with discipline and practice. As a designer, this is an incredibly powerful tool of practice. As a non-designer, this is an equally powerful tool of understanding.

Here is how Professor Dittmar outlines the exercise: Design is a game of find and seek, where the seeker does not know what he/she is looking for until he/she has found it (paraphrased from the Introduction to H. Janson's *History of Art*).

OBJECTIVES

To investigate design as a synergistic process of creativity and logic; a process of systematic inquiry, exploration, "discovery," and "unfolding;" a discourse and a dialogue between emerging thought and simultaneously emerging physical form.

TASK/METHOD

Beginning with a planar, square, or rectangular sheet of paper, you are asked to perform an "operation" on it (which subsequently will become the basis for a whole sequence of moves). The operation may consist of one, or several, cuts and/or folds of your own choosing. However, after you have executed this operation on the paper, it remains topologically the same for the remainder of the sequence (i.e., you have visually "defined" *the nature of the operation*: its general form vocabulary, its geometric order, and its rules of execution).

You are then asked to generate a sequence of models by repeating this operation in such a way that the series forms a progression. Each time you execute a new operation, you are required to start with a new sheet of paper and repeat all previously performed operations before adding the new one. Thus, sheet 0 is the plain sheet of paper you started with, sheet 1 shows the execution of operation 1, sheet 2 operation 1 + 2, sheet 3 operation 1 + 2 + 3, etc. After operation 1, you are free to add the next operation either by executing it on the base sheet of paper, or by performing it on a previously made operation. You are free to change the dimensions and proportions of the cuts and/or folds that constitute your operation. But after you have defined the operation you cannot change its formal character or order (e.g., if your operation started out with rectangular cuts and/or folds you cannot, all of a sudden, arbitrarily insert a diagonal cut or fold later on in the sequence).

There should be at least six steps (models) within one sequence (not counting sheet 0), and the whole series should aim at a rich but coherent, evolving, formal logic with a definite end to it; that is, like a story come to some sort of formal resolution or conclusion (however many steps this takes). In Figure A we see a simple example of the end sequence.

So what's the big deal? If you do this exercise, you'll quickly become engrossed in a dialogue with the paper and your own set of decisions. You'll realize you're making informed decisions based on the rules and your previous move, you're executing with intention but not with a premeditated end in mind, you're actively considering and reconsidering the decisions you make (reflective awareness), you're understanding and developing strategies based on consequences and opportunities that your decisions provide you with . . . the richness goes on. (Note: this is not a methodology or prescription or any kind of formula.)

II. Process + Design Sensibility: There is no right or wrong, but there is better or worse

How do we judge better or worse? This is part of the design culture known as the design critique. We get together and talk over the design decisions and strategies employed to get to a particular design. The designer explains the process and decisions and the discussion about the quality of those decisions ensues. How did the designer use design elements? Do the design strategies achieve the designer's goals (as well as serve the stakeholders' and users' needs)? What rules did the designer work with and to what extent did the treatment of those rules achieve an elegant form or experience? The application of design sensibility is not arbitrary and is unique to designers. Designers actively consider things like composition, light and shadow, proportion and scale, spatiality, repetition and interruption, shape, contrast, grouping and proximity, flow, orientation, sequencing, etc. They are taught to consider these things and execute a sensible consideration of them. Truth be known, I forget the "design principles" that I was taught—I can't list them, but I use them all the time. They have become ingrained into my subconscious, and with practice, they've become part of my intuition. It's my job to articulate this intuition to others so they understand the meaning of the decision.

Design sensibility can be achieved in personal practice, on an individual level. The critique pulls the design into the social realm, and makes the assessment aspect of designing more explicit, overt, and tangible. Critiques help weed away some of the unhelpful thoughts and decisions, and recognize the more successful ones. The critique isn't just about the product, but also about the decisions regarding how it got that way (T. Vetting-Wolf, Design Notes Part I and II, 9/17/2007).

Figure A • Example of a paper-folding exercise

continued on the next page

continued from the previous page

If we look at other examples of this same exercise, we see different manifestations of the same set of objectives and project directives.

Figure B • Example of folding exercise

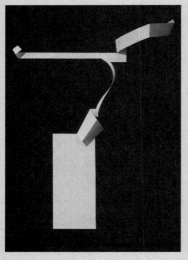

Figure C • Example of folding exercise

relationship between gender and space is what creates power relations. She suggests that:

> Spatial arrangements between the sexes are socially created, and when they provide access to valued knowledge for men while reducing access to that knowledge for women, the organization of space may perpetuate status difference . . . To quote geographer Doreen Massey, "It is not just that the spatial is socially constructed; the social is spatially constructed too." (pp. 3–4)

Spain argues that space is socially constructed geographically, architecturally, and institutionally, in the sense that, as she suggests:

> Over the course of the life cycle, everyone experiences one or more of the institutions of family, education, and the labor force. . . . Equally important are the spaces within which these institutional activities occur. Families must be analyzed in the context of dwellings, education in the context of schools, and labor in the context of workplaces. (p. 10)

Spaces impose on us and create the social constructions that govern social and power relations between men and women (Poldma, 1999). It is for this reason that we must understand how social institutions are manifested through how we design interior spaces.

Conversely, as we have seen throughout this book, people have the capacity to make sense of their surroundings, and with the changing times, are more apt to define and create their lived spaces around what they need, as situated in their values, their gender, or their particular cultural contexts. Thus, the user and their "voice" (expressed as needs) become vital in the design process. The interior designer can identify the personal and subjective needs of people, and situate the power relations when aware of them, framing these experiences within interior designs that support people and understand what institutional constructions are at work, or even perhaps breaking down the social relations in favor of a more equitable solution (Poldma, 1999; Vaikla-Poldma, 2003).

The Modern Fast Food Concept

The aim of this design project given in a second-year interior design studio was to design a booth for a trade show for a hospitality industry conference in a large exhibition hall. Students had to choose the trade show booth location and size, and create a concept for either a food concession chain, a hotel chain, or service, all promoting the idea of well-being and healthy lifestyle choices.

The student chose to develop a food concession concept based on healthy eating with the idea of selling the product to hotel chains to include in their food service program. After doing extensive research and program development, she created a concept of "goodness" of healthy food, and designed the trade show booth as a place where people could come and experience this goodness.

Figure A • Initial concept sketches of the walk-through of the space

Figure B • Model development of the walk-through of the space; view 1

continued on the next page

continued from the previous page

To be able to visualize and construct the experience, the student created a small model of the idea that she had in her head, which she then photographed from the scale and eye view of the user.

Here we see the views of her space as a user might experience it, and the resultant perspectives drawn from the abstract model development.

Finally, she documents the concept through plan, elevation, and perspective views.

Figure C • Model development of the walk-through of the space; view 2

Figure D • Plan layout of proposed fast-food kiosk concept

Figure E • Typical elevation of the proposed fast-food kiosk concept

Figure F • Perspective walk-through of Raphaelle's final concept

Understanding the Voice of the User/Client

Design solution possibilities begin with the client/ designer relationship. This is uncovered during the collaboration and dialogue between the designer and the client, allowing the appropriate contexts for the project to emerge. Designer and user become co-participants in the production of the design concept through the elaboration of the necessary contexts that are uncovered. Designers must have the tools and capabilities to judge and determine how user needs might be expressed in the exploration of new design possibilities.

While the first part of this process is speaking with the client to understand their needs, the second part of this process is the collaboration, wherein the voice of the client is integrated with the design intent. The interior designer gives the client informed and ethical choices, and they both work together to for-mulate a functional and pleasing spatial environment. The resulting space reflects the values intended by both client and user, as interpreted by the interior designer as an agent of the client's needs and desires (Poldma, 1999, pp. 98–99).

A Cultural Approach to the Design Process

When discussing values, we inevitably arrive at the impact of culture on design contexts. Cultural aware-ness means situating the design process within an understanding of the particular cultural milieu the design must exist and adapt in.

Culture is a broad concept that encompasses spe-cific groups of which we are all a part, as well as the cultural realities of a global world. Individuals carry their cultural influences with them wherever they go, and sometimes, whether through immigration, war, or famine, entire populations can shift from one country to another. Although relocation can be forced, more often people move to seek a better life for themselves and their loved ones. Whatever the reason, the movement of people is increasing as borders become more open and economies boom in certain parts of the world.

Increasingly, students at the bachelor's and mas-ter's level are investigating the impact of cultural practices and cultural awareness on design decisions and aesthetic choices. For example, if you study the concept of "feeling at home," be it in the personal sanctuary of the home or within the cultural community, this will change with your identity within the cultural milieu. Whether it be a Somali family trying to integrate in the Midwestern United States (Hadjiyanni, 2007) or the Muslim community trying to adapt to the local, foreign urban milieu (Dubois, 2006), students study how each cultural adaptation informs and creates new issues and contexts within the design process. For example, as Cherif Amor (2006) states when studying the Arab-American home interior: "Space appropriation and use of artifacts illustrate the rooted sensory need to reaffirm the attachment to the homeland's social and cultural values; additionally, these trends symbolize the enduring values of the group and render the home interior a space apart" (p. 1).

A culture and its values are inseparable, and each culture derives its meanings from objects and environments in very different ways.

Social Responsibility and Interior Design

One problem with the new global world and today's technological revolution is the increased disparity between those who do and those who do not live this type of existence. This exciting realm of worldwide communication and flexible environments depends on the virtual and physical components that transform spatial dimensions. But for some, this world is a distant one, in particular for those outside the work world or without the means to achieve financial independence. I spoke about this when considering how to build "human issues" into design studio experiences:

> Design is usually linked to new products, technologies, and aesthetics that respond to economic well-being, and while these new modes of living and working are redefining our spatial experiences when we are engaged with technology and the global milieu, concurrently there is also an increased global, social and cultural disparity between people who do and do not live this type of existence. (Poldma, 2006, p. 48)

Building human issues into the design process means thinking about the more human aspects of the design, such as how to empathize with people in different situations in life, be they economic, physical, or social. It means understanding different social contexts throughout one's design career. If we are to be ethical designers, the social role of what we do cannot be ignored.

One way to understand early on what it means to live differently is through the design project experience itself. For example, in Chapters 2 and 3 we looked at first-year students who were researching life in an urban environment very different from their own, while designing for three generations in a working-class part of the city. Students examined the idea of "family" by exploring different family types, such as a single mother living with her daughter and mother, or three university students living together. Theoretical and aesthetic concepts were studied with regards to housing types, the urban milieu, and the historical context of the older neighborhood. The students explored the local cultural dynamics and complex social issues of the area, alongside aesthetic and functional considerations (Poldma, 2006).

Ethical Design Process

In Chapter 8 we introduced the idea of ethics as this relates to the considerations given to the transformation of the design concept into the built project. Here we will consider other ethical choices we make

> **BUILDING BLOCK** • *A great way to get involved in interdisciplinary and cross-disciplinary design contexts is to use your own experience to guide you. Developing your own sense of community is one way; volunteering to help others in a different economic or social situation is another. For example, volunteering in a seniors' home or community center is a great way to meet people in different stages of life, especially if you do not know many older people. Creating new experiences that give you perspective help you to evolve as a person and as an interior designer.*

as designers, such as being transparent with the client and by making sure that the integrity of the agreed-upon design is maintained. How can you (and should you) develop an ethical approach within your design process?

At the outset of your meetings with a client, you listen and learn about the user and client needs, and document the ways that they use and occupy the space. This helps you, as the interior designer, to understand who they are, how they live, and what is of importance to them. However, this also means that you have a means to see what they need in a somewhat different light. You can temporarily step into their shoes and empathize with their situation. Ethical considerations begin when you situate your design thinking within their contexts, however temporarily, to try to grasp how your designing might help the user better adapt to his interior environment. Let's illustrate this idea with an examination of how we bring about change through the design process.

This begins to touch on the concept of "intentional change." In *The Design Way*, Harold Nelson and Erik Stolterman (2003) speak about designing as intentional change when they discuss how a design approach includes several fundamental elements, including the concept of "desiderata" and "care taking" (p. 131).

First, they present the idea of desiderata with the argument that problem solving in and of itself to produce change is not enough, and that good intentions can land one in trouble. To be effective, design intentions invoking change must be produced to create the conditions for an "imagined and desired situation" (p. 133). Here they talk about this dilemma:

> Too often, good intentions that arise from the recognition of a need for change lead to paralysis . . . strategies for change . . . lead to dead-ends, rather than next-best steps. Some of these dead ends include analysis paralysis, value analysis and holistic analysis (i.e., attempting to be comprehensive). Analysis paralysis occurs when too much divergent information is generated, without any effective means for convergence. (p. 133)

If you recall from Chapters 3 and 4, although we look at all possible contexts, we do so collecting specific information. We need to understand how to sift out the unimportant elements in order to zero in on what is important and what is not. We ask specific questions to get the responses that we need.

Let's continue with Nelson and Stolterman's ideas:

> Value paralysis occurs when any and every value system is taken into account without any means of transcending the differences and diversity. The paralysis of holism occurs when there is no automatic means for bounding or limiting comprehensive expansion.
>
> This unfortunate situation exists because all of these strategies have a common foundation in "problem solving." Their focus is on *that-which-is* (description and explanation), versus *that-which-ought-to-be* (ethics and morality), without consideration for *that-which-is-desired* (desiderata).
>
> . . . [T]hese three approaches to intentional change have the following correspondence. What we *want* can be seen by our aesthetics. What we believe ought to be related to our ethics. What is corresponds to reason. In any particular situation, however, there is never just one approach. Depending on what we perceive as the basis for intentional change, there will be different proportions among the three, aesthetics, ethics, and reason. In real-world contexts, everything is a blend . . . desiderata are about what we intend the world to be, and is the *integrative outcome of all three approaches in concert*. (pp. 133–135)

It is very important to understand this concept because we make choices when we design in order to respond to these three different aspects of the design process. In essence, we use our reason to functionally lay out the interior space and make sure that everything fits, while using our ethics and sense of empathy for the user to create the best possible design concept. This parallels our earlier ideas about the real, the possible, and the ideal when we examine what is actual, what is possible, and what is the best, ideal situation that we can conceive of for our clients and users. We must design the space by expanding our vision of the concept, but yet not get trapped by the elements that might cause us to get swallowed up in the idea or aesthetic concept at the expense of other vital aspects such as cost or time. Conversely, we need to be sure that the functions and needs are met, and allow aesthetic ideas to frame these as well, striking a balance between meeting needs and allowing the ideal and possible to emerge.

Secondly, Nelson and Stolterman develop the idea of "care taking." This parallels our discussion in Chapters 7 and 8, where we tackled the job of turning our ideas into built design solutions. We spoke about design production, which includes transferring a design idea into a built project with complex technical and contractual elements. Nelson and Stolterman suggest that this production is integral to the design process as a form of care taking in that we take care to choose appropriate materials, ensure the production process is respected and controlled, and understand the production process early on in our initial design decision making (pp. 230–231).

Understanding Universal Approaches in Interior Design Process Thinking

A third element of the design process is the recognition of universal design approaches. This means that we design considering all types of people in all situations. For example, when we first discussed the design of a doorknob in Chapter 1, we compared how an industrial designer, an architect, and an interior designer might look at the problem. If we turn our attention to the person who will use the doorknob, we can consider the round knob versus the lever-style handle. In a universal approach, a lever handle will be usable by everyone at any age, whereas a round knob would be impossible for someone to turn if they have severe arthritis, thereby not adapting to the user and their real, actual physical needs.

A universal approach to designing considers how design can be better integrated into the needs of all types of people in society through universal principles (Mace, 1997; Lidwell, Holden, & Butler, 2003). If we

apply this concept to interiors, they can be conceived from the outset, by understanding situations and needs of people in all walks of life. For example, as our population ages, universal design decisions can be made to help people adapt longer within their own environment, thereby diminishing health care costs as people who can live at home longer are not a cost nor burden on society (Poldma, 2006). When we consider design intentions as part of a universal design approach, we broaden the discourse of design for all types of people within a variety of contexts and situations.

A Sustainable Design Approach

Throughout this book we have considered sustainable approaches. This can be as simple as selecting materials that are ecologically sound choices or recycling a building's interior for a renovation project. On a more complex level, a sustainable design begins with a thorough understanding of the issues facing our planet, and understanding the full impact of our choices on ecological issues (Winchip, 2007). In *Sustainable Design for Interior Environments* (2007), Susan Winchip suggests how we can build a design process around sustainable strategies through proper management. She contends that an understanding of how sustainable projects are built is an essential context of the design process. As she notes, "To successfully design sustainable interiors requires an interior designer's commitment to the principles of sustainability" (p. 261).

This requires more than just selecting green materials. This means rethinking how we design, and what we do to give back in what we place into the environment. No matter what type of interior, whether within a "green" building or a building being renovated that is over 100 years old, everything you select and use—from the environmental systems to the lighting to the materials and furnishings—should be chosen with consideration toward the impact on the environment.

Current non-sustainable building practices, such as demolition of an entire space to fill it with something new, are no longer acceptable even in large commercial buildings. Increasingly, existing buildings demand recycling and reusing as a fundamental element of the design process.

The depletion of world resources is evident every time we select a material that is not sustainable or ecologically sound. This is fundamental to our work as interior designers and the choices we make. Whenever we make design decisions, we impact on the built environment. These, too, are ethical considerations. A sustainable approach to the design process means incorporating essentially two things:

1. Making ethical choices that do not create waste for the planet when possible
2. Considering the "bigger picture" of the built interior and its impact on the environment

Considering the bigger picture means integrating the sustainable approaches in more fundamental ways into societal structures (McDonough & Braungart, 2002). McDonough and Braungart, in their seminal book *Cradle to Cradle—Remaking the Way We Make Things*, suggest that everything we produce is part of a larger ecosystem, and that we must incorporate social and political decisions alongside economic and aesthetic ones when we design, whether it be products, buildings, or interiors. Their concept of cradle-to-cradle is a fundamental concept we need to understand and integrate into our design process thinking.

DEVELOPING A HOLISTIC DESIGN PROCESS

Let's return here to the fundamental components of the design process: space and its occupants. We have examined the more physical components of space and how we construct an environment physically and virtually. We have also discussed how we respond to the spatial environment within other contexts such as:

- our personal perceptions and reactions
- our experience of the space, its surround, the virtual realms associated with it
- the social relations that we may have within a space
- our capacity to perform certain tasks and activities
- the social, political, and economic contexts within which the space is designed
- the material and systems choices that we make, and how these impact on the built and natural ecological environment
- the aesthetic, psychological, and physiological contexts within which the space is conceived

Whereas we have explored design sensibility, social issues, sustainability, and ethics as separate concepts, try to think of them as parts of a whole. Any holistic design process must incorporate multiple understandings and contexts. We always use our intimate view of people and their needs, along with the multiple aspects of designed interior space, as our guide. The contexts that we have evolved round out the design process, add complexity to the overall design considerations, and hopefully make the resultant design solutions richer.

Developing a design sensibility is the foundation of our aesthetic capacity to consider the design problem, ethical considerations are vital and sometimes challenge taken-for-granted ways of designing, and sustainable practices should form the foundation of design thinking rather than being added on at the end, collapsing ethics and sensibility within its context each time we begin a design project.

We will now complete our understanding of the design process by looking at what lies in the future. How can we as interior designers continue to move the design process forward? Design as a process and as research will be explored next.

BIBLIOGRAPHY

Amor, C. M. (2006). Arab-American Muslims' home interior in the U.S.: Meanings, uses and communication. *Journal of Interior Design, 32*(1), 1–16.

Brawley, E. (1997). *Designing for Alzheimer's disease.* New York: John Wiley & Sons.

Dittmer, G. (2007). *Developing a design sensibility.* Design projects from course given by professor Gunter Dittmar, College of Design, Department of Architecture, University of Minnesota; http://cdes.umn.edu/faculty/Roster/GunterDittmar.html

Dubois, J. (2006). La complexité de l'aménagement des lieux de culte muselman à Montréal : au déla de la materialité de l'objet et de l'organisation spatiale. Unpublished master's thesis. Montreal: University of Montreal, Author, 2006.

Friedman, A. T. (1998). *Women and the making of the modern house: A social and architectural history.* New York: Harry N. Abrams.

Gedenryd, H. (1998). *How designers work.* Retrieved from http://asip.lucs.lu.sc/People/Hendrik.Gedenryd/HowDesignersWork/

Hadjiyanni, T. (2006). Bounded choices: Somali women constructing difference in Minnesota housing. *Journal of Interior Design, 32*(2), 17–27.

Hall, E. T. (1981). *Beyond Culture.* New York: Anchor Books.

Mace, R. (1997). *Universal design: Housing for the lifespan of all people.* New York State University, New York: The Center for Universal Design.

McDonough, W., & Braungart, M. (2002). *Cradle to cradle: Remaking the way we make things.* New York: North Point Press.

Mitchell, C. T. (1993). *Redefining designing: From form to experience.* New York: Van Nostrand Reinhold.

Montouri, A., & Conti, I. (1993). *From power to partnership: Creating the future of love, work, and community.* New York: HarperCollins.

Nelson, H., & Stolterman, E. (2003). *The design way: intentional change in an unpredictable world.* Englewood Cliffs, NJ: Educational Technology Publications.

Paperzak, A. (1986). Values: Subjective-objective. *The Journal of Value Inquiry, 20,* 71–80.

Poldma, T. (1999). *Gender, design and education: The politics of voice.* Unpublished master's thesis. Montreal: McGill University, Author.

Poldma, T. (2006, July/August). Adapting the interior environment: A case study using light, color and research as catalysts for interior design problem solving. *Interiors and Sources,* 58–59.

Poldma, T. (2006). Building human issues into design studio experiences: Empathy, humanity and social responsibility. *In-form: The Journal of Architecture, Design and Material Culture, 6,* The Human Aspect of Design, 47–57.

Ross, S. D. (Ed.). (1994). *Art and its significance: An anthology of aesthetic theory.* Albany, NY: State University of New York Press.

Spain, D. (1992). *Gendered spaces.* Chapel Hill, NC: University of North Carolina Press.

Vetting-Wolf, T. (2007, September). *Design notes,* New York: Author.

Winchip, S. (2007). *Sustainable design for interior environments.* New York: Fairchild Books.

Chapter Ten

FROM PROCESS TO PRODUCT TO RESEARCH

Objective

Throughout this book, we have explored the design process from the perspective of creating designs. Whether developing an aesthetic design sensibility, understanding ethical and sustainable issues, or integrating functional elements and requirements into the design process, interior designers seek to better the human condition through holistic process thinking.

In this last chapter we will consider the questions we ask that require more in-depth inquiry. What is design research and inquiry for interior designers? Whether you are a practicing interior designer, a new graduate getting started in the field, or someone interested in post-design research at the master's and doctoral level, you may be interested in asking questions that consider issues of importance to the development of interior design as a discipline. The practices of any evolving profession are grounded and articulated through the theory and processes that it develops.

We have explored concepts of research as this pertains to investigating aspects of the design project, and how we might include evidence-based research in our design project work. This chapter will explore design research from a broader perspective. What is design research? What is design research within the practices and processes of interior design? We will look at different ways to theorize about design and how to go about developing design research through inquiry.

We will evolve three main ideas throughout the concepts we will explore in this chapter:

- What is practice-based inquiry and how does this inform interior design practice?
- What is design research?
- What are different forms of research, and how might we understand the complexity inherent in design and its processes through research?

This is by no means authoritative or definitive; our goal in this chapter is to open up several different ideas about interior design inquiry, research, and design approaches that help explain the nature of the complexity we experience when using the design process, with the aim of opening new avenues for further exploration.

RESEARCH IN PRACTICE AND PROCESS

To fully understand and appreciate interior design practices and processes, we must, as interior designers, reflect on what we do and how. One way to understand issues within design is to study the design problem within the environment where it occurs. This is a type of practice-based research, where we examine and research the conditions surrounding the designed interior space, its surrounding interior/exterior, and broader urban, social, and cultural contexts, and its users and their real-world lived experiences of the space once it has been built. Michael Peters (1997) suggests that we must find "ways of studying our own practices." This means placing the responsibility of questioning practices and exposing meanings squarely on the shoulders of research (Vaikla-Poldma, 2003, p. 116). This is done by situating research in the concrete experiences and situations of practitioners where the situations arise, as in when educators study their school learning environments (Carr & Kemmis, 1986).

When we seek to understand what we do and how, we enter into forms of design inquiry, where we question and develop the specificity of a discipline. Interior design problem solving can be studied and understood within a broader context of design inquiry, where questions are asked and issues are studied.

One way we can advance our profession is by reflecting upon our practices. In the profession, interior design has made great gains in creating licensing guidelines and practices through various initiatives, especially in North America (Guerin & Martin, 2001), including professional accreditation of interior design programs and licensing in some countries. However, on the more theoretical side of interior design education and practice, there are many aspects of interior design knowledge that can still be developed, in particular when it comes to developing theory situated within the specificity of the interior design process as it is informed by other disciplinary theories and practices (Chalmers & Close, 2007). And whereas interior design is an evolving profession moving rapidly toward becoming a discipline, the popular media (in North America particularly) still sends counter-productive images of what interior design is to the public, creating confusion and a muddled idea of who we are and what we do (Vaikla-Poldma, 2003; Caan, 2007; Mitchell & Rudner, 2007). This is due in part to the historical evolution of the profession from diverse backgrounds and disciplinary stances (Turpin, 2001), and in part to the recent development of interior design as a profession in its own right in some parts of the world but not in others.

DESIGN PROCESS AS INQUIRY

Design as inquiry includes studying interior design processes and practices using diverse research methods. Practice-, inquiry-, and evidence-based research as well as the development of a pragmatic or philosophical stance are all ways to document interior design processes and practices, and to document and advance interior design knowledge. The profession of interior design can define its own specificity by studying what makes the profession unique within the built environment disciplines.

Interior designers have a unique way of understanding intimate human experiences, designing spaces to fit people, and understanding how this is integrated with the scale of the interior environment. As John Weigand (2006) suggests:

> It is the *design process* that defines the unique contribution of the interior designer. The process requires knowledge that is both uniquely broad and also not very pure in the sense that it intersects frequently with other disciplines. . . . It is a knowledge based not on the parts but on the whole. . . . Interior designers apply their knowledge of design and the built environment to solving problems at the interior scale and at the level of direct human experience. (p. 30)

A full range of design research that is situated within interior design practices and processes can be studied looking at the interdisciplinary contexts and how these add richness to the discipline. We can develop new knowledge and stimulate thinking specific to interior design methods, processes, and ways of doing. This type of research includes understanding the underlying values and ideas that frame what interior designers do and how. Capturing and promoting our own specificity goes a long way to getting out messages to stakeholders about who we are and what we do, as integral players in the built environment.

As interior designers, through the design process we naturally construct knowledge through our design practices. This reflects what Donald Schon and others refer to as reflective practices (Schon, 1987; Weigand, 2006), reflective thinking situated in practice-based research. We infuse the design process with inquiry and judgment, much like the "figuring out" of scientific inquiry.

PRACTICE-BASED RESEARCH

Interior design is a practice that uses research and inquiry in many ways. One way to understand the methods and processes that inform interior design and its practices is to do practice-based research. In simple terms, this means being critically reflective and situating the research within the practices that give rise to the situations wherein design is done. Practice-based research is common in education and disciplines such as architecture, where practices are examined with a critically reflective or humanistic stance (Schon, 1987).

When we talk about research for interior design, we want to study interior design methods and processes, history and theory, thinking and doing, and practices situated in designing interior spaces, to name but a few areas of interest. Practice-based research allows us to move further in our design thinking, and to move beyond design itself into understanding and knowledge creation.

Interior Design as Process and Research

Throughout this book, you have seen how the design process is used to conceive and build interior space. What you have learned is somewhat pragmatic in that we design physical space using material and immaterial elements. Material elements include the finishes, forms, and means by which we offer safe, clean, functional, and detailed interior spaces. We consider functional layouts, the health and well-being of users

through the choices that we make in the environmental systems, and look and feel through the aesthetic aspects of the project.

We create designs and infuse design concepts with iterative thinking, judgment, and criticism. Research-based practices help to give the design depth and context. These aspects of interior design add to the way we conceive spaces that help us to create our specificity. But this is not enough. These very pragmatic situations and practices need theoretical foundations. Let's examine some thoughts on this next.

Examining the Role of Theory in Interior Design Education and Practice

When we consider theory in our education, we consider why we do the things that we do. One of the things you might want to examine when you design is how you do what you do. Whether we are teaching interior design, practicing, or doing both, this aspect of designing is reflective and requires a theoretical underpinning. Chalmers and Close (2007) suggest that:

> interior designers should use theory to enrich both its disciplinary education and its practice. . . . The place of theory is significant as it encourages both students and practitioners to think critically about the creative design process. It is not enough to merely consider what to make but it is necessary to reflect upon how and why it is made. The future relevance of design theory is to inform and encourage designers to think about significant concepts related to contemporary society.

Theory thus informs practice, and practice can subsequently inform theory. Reflecting on our designs, as we have seen thus far, is a natural part of the design process, whether it is making critical judgments or deciding which design merits development. We judge and critique our work before, during, and after it is transformed into the built reality, and then once again when we see how the design recipients use and appropriate the spaces we have designed. Critically reflecting on design practices and documenting and studying these practices and processes help us to develop theories specific to interior design.

A PRAGMATIC AND SYSTEMATIC DESIGN PROCESS APPROACH

The design process described in this book allows you, as a professional interior designer, to develop the knowledge and skills you will need to be able to solve pragmatic problems using both theory and practice-based skills. You acquire knowledge that is explicit, by using the different tools of the design process learned throughout this book, to formulate appropriate design solutions and responses.

You can also develop critical reflection tools to judge your ideas and their worth, develop post-design evaluation processes, and improve your design skills through the iterative design process and more formal mechanisms such as the post-occupancy evaluation (Guerin & Martin, 2001; Winchip, 2007, Vaikla-Poldma, 2003). These mechanisms are a first step in developing inquiry-based design-process thinking, and basing designs on more systematic thinking.

A Pragmatic Design Process Informed by Theory

A pragmatic design process acknowledges several real components. When designing, you are concerned with the real, physical attributes of interior space. You are also concerned with the more sensual and immaterial aspects of the environment, such as lighting, how people feel, what they experience, and so on. These are ideas that are based on pragmatic ways of solving design situations: We explore, we examine, and we design both with our ideas and within the real-world situations in which the designs are located.

Part of this pragmatic approach is the research and analysis of the design situation or the problem at hand. You research all the contexts of the project and ask questions about the relative issues, reflecting upon the situation you are faced with. Whether it is children in a cancer ward or the elderly who have trouble seeing and negotiating their way, each user has specific needs and contexts that you must reflect upon.

Another part of this pragmatic approach is how you deal with the contexts and problems during the design process. Quite often we see how people live and want to improve on their condition in ways that we may not necessarily yet understand. You question how we have provided environments for these people in the past, how we can improve the spaces through the designs that we provide, and how we can create something that the user or client could not have imagined. The desire that we have as designers pushes us to conceive of new ways of doing things, or to improve our design practices through knowledge.

Broad Research Methods and Processes Used in Interior Design

There are a variety of ways that we can develop design research for interior design questions, and we will introduce a few current design research practices and emergent ways to develop design research and inquiry approaches next.

Environment-Behavior (E-B) Approaches

In Chapters 3 and 4 we considered the psychological perceptions that we have of spaces and how we deal with our own personal space. We looked at ideas first developed almost 40 years ago by Robert Sommer (1969), and how Sommer developed a theory for explaining knowledge within the environment from an architectural perspective framed in behavioral psychology, where user behavior is considered as two types of spaces:

> The first refers to the emotionally charged zone around each person . . . which helps regulate the spacing of individuals. . . . The second usage refers to the processes by which people mark out and personalize the spaces they inhabit. (Sommer, 1969, p. viii)

Sommer suggests an exercise to determine a person's "invisible boundary" by moving closer to them until they complain (Sommer, 1969, p. 26). As a student you learn about personal boundaries through spatial proximities and ideal spatial relationships, and plan arrangements for typical interpersonal and personal relationships with space. For example, you might learn about spatial proximity, or "touch and comfort zones" as developed by Dr. John Fruin (Ching, 1987, pp. 64–74; Panero & Zelnik, 1979, pp.

40–41). This is but one simple example of how we can use theories to help inform our design process choices.

With regard to environment-behavior (E-B) theory, John Zeisel, in his seminal book, *Inquiry by Design*, asks, "What happens when designers test the responses they present? What do designers image? How do designs develop once conceived?" (p. 26). Zeisel develops theories about how we inquire using design as the foundation. As a research-based methodology from an E-B perspective, Zeisel advocates creating and testing hypotheses as a means of understanding how people behave in spaces, and how the environment can be modified to encourage certain behaviors. Zeisel suggests that we do this type of testing to make a design explicit, and links how we think as creative designers to how we can transfer this creativity through empirical testing:

> Most images are developed and refined by means of modest "creative leaps." . . . Testing triggers creative leaping. Testing a tentative design response against quality criteria within the situation and its context to find out where the presentation is strong and where it is weak forces the designer to respond creatively.
>
> Making tacit attributes of a design explicit through testing helps designers re-image and re-present their designs with greater precision. (Schon, 1974, in Zeisel, 2006, pp. 26–27)

When we test and compare along with the designing, we enter into a designing process that is situated in inquiry and becomes evidence-informed.

Qualitative, Quantitative, Mixed Methods, and Theoretical Approaches

Over the past decade, different research approaches have emerged as useful for studying interior design processes and practices. Although there are multiple ways to engage in scientific inquiry, three fundamental ways to develop research based in empirical inquiry are theoretical, qualitative, quantitative or mixed method approaches (Creswell, 2003). Although both qualitative and quantitative methods allow for hypotheses, these are framed quite differently depen-

ding on whether you develop research questions using a quantitative, or qualitative (or alternative) research paradigm (Friedman, 1997; Creswell, 2003). Mixed method approaches mix together components of qualitative and quantitative inquiry methods, while theoretical approaches have as their basis other types of paradigms.

We bring back this idea of paradigm, this time with regards to research inquiry types. A *paradigm* is a way to understand the object of research, and is described by Kuhn as "any new way of thinking" (Nelson & Stolterman, 2003, p. 27). More precisely, "the concept of paradigm creates coherent frames of reference by defining the epistemological rules of the game for any particular system of inquiry" (p. 90).

In this sense, any theoretical, qualitative, or quantitative "method" is supported by a particular paradigm. Using the example of qualitative and quantitative methods, Glesne and Peshkin (1992) provide a simple description of the differences between these two inquiry methods using this idea of paradigm:

> Quantitative methods are, in general, supported by the positivist . . . paradigm, which leads us to regard the world as made up of observable, measurable facts. In contrast, qualitative methods are generally supported by the interpretivist paradigm, which portrays a world in which reality is socially constructed, complex, and ever changing. (pp. 5–6)

There are many different ways to study a phenomenon and situation in research. Let's look at the foundations of research through an understanding of qualitative, quantitative, and mixed method approaches. We will also consider theoretical research approaches as a fourth way to study design from a more philosophical or historical perspective.

Quantitative Research Methods

In quantitative research, theories are tested using variables and are supported by scientific method. Questions are framed in the form of hypotheses that are based on the reduction of the object studied into variables (numbers). You begin by setting up a question, choosing the objects of study, and then collecting the information required to substantiate your hypothesis (Creswell, 2003). This form of research objectifies the object of study, thereby separating it from the researcher and other environmental elements to generalize the findings to a broader situation. This type of research stems from a positivist tradition located in the natural sciences (Creswell, 2003; Glesne & Peshkin, 1992).

Qualitative Inquiry Approaches

Alternatively, another type of inquiry approach for evidence-based research is qualitative research. With qualitative inquiry methods, we study the tacit, subjective qualities of people's responses to their environment, and seek to make meaning from what they say and experience. This can be evidence of how people respond to the designer's creative- and process-oriented approach, or on how they respond to environments through a more phenomenological real, lived experience. Qualitative inquiry methods focus on what people say, how they use their environment both functionally and also subjectively as active, dynamic users, and how we document these responses in a more direct manner through conversation and open-ended questions and conversations.

A qualitative approach in theory and method means that we ask questions of a broad nature that are situated in the design process itself before, during, and after the design of an interior environment. The object of study and the researcher are not separate, meaning that the study of the phenomena, situation, or environment studied is not done as separate from the researcher. *Qualitative* means that we understand design situations and problems from the larger phenomena we observe and record them through the unfolding activities of the phenomena itself. We are interested in the stories of the people using the space, what they say, and how they say it.

Qualitative methods begin with the asking of questions situated in the social constructions that we observe, whether a designed interior space or within a larger society. They continue when we interpret what people say and how they say it, and when we interpret what we see as responses within the interior environments that we study (Ely et al., 1997; Vaikla-Poldma,

2003). When we use qualitative approaches, we seek to interpret and understand narrative. Narratives are the recorded stories, interviews, and anecdotes that people tell us in open-ended interviews that provide insight into their intimate thoughts regarding environments and their perceptions of them, or the social relations that they have within them.

Mixed Methods Approaches

A third possibility is using mixed method research (Creswell, 2003), whereby we explore pragmatic knowledge claims and study the sequences of events using both qualitative and quantitative approaches. Research questions are constructed with a constructivist paradigm, meaning that the research is framed in a constructed, scientifically supported framework.

Theoretical Approaches

Finally, interior designers can situate their inquiry in historical or theoretical perspectives that are neither solely qualitative nor quantitative in approach. Philosophical or theoretical inquiry might ask questions situated in documented history or theory, and may not study the live, active situations of people in the built environment. Research about interior design knowledge, about its epistemological grounding, about its history or theory, is of a more theoretical nature.

Summary

These delineations and clarifications are necessary if one is going to conduct research of any kind. For interior designers, understanding these basic paradigms is a first step to understanding what choices are available, and how design research choices are underpinned by paradigms and values about the research subjects as objects of study (Creswell, 2000; Creswell, 2003).

Whichever research methods you choose, you must research the paradigms related to the methods chosen, and understand how what you study fits with the research methods you have selected. Mixing methods is dangerous if you are not well versed in the different paradigms. Although some researchers suggest that mixing methods is possible and useful

(Creswell, 2003), others suggest that this is not viable, as the paradigms are quite different. For example, Ely et al. (1997) suggest that the issue of paradigms is fundamental and cite Lincoln and Guba in this regard:

In this time of shifting and emerging paradigms, certain writers have also suggested that researchers should feel free to combine features of the quantitative and qualitative paradigms or to adopt the desired features of each at will. Lincoln and Guba (1985; Guba, 1990) have argued forcibly that there is a basic incompatibility between these research paradigms because of their conflicting philosophical positions, or worldviews. . . . We believe that a researcher's clarification of his or her posture or postures within a research paradigm works to reveal epistemological assumptions . . . the researcher owes readers a sound rationale for such choices as well as a comparative discussion of the underlying assumption of each technique and set of results. Without such, we have seen many combinations of techniques misused and misunderstood. (pp. 229–230)

Whereas designing interior space means understanding its specific contexts, so studying it and researching it means understanding the world views of the researcher and the researched.

Let's examine how we might research interior environments through design inquiry.

COMPLEXITY IN THE DESIGN PROCESS

Another way to understand how people use interior environments is to understand people and the environment itself as a whole entity. Nelson and Stolterman (2003) develop the idea of "complexity" as a distinctive attribute that describes real-world human relationships:

Nature is not merely a collection of organic and inorganic elements or compounds, possessing attendant qualities and attributes, which exist in isolation. Nor is humanity merely a collection of individuals in isolated proximity to one another.

Everything is in relationship to everything else at varying levels of criticality and intensity. These relationships produce qualities and attributes at multiple levels of resolution. Complexity, a distinctive attribute arising as a consequence of the dynamic interactivity of relationships, is the rule in the real world. (pp. 72–73)

This idea of complexity is useful for interior design process inquiry when we require an understanding of multiple contexts for a design, or when we study how we design in complex situations. As we develop design projects, we contextualize our designing within notions of complexity, as we integrate multiple contexts and issues simultaneously, designing interior spaces that are dynamic and changing. For example, if I am designing an elder-care facility, I am concerned with the people who live there and use the environment both as a personal space (their room) and as a public space (eating with others, playing games, socializing), and am also concerned with their particular status (healthy, with dementia or Alzheimer's). I also consider the caregivers and their role (family, volunteers, nurses, doctors) and the administration of the required care. At this point I may not have even looked at the design of the space itself. These stakeholders are all concerned with dynamic relationships and the ways that the designed spaces serve the various users, including the caregivers and those who call these institutional spaces "home." As we have seen, concepts of home also play a part in this dynamic series of relationships, and this is particularly true in an elder-care facility where people live out their lives, as an example.

A Systematic Approach to Design Research

Nelson and Stolterman (2003) suggest that these ideas about complexity are grounded by the dependence of environmental elements within a holistic system. They suggest:

Everything exists in an environment and within a context. Everything depends on other things for something, whether it is food, protection, or other basic needs. Such assemblies of functional relationships lead to the emergence of phenomena that transcend attributes and qualities of the things themselves. Ecosystems are one example of this. An ecosystem, as a community of living things in close interaction with one another, displays qualities that are experienced only in aggregation, as in the case of wetlands. . . . Another example of emergence is a house, a functional assembly of construction materials, until it is experienced as a home—not merely a building. (p. 73)

We must design interior spaces considering the ways that our designs impact upon, and are impacted by, other systems that surround us. For example, if we speak of work environments or leisure spaces, these are bound by the functional systems inherent to a building that serve to satisfy human needs, including:

- the building system (construction type, spatial movement, material attributes)
- the environmental systems of that space (heating, ventilation, air-conditioning, and human comfort attributes)
- the acoustic systems (wall thicknesses, material choices to help or hinder the transmission or absorption of sound)
- visual systems (lighting systems as task guides, color systems for visual movement and navigational ability)
- the sustainable aspects of the environmental systems and materials chosen
- the social and human aspects as integral components of the total environment

A Systems Approach in Design and Design Inquiry
When we inquire and design integrating trying to solve problems of how the systems and people interrelate with one another, we are doing what Nelson and Stolterman refer to as a "systems approach:"

When we view nature and human activity as inter-related and inter-relating, we are taking *a systems approach*. . . . Such an approach requires that close attention is paid to relationships and the phenomenon of emergence when evaluating any subset of existence. If the designer's objective

is to create something new, not to just describe and explain, or predict and control, it is especially important to take a systems approach. . . . There is no way around the fact that any design created will be in relationship to, and interrelated with, the real world. (p. 74)

When we design spaces, we contextualize the design within the particular situation within which it exists, with varied and multiple contexts, and each time with different systems, approaches, and variations. The people will be different and the ways we implement the design will differ each time we do a design.

SOCIAL THEORIES AND THEIR USEFULNESS IN DESIGN INQUIRY

Another important way to theorize the design process is to understand the social meanings and ways that people act when in public situations. When we design bars, nightclubs, institutions, restaurants, workspaces and kitchens, or living rooms, we design space around the social situations in which people find themselves. We become concerned with personal spaces, the social relations that people engage in, and how to best support these activities through the spatial design.

There are many theories that accompany this type of thinking. Some are more directly attributed to people as actors, as in actor-network-theory (Latour, 2005), whereas others are situated in social concepts about space (Ardener, 1981) or geographical space concepts that examine social relations (Spain, 1992). The most pivotal theory currently in use is actor-network-theory, developed by Bruno Latour, which attempts to decipher the role of "social" in the world by breaking down what we consider to be "society" (Latour, 2005, p. 3). Too complex to treat appropriately within the simple confines of this book, actor-network-theory nevertheless provokes ideas about how we deal with social interactions on broader levels.

At the moment in interior design, our understanding of concepts such as "social" is limited generally to what we identify as the social relations of people within environments. For example, when we design

ENTERTAINMENT ENVIRONMENTS

In the following two examples, the designer shows us how the design for a club has a certain atmosphere that draws people into the place for a drink. The space supports an event, whereas the creation of that space is composed of multiple elements. The designer creates a concept for the client, developing complex systems for each function and requirement, evolves the appropriate aesthetic, and then situates the design within the local cultural milieu of the country where they open the store. In Figure A we see a concept for a bar in North America, and in Figure B we see an entrance to a virtual environment in Kuwait.

There are always inherent complexities to design projects: the client and user as players, the particular location, the cultural contexts, the particularities of the design project itself, and how all these factors play out in the specific situation of the project.

The design process here is holistic, systematic, and complex, engaged in multiple contexts relative to the client's goals and the user's needs and desires. As an interior design student, you could examine this case study as a precedent for designing; as a designer, I might be interested in how this design has been conceived, built, and appropriated by both client and user alike. As a design researcher, I might be interested in developing critical theory about the way the design is done, or doing a qualitative research project that compares the different spaces to see where the design is more appropriate to the community where it exists. Or perhaps I would like to test variables by examining people's reactions in day versus night when doing a specific activity. In each case I am interested in examining the design and in each case for very different reasons.

Figures A • Bar in North America

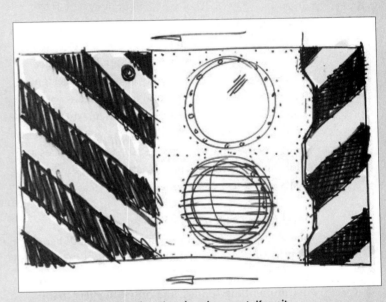

Figures B • Entrance detail to virtual environment, Kuwait

offices or open workspaces, we may be neglecting many social practices in favor of personal or political practices. And yet each social practice we design for is loaded with political messages. We tend to apply ideas quickly rather than study how people work together intimately, what they actually do and how. What we "construct" as social relations become political decisions that are implemented through the walls, partitions, or other structures we construct to put people together within an environment. This is an area where design research can be explored on multiple levels, where design criteria can be evolved further, and where we can change design practices through design research discoveries.

Developing Theories

When we use the design processes put forth in this book, we become producers of design knowledge. We develop a design sensibility and use the design process to solve problems, and in essence, as we think about designing spaces, we also question what is done, how, and why. We develop new and different ways of designing, while respecting best practices and good ways of creating appropriate interior environments. These are complementary practices.

Developing Design as a Science

John Zeisel's idea of "inquiry by design" (2006) and the other approaches listed herein suggest that we can and should develop "a design science" for the built environment disciplines, and others suggest that it is time that we as designers develop our own science situated in our practices (Zeisel, 2006; Friedman, 1997; Krippendorff, 2006). In another example, Klaus Krippendorff in *The Semantic Turn: A New Foundation for Design* (2006) suggests that design needs to develop its own research "semantics." Using product design as his context, Krippendorff defines product semantics (with Reinhart Butler) as:

- a systematic inquiry into how people attribute meanings to artefacts and interact with them accordingly

- a vocabulary and methodology for designing artefacts in view of the meanings that they could acquire for users and the communities of their stakeholders (p. 2)

He suggests that developing research in design means understanding a "semantic turn" for industrial design. We can look to researchers such as Krippendorff, and be inspired by how design research is situated within the practices and ideas of a particular discipline, such as industrial design. My own work is on what we do and how interior designers ask similar questions in interior design from the perspective of the design process and the perspective of the interior designer (Poldma, 1999; Vaikla-Poldma, 2003).

New ideas about the design process are being explored constantly. For example, Chris Heape (2007) provides a compelling way to understand the design process as "conceptual space" where he describes the "design process as the construction, exploration and expansion of a conceptual space" and this open-ended conceptual space is explored by students and captured in his doctoral thesis (Heape, 2007).

CONSIDERING INTERIOR DESIGN PROCESS AND PRACTICE AS RESEARCH

When we develop an understanding of the interior design process using theory-based thinking, we move toward understanding it as the basis for how we understand the world. This means knowing what we do and how, and making sense of the design process, as it is experienced by interior designers.

It is important for interior designers and researchers to find the specificity that makes interior design unique, evidence-based, and relevant. Interior spaces are lived-in, dynamic places, and this forms the basis for our design process and how we make interior space come alive (Vaikla-Poldma, 2003). Interior design is informed by multiple stances, practices, and inquiry modes, some of which are documented and many more that need full documentation, further research, and development.

Developing Attributes

Let's look at the attributes that make interior design and its methods and processes unique:

1. We develop a systematic inquiry about what people need in spaces, how they function to perform better, enjoy their activities longer, or experience space better.
2. We design interior spaces that support lived experiences in the real world.
3. We design spaces supported by inquiry-based methods, research, and analysis of situations requiring change, and understanding the issues that give rise to the intimate needs of users.
4. We create interior environments with an intimate view of the user-space-object interrelationship, and how this supports and is informed by other views (user-product, user-building, user-exterior spaces, user-urban environment).
5. We are concerned with the intimate ways that people appropriate spaces through the meanings they attribute to things found within spaces, and how these are qualities of the spatial design.
6. We are care-based in our approach, in that we offer both a service that cares for its users, while also "taking care" (Nelson & Stolterman, 2003, p. 225) in how we take the design from idea to built reality.
7. We offer detailed and developed ways for a design concept to become a reality that is user-centered and based in knowledge of materials, processes, details, and systems designs that are sustainable and ethically based.
8. We are interested in innovation—in creating something new and different, yet supporting the first seven attributes listed.

All of these attributes form part of design as process and allow interior designers to solve design problems and situations.

DOCUMENTING THE DESIGN PROCESS THROUGH POST-DESIGN RESEARCH

Klaus; Krippendorff (2006) carefully makes the distinction between design process and design research when he suggests that post-design research is another way to reflect on one's design practices, also in the systematic thinking. He states:

> It may be convenient to designers to stop any concern for their design on its delivery to their clients, but this would terminate the learning process. . . . [D]esigners could make the additional effort to learn from their own successes and failures. A science for design suggests doing so not merely anecdotally but systematically. Post-design research inquires into what happened after a design was delivered, how it worked its way through the network of stakeholders or not. Post-design research is research proper as it examines and seeks to generalize from what happened in the recorded past of design practices. (p. 269)

Krippendorff also puts forward the idea that "[w]ritten design discourse is the re-examinable repository of knowledge of design" (p. 269). The more we document and identify good practices, develop and explore theories and philosophies specific to design processes and practices, and criticize what we do and how we do it, the more we develop design knowledge. As we have seen in this book, interior design processes and practices exist in multiple forms of knowledge: explicit and tacit, real and unreal, material and immaterial, and all of these forms bear investigation further through design research.

New ways of thinking about the design process are evolving daily. You have experienced only a few different ways of thinking about the design process in this book. The design process and interior design will continue to evolve, change, and develop as the world changes and evolves.

BIBLIOGRAPHY

Caan, S. (2007). Consensus or confusion? Conference proceedings abstract, *Thinking inside the box, Interiors forum Scotland*, p. 8. Retrieved from http://www.interiorsforumscotland.com/page8.htm

Carr, W., & Kemmis, S. (1986). *Becoming critical.* London: The Falmer Press.

Chalmers, L., & Close, S. (2007). But is it interior design? Considering the intervention of theory in interior design education. Conference proceedings abstract, *Thinking Inside the Box, Interiors Forum Scotland*, p. 9. Retrieved from http://www.interiorsforumscotland.com/page9.htm

Creswell, J. (2003). *Research design, qualitative, quantitative and mixed method approaches* (2nd ed.). Thousand Oaks, CA: Sage.

Denzin, N. K. & Lincoln, Y. (Eds.). (1994). *Handbook of qualitative research*. Newbury Park, CA: Sage.

Ely, M., Vinz, R., Downing, M., & Anzul, M. (1997). *On writing qualitative research: living by words*. London: The Falmer Press.

Franz, J. (2000). An interpretive-contextual framework for research in and through design: The development of a philosophically methodological and substantially consistent framework. In D. Durling and K. Friedman (Eds.), *Foundations of the future: Doctoral education in design*: Proceedings from the Conference held 8–12 July in La Clusaz, France. UK: Staffordshire University Press.

Giroux, H., Lankshear, C., McLaren, P., & Peters, M. (Eds.). (1996). *Counternarratives: Cultural studies and critical pedagogies in post-modern spaces*. New York: Routledge.

Guba, E. G. (Ed.). (1990). *The paradigm dialog*. Newbury Park, CA: Sage.

Guerin, D., & Martin, C. (2001). *The interior design profession's body of knowledge; Its definition and documentation*. Original report prepared for the Association of Registered Interior Designers of Ontario (ARIDO). Toronto: ARIDO, 2001.

Heape, C. (2007). *The design space: The design process as construction, exploration and expansion of a conceptual space*. Ph.D Dissertation, University of Southern Denmark, Sondenborg, Denmark: Mads Clausen Institute, Author.

Krippendorff, K. (2006). *The semantic turn: A new foundation for design*. Boca Raton, FL: CRC Press, Taylor & Francis.

Latour, B. (2005). *Reassembling the social: An introduction to actor-network-theory*. New York: Oxford University Press.

Lincoln, Y., & Guba, E. G. (1985). *Naturalistic inquiry*. Beverley Hills, CA: Sage.

Mitchell, C. T. (1993). *Redefining designing: From form to experience*. New York: Van Nostrand Reinhold.

Mitchell, C. T., & Rudner, S. (2007). *Interior design's identity crisis: Rebranding the profession*. Conference proceedings abstract, *Thinking Inside the Box, Interiors Forum Scotland*, p 27. Retrieved from http://www.interiorsforumscotland.com/page27.htm

Nelson, H., & Stolterman, E. (2003). *The design way: Intentional change in an unpredictable world*. Englewood Cliffs, NJ: Educational Technology Publications.

Poldma, T. (1999). *Gender, design and education: The politics of voice*. Unpublished master's thesis. Montreal, QC: McGill University, Author.

Poldma, T. (2008). Interior design at a crossroads: Embracing specificity through process, research, and knowledge. *Journal of Interior Design, 33*(3), vi–xvi.

Turpin, J. (2001). Omitted, devalued and ignored: Re-evaluating the historical interpretation of women in the interior design profession. *Journal of Interior Design, 27*(1), 1–11.

Vaikla-Poldma, T. (2003). *An investigation of learning and teaching processes in an interior design class: An interpretive and contextual inquiry*. Unpublished doctoral thesis. Montreal: McGill University, Author.

Vetting-Wolf, T. (2007 September). *Notes about design sensibility*.

Weigand, J. (2006 Winter). Defining ourselves. *Perspective*.

Zeisel, J. (2006). *Inquiry by design: Environment/behaviour/neuroscience in architecture, interiors, landscape, and planning*. New York: W. W. Norton & Company.

Credits

Chapter 1

Sketch on p. 2: Courtesy of the author

Figure 1.1: Courtesy of Margaret DaCruz

Case Study 1.1—Figures A and B: Courtesy of the author

Figures 1.2–1.5: Courtesy of the author/Bélanger

Figure 1.6: Courtesy of the author

Case Study 1.2—Figures A and B: Courtesy Michel Raynaud

Figure 1.7: Courtesy Michael Joannidis

Figure 1.8: Courtesy of the author

Figure 1.9: Courtesy of the author

Case Study 1.3—Figure A: Courtesy of the author

Case Study 1.3—Figure B: Courtesy of R. Girard

Case Study 1.4—Figure A: Courtesy of Faye Dea-Jalbert and Émilie Richer-Groulx

Case Study 1.5—Figure A: Courtesy of Anne-Joelle Chamberland

Chapter 2

Figure 2.1: Courtesy of the author

Figure 2.2: Courtesy of the author (and from other sources)

Figure 2.3: Courtesy of the author (masters' thesis)

Figures 2.4–2.8: Courtesy of the author

Case Study 2.1—Figures A and B: Courtesy of Nathalie Briere

Case Study 2.1—Figure C: Courtesy of Julie Girard

Figures 2.9 and 2.10: Courtesy of Manon D'Alencon

Case Study 2.2—Figure A: Courtesy of Julie Girard

Figure 2.11: Courtesy of the author

Case Study 2.3—Figures A and B: Courtesy of Debra Lerner

Case Study 2.4—Figures A–C: Courtesy of Faye Dea-Jalbert and Emilie Richer-Groulx

Figures 2.12 and 2.13: Courtesy of the author

Figure 2.14: Debra Lerner

Figure 2.15: Julie Girard

Figure 2.16: Courtesy of the author

Figures 2.17 and 2.18: Courtesy of Veronique Lalande

Figure 2.19: Courtesy of Julie Girard

Figure 2.20: Unknown (student)

Figure 2.21: Courtesy of Caroline Joly

Chapter 3

Figure 3.1: Courtesy of the author

Case Study 3.1—Figures A–C: Courtesy of Louise Mathieu

Case Study 3.2—Figures A and B: Courtesy of Jacinthe Leduc

Case Study 3.3—Figures A and B: Courtesy of the author

Case Study 3.4—Figure A: Courtesy of the author

Case Study 3.5—Figure A: Courtesy of the author

Case Study 3.5—Figures B and C: Courtesy of Pierre-Marc Savoie

Case Study 3.6—Figures A–D: Courtesy of the author

Figure 3.2: Courtesy of the author

Figure 3.3: Courtesy of Caroline Joly

Figures 3.4–3.10: Courtesy of the author

Figures 3.11 and 3.12: Courtesy Nicolas Ruel/George Reeleder

Figure 3.13: Courtesy of the author

Chapter 4

Figure 4.1: Courtesy of Nicolas Ruel/George Reeleder

Figures 4.2–4.8: Courtesy of the author

Case Study 4.1—Figure A: Courtesy of Faye Dea-Jalbert and Émilie Richer-Groulx

Case Study 4.1—Figure B: Raphaelle Parenteau

Figure 4.9: Courtesy of the author

Case Study 4.6—Figures A–D: Courtesy of the author/client space courtesy JP Janson

Case Study 4.7—Figure A: Courtesy of Debra Lerner

Figures 4.10 and 4.11: Courtesy of the author

Figure 4.12: Courtesy of Debra Lerner

Figure 4.13: Courtesy of the author

Figures 4.14–4.17: Courtesy of Debra Lerner

Figure 4.18: Unknown (students)

Figure 4.19: Courtesy of Debra Lerner

Figure 4.20: Courtesy of Caroline Joly

Figure 4.21: Courtesy of Veronique Lalande

Chapter 5

Figures 5.1–5.3: Courtesy of the author

Figures 5.4–5.15: Julie Girard

Figures 5.16 and 5.17: Manon D'Alençon

Figure 5.18: Julie Girard

Figure 5.19: Unknown (student)

Figure 5.20: Unknown (student)

Figure 5.21: Unknown (student)

Figure 5.22: Courtesy of the author

Figure 5.23: Manon D'Alençon

Chapter 6

Figure 6.1a–d: Courtesy of the author

Figure 6.1e: Courtesy of Manon D'Alençon

Figures 6.2 and 6.3: Courtesy of the author

Figure 6.4: Courtesy of Julie Girard

Figures 6.5–6.7: Courtesy of the author

Case Study 6.1—Figures A–C: Courtesy of Myriam Alarie

Figures 6.8–6.10: Courtesy of the author

Figure 6.11: Courtesy of the author/student and teacher discussion

Figure 6.12: Courtesy of Michael Joannidis

Figures 6.13 and 6.14: Courtesy of Julie Girard

Figure 6.15: Courtesy of Justine Maassen

Figures 6.16 and 6.17: Courtesy of Michael Joannidis

Chapter 7

Figure 7.1: Courtesy of Manon D'Alençon

Case Study 7.1—Figures A–I: Courtesty of Julie Girard

Case Study 7.2—Figures A–D: Courtesy of Manon D'Alençon

Case Study 7.3—Figures A–I: Courtesy Julie Girard

Chapter 8

Figure 8.1: Courtesy of the author/A. Jones

Figure 8.2: Courtesy of Josiane Pouliot

Case Study 8.1—Figures A–C: Courtesy of the author

Figures 8.3–8.20: Courtesy of Josiane Pouliot

Chapter 9

Case Study 9.1—Figure A M. Haller (Courtesy of G. Dittmar, professor)

Case Study 9.1—Figures B and C: Blaisdell (Courtesy of G. Dittmar, professor)

Case Study 9.2—Figures A–F: Courtesy of Raphaelle Parenteau

Chapter 10

Case Study 10.1—Figures A and B: Courtesy of Michael Joanndis

Index

narrative analytic tools, 83, 86
nature, 54
    applied to man-made things, 201
    inspiration from, 54, 194, 197f
needs assessments, using, 140
neighborhood exterior view, 74f
Nelson, Harold, 59, 259, 260, 269, 270

observation, 82
off-angle plan, 157f
office design, corporate, 115
office project, gathering information
    for, 113
offices
open *vs.* closed, 107f, 108f, 167–68
optimal space between people in, 107f
organizational lists, 85f, 120, 122t
organizational principles, 180f
organizing principles, 189–90
Ornstein, Robert, 183

Paneiro, Julius, 108
paper-folding sequence, 253–54f
paradigm shift. *See also under* design
    process
    defining the concept of, 250
paradigms. *See also* research methods
    defined, 250, 267
participatory concept (building ideas),
    54
partitions, 164
patterns
    for generating ideas, 192
    as motifs, 192
    in nature and design, 151–52
personal analogy, 200
Personal Space (Sommer), 105
perspective, sketching in. *See* modeling,
    the interior virtually
perspective sketches from models, gen-
    erating, 127
perspective view of design concept, 130f
perspectives, trying things out from
    multiple, 189
phenomenological design approach, 233
    designer and design act as phenom-
    enological, 244–47
phenomenological idea of real, lived
    experience, 232–34
phenomenology, understanding the
    philosophy of, 244–46
philosophical approaches, 93, 97
photography, 197, 199
plan development, two-dimensional, 141
planning process components, 63
playroom concept, 110f
"po," 177

Poldma, Tiiu, 234, 258
possibilities, 177
    exploring, 178
possible, the, 46, 47, 49f
post-design process(es), 63, 220–21,
    225, 228, 232. *See also* building the
    design; phenomenological design
    approach; space, taking up
    changing and shifting design founda-
    tions, 232
    designer and design act as phenom-
    enological, 246–47
    transformation of the spatial experi-
    ence, 246
    various players involved in, 226–27
post-design research, documenting the
    design process through, 273
post-design responses and thinking, 45
post-occupancy evaluations (POEs),
    228, 232
post-project/post-occupancy phase, 42
prejudice, 92
pre-lease space concept, 116f
pre-process stage, 62, 69, 72, 224–25
problem solving, 16, 19, 44. *See also*
    design problems
    creative, 199–201. *See also* creative
    component of design process
    environment and, 185
product semantics, 272
programming, 37
projects. *See* design projects
proportion, scale and, 154f, 165
punch lists, 228
Pye, David, 5, 16, 18

questions. *See also* design inquiry;
    inquiry
    asked at outset of project, 62, 65, 69,
    71
    asking, 187

radial patterns, 191
Rao, Satish, 69
"real, lived experience," phenomenologi-
    cal idea of, 232–34
real, the, 46, 49f
rectilinear patterns, 191
reflective practices, 265
Reiwoldt, Otto, 235
Rengel, Roberto, 17
repetition, 191
research, 36, 37, 75. *See also* design (pro-
    cess) approach
    and analysis, 43–44, 102
    early, 53–54

matched to clients and their needs,
    91–93, 97
tools and methods, 76, 82–83
design process and practice as, 272–73
documenting the design process
    through post-design, 273
in practice and process, 264
practice-based, 265
a systematic approach to, 269–70
research methods, 268–69
    mixed methods approaches, 268
    qualitative inquiry approaches, 267–
    68
    quantitative, 267–68
    theoretical approaches, 268
restaurants, 68, 68f, 168, 170–71. *See
    also* fast-food kiosk concept; food
    courts
retail environments, 171–72
retail space, interior concept for, 3f
Rewi, Adrienne, 235
rhythm, 154f
Roscoe, Tara, 235
round table and chairs, 106f, 107f
Roy, M., 184

scale and proportion, 154f, 165
schematic analytic tools, 120
schematic diagrams, 120
school design, an alternative, 215,
    215–19f
science center, interactive, 48–49
sculptural form development, 130
second-level design problems, 65
self, space as representation of, 166
senses, visual inspiration from the five,
    54
shapes and forms in interior spaces, 158
Shoskes, Ellen, 58
Shusterman, Richard, 93
sight lines, movement and, 158
sketch, rough, 147f
sketching in perspective. *See* modeling,
    the interior virtually
social construction of space, 233–34
social responsibility and design, 258
social spatial concepts, 106
social spatial requirements, 105–8
social theories and their usefulness in
    design inquiry, 270, 272
    developing design as a science, 272
    developing theories, 272
Sommer, Robert, 104–5, 266
space. *See also* distances between people
    changing concepts of time and, 234
    3-D sketch of concept for, 118f
    as design principle and element, 158